Published 2014 by

Applied Research + Design Publishing

with the University of Pennsylvania, School of Design

www.appliedresearchanddesign.com

info@appliedresearchanddesign.com

terrain.design.upenn.edu

www.design.upenn.edu

Book Design: Anuradha Mathur, Dilip da Cunha,
Rebekah Meeks and Matthew Wiener with Pablo Mandel

Edited by: Anuradha Mathur, Dilip da Cunha,
Rebekah Meeks and Matthew Wiener

Color Separations and Printing: ORO Group Ltd.

Cover Design: Karl Peters, DIE Creative, Inc.

ISBN: 978-1-941806-24-1

First Edition

Applied Research + Design Publishing makes a continuous effort to
minimize the overall carbon footprint of its publications. As part of this
goal, Applied Research + Design Publishing, in association with Global
ReLeaf, arranges to plant trees to replace those used in the manufacturing of the paper produced for its books. Global ReLeaf is an international
campaign run by American Forests, one of the world's oldest nonprofit
conservation organizations. Global ReLeaf is American Forest' education
and action program that helps individuals, organizations, agencies, and
corporations improve the local and global environment by planting and
caring for trees.

Library of Congress data: Available upon request.

For more information on our distribution, please visit our website:
www.appliedresearchanddesignpublishing.com

DESIGN in the terrain of water

ANURADHA MATHUR / DILIP DA CUNHA

LINDSAY BREMNER

TEDDY CRUZ

NATALY GATTEGNO

ALISON HIRSCH

ANNE WHISTON SPIRN

KONGJIAN YU

SIMON RICHTER

DOUG JEROLMACK

WALTER HOOD

KAZI ASHRAF

PETER HUTTON

ELIZABETH MOSSOP

ILA BERMAN

CHRISTIAN WERTHMANN

MARION WEISS

WILLIAM BRAHAM

ANNA HERINGER

DAVID LEATHERBARROW

HERBERT DREISEITL

MARGARITA GUTIÉRREZ

IÑAKI ECHEVERRIA

TILMAN LATZ

PIETRO LAUREANO

DIÉBÉDO FRANCIS KÉRÉ

JOHN TODD

DESIGN in the terrain of water

Edited by

ANURADHA MATHUR / DILIP DA CUNHA

with REBEKAH MEEKS
MATTHEW WIENER

NATALY GATTEGNO

KAZI ASHRAF

ELIZABETH MOSSOP

SIMON RICHTER

ANURADHA MATHUR / DILIP DA CUNHA

TEDDY CRUZ

PETER HUTTON

ANNE WHISTON SPIRN

WALTER HOOD

KONGJIAN YU

DOUG JEROLMACK

ALISON HIRSCH

LINDSAY BREMNER

FOREWORD

"Water is everywhere before it is somewhere..." With these seven words set in fluid meter, Anuradha Mathur and Dilip da Cunha launched a dialogue that grew and then swelled as others rushed to join in. Colleagues known and not yet known came from places far away along the dimensions of space, time, and discipline, to convene at the School of Design, University of Pennsylvania, and when the last of the presentations and papers had vanished from the air of the gallery in Meyerson Hall, still no one wanted to leave.

The lingering allure of that collective event has persuaded the conveners to reassemble the moment, the words spoken and the ideas exchanged, in printed form, in order to extend a philosophical and cultural conversation that is already changing our shared perspectives—on lines drawn on maps, on territorial borders, on the disappearance of boundaries we ourselves have established—in favor of a regenerative rethinking of the terrain of water.

The work presented in this book distills and reframes the remarkable latent energy and the untapped potential of questioning the boundaries between water and land. Just as society struggles to replace balkanization with inclusion and to supplant place of origin with new inhabitation, just as across the fields of design we explore the reduction of barriers between disciplines in order to improve our response to seemingly intractable social and cultural problems at local and global scales, this exploration of terrain becomes newly and critically important.

In the opening contribution to this book, Mathur and da Cunha address the question of the line as a tool to gain literacy about terrain and as a way of projecting ourselves into the future rather than acting only within the bounds of more time-proximate determinants. They describe the centuries-old invention of river-based maps that defined locations even though the river and its locations were always changing and will continue to change.

So, too, the convening they called *Design in the Terrain of Water* and this publication represent a singular moment amidst a water-challenged decade that both inspires and necessitates an interweaving of science and culture, of design and poetics, of activism and advocacy, to respond to a world that is more inconstant and risk-filled than we want it to be.

Water inundates. It also challenges us to think in four dimensions, not three, where the impulse of time-based thinking can enable a realignment of resources in favor of the longer-term, not that shorter one in which we simply build exactly what we have lost, not realizing how truly impossible that is. Traveling along this new dimension we may inhabit not just again, but better, and with greater resilience, as we embrace the indeterminate nature of design in the terrain of water.

MARILYN JORDAN TAYLOR

Design in the Terrain of Water makes room for water that is *everywhere* before it is *somewhere*: water that is in rain before it is in rivers, soaks before it flows, spreads before it gathers, blurs before it clarifies; water that is ephemeral, transient, uncertain, interstitial, chaotic, omnipresent. This is water to which people are increasingly turning to find innovative solutions to water scarcity, pollution, aquifer depletion, and other problems that are assuming center stage in local and global politics, dynamics, and fears. It is also water that is celebrated and ritualized in ordinary and everyday practices across many cultures.

This book brings together the work of eminent professionals, designers, artists, scientists and theorists, who respond to the challenges that water everywhere poses: its visualization, infrastructure, politics, and science.

At a moment when design disciplines are beginning to embrace measures such as flexibility, agility and resilience, we believe this book will make a timely contribution. These are measures that we associate more closely with water and watery imagination than with the terra firma that grounds aspirations of prediction and control that have proved elusive, perhaps even detrimental. The book asks if in this time of uncertainty and ambiguity brought on by increasing openness of economies, cultures, and ecologies, we need to re-invent our relationship with water. Should we look to the past, present and future and ask if in seeing water somewhere rather than everywhere we miss opportunities, practices and lessons that could inform and transform the design project? What role does representation and visualization play in confining water to a place on land? Can we look at projects in history and projects emerging today—cities, infrastructures, buildings, landscapes, artworks—with a cultivated eye for waters everywhere? What is it to see water as not within, adjoining, serving or threatening settlement, but as the ground of settlement?

This book is structured as a dialogue between two waters – water that is somewhere, framed, held in place and distinguished from land; and waters that are everywhere, challenging conventional representation and demanding invention. These two waters are visualized as horizons in the works and reflections of the contributors to *Design in the Terrain of Water.* In the horizontal structure of this book these two horizons run a parallel course, breaking occasionally with ambiguity, complexity, and measures that are not easy to define, separate, or delineate. Water here simmers as a force within political and geographic dynamics, even as it submerges boundaries between places and disciplines. As a collection of visual and textual essays, this book presents a way to image, imagine, build, and advocate design in the terrain of water.

The idea of this book comes out of a symposium at PennDesign in April 2011 that gathered a unique spirit and momentum that we have tried to sustain and advance through this publication. The symposium itself was structured by the themes of activism and advocacy; imaging and imagining; and structure and infrastructure. In the process of developing this publication we became acutely aware that many contributors' works and ideas are exemplary of more than one of these themes and that these themes are too often inseparable. We then took the more chaotic path of assembling individual contributions united by a drive to engage water, not as an element to extract, an embellishment to design, or a commodity that is scarce. Rather, it is a terrain that challenges assumptions, reminds us of our fallibility, accomodates complexity, and locates our horizon.

We have many people to thank for their support and work in making this book possible. Dean Marilyn Taylor put her faith and energy behind us from the very start, encouraging us to conceive and curate the symposium in 2011 and then to make this book. Many of our colleagues at PennDesign, in particular David Leatherbarrow and William Whitaker were generous with their time and advice at critical stages of this project. We would also like to thank the staff in the Dean's Office and the Landscape Architecture Department, particularly Megan Schmidgal, Chris Cataldo, and Diane Pringle. We would like to acknowledge the symposium core team who initiated this project with us and were engaged in multiple aspects of the event and exhibition that opened in conjunction with it: Catherine Bonier, Michelle Lin, Jessica Ball, and Yadiel Rivera-Diaz.

We are especially indebted to Rebekah Meeks and Matthew Wiener who brought extraordinary skill, dedication, and insights to the book. Reva brought energy and an eye to developing with us the initial structure and layout of the book and Matt brought a focus, diligence, and design ability to seeing it to a finish. We are grateful to Gordon Goff for his enthusiasm for the project, and to his team for coordinating with us to make this a quality publication. Most of all we would like to thank all our contributors who were willing to indulge our many requests and worked closely with us to not just present their projects and research, but to draw out particular qualities and ideas that would advance the conversation on how water is imaged, imagined and engaged in design.

Last, but not the least, our daughter Tara. She is now thirteen and has been with us in many terrains of water, most recently the Himalaya Mountains in June 2013 when waters were everywhere, washing away mountain sides, settlements, infrastructure, and people, seemingly in defiance of being placed somewhere. We were fortunate to return unhurt; many thousands did not. This book is dedicated to them and the many others who experience the fury of confined waters.

ANURADHA MATHUR / DILIP DA CUNHA

ANURADHA MATHUR / DILIP DA CUNHA
WATERS EVERYWHERE

WHY IS IT THAT DESPITE WATERS EVERYWHERE PRECIPITATING,
SEEPING, SOAKING AIR, SOIL AND VEGETATION, COLLECTING IN INTERSTICES, PORES,
TERRACES, CISTERNS, AND AQUIFERS, EVAPORATING, TRANSPIRING, AND SUBLIMATING, WE
SEE WATER SOMEWHERE, CONFINED WITHIN OR BEHIND LINES AND GENERALLY COLORED BLUE
IN MAPS? IS IT THAT WE PRIVILEGE A MOMENT IN TIME, A WISHFUL MOMENT PERHAPS, WHEN
THE EARTH SURFACE PRESENTS ITSELF AS DIVIDED BETWEEN LAND AND WATER? THE FACT
IS THAT IN THE TIME OF THIS MOMENT MAPS ARE DRAWN, PROPERTIES ARE DEMARCATED,
DECISIONS ARE MADE, THE PAST IS DESCRIBED, AND THE FUTURE IS CONSIDERED. MORE
SERIOUSLY, IN THE TIME OF THIS MOMENT, THE LINES THAT DIVIDE WATER FROM LAND ALSO
DRAW OUT CLEAR AND DISTINCT 'THINGS' THAT ARE GIVEN THE STATUS OF BEINGS, BEINGS
THAT ARE PERSONIFIED, EVEN DEIFIED, BUT MORE SERIOUSLY TAKEN FOR GRANTED TO BE
'NATURAL' ENTITIES WITH A SIGNIFICANT ROLE TO PLAY AS AGENTS OF CHANGE ON THE
SURFACE OF THE EARTH AND IN EVERYDAY LIFE. NOTABLE AMONG THESE ENTITIES IS THE
RIVER. IT IS INCONCEIVABLE WITHOUT THE DRAWN LINE, A PRODUCT OF A VISUAL LITERACY
RATHER THAN A NATURAL FEATURE OF THE EARTH SURFACE, AN EXTRAORDINARY WORK OF
ART BEFORE IT IS A TAKEN FOR GRANTED OBJECT OF SCIENCE.

The hydrological cycle portrays water circulating endlessly, changing states, evaporating, condensing, precipitating, transpiring, flowing, seeping, and soaking. But very early on in the 5th century BCE, academics of the School of Miletus led by Anaximander and Hecataeus fixed on one moment in this cycle when water gathered and flowed on the surface of the earth. In this time, they could confine water with lines in the world map, which they are credited with inventing.

Lines feature prominently in the image of rivers. They flow alongside the waters of rivers as 'banks' from high ground where they meet in a point, or points, that are generally springs or the starts of rills where runoff first gathers, to what in most cases is the sea where they mysteriously transform into lines of the coast. On route, these lines perform three tasks: they separate the space of water from the space of land; they calibrate time along their length in keeping with a flow from an 'origin' to a 'end' or at least an earlier to a later; and they hold water to a channel.

Endowed with the ability to separate, calibrate, and contain, the lines of rivers can be traced to Anaximander of Miletus, among others. This early academic of the Milesian School is widely credited with 'inventing' the world map in the 6th century BCE, but also with calling out rivers as a particular moment in the extended time of water, a time that Aristotle believed was known to the 'ancients' as Oceanus. In this extended time, according to him, moisture about the earth is evaporated by the sun, raised into clouds, and cooled and condensed to return from air to water to evaporate again. One should think of it, he says, "as a river with a circular course" that "continues indefinitely."[1] Today, we know this extended time of water as the hydrological cycle: "The grand circle of movement of water from ocean to atmosphere to continent and back to ocean [that] is the essential mechanism that allows organisms—including humans—to emerge, to develop, and to live on Earth."[2] This circle, it is said, has been going around for many million years with ordinary terrestrial rivers serving as a particular moment in it, a moment when water appears to occupy a clear and distinct space

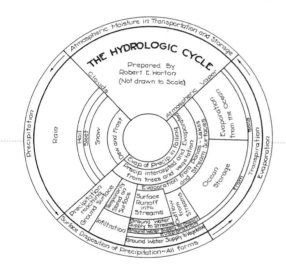

Water is everywhere before it is somewhere. It is rain before it is in rivers, it soaks before it flows, it spreads before it gathers, it blurs before it clarifies. Water, at these moments in the hydrological cycle, is not easy to picture in maps or contain within lines.

2

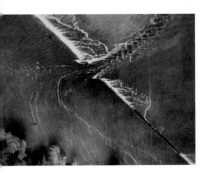

The human eye is cultivated to see rivers through experience, stories, facts, and definitions such as "flowing water in a channel with defined banks,"[12] but most significantly through the art of drawing a line: beginning it in a point, extending it with a stroke, and deleting or changing it with erasure. These acts correspond to three essentials of a river: source, course, and flood. Rivers begin, flow, and violate their banks.

on the surface of the earth. Anaximander drew this space with an eye positioned high above the earth, giving him a view that philosopher Charles Kahn observes "lends itself directly to geometric representation." As such he says, Anaximander could diagram the earth in a way that poets like Homer did not and perhaps could not or maybe resisted because diagramming as Kahn says "requires not drama but a precise geometric arrangement, and nothing could be more alien to the poet's state of mind."[3]

There is no record of Anaximander's map, but it reportedly depicted the earth surface in terms of points related by distances that he could reproduce to scale. The points did not interfere with the translation from surface to representation, as points had neither length nor breadth, and as such transcended scale. These points connected to each other with lines of measurable length but no breadth, so that they outlined 'things' that remained true to form in the transfer from earth surface to drawing. Anaximander may not have been the first to use points and lines in this manner, i.e., to construct a map, but he is widely believed to be the first in a tradition that sought to capture the entirety of the earth surface in a 'world map'. He saw this surface from high above as a circular landmass inscribed by rivers and enveloped by Oceanus, the extended time of water which circulated everywhere endlessly but also formlessly, except, that is, when it was in the clear and distinct courses of rivers on the earth surface. These terrestrial rivers, then, had a special place as finite anchors of what classicist James Romm describes as a vastitude marked by "a formlessness and diffusion that are the enemies of order and hierarchy."[4]

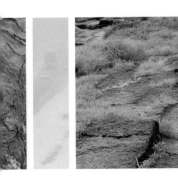

Today, Anaximander's lines, with attributes of form and scalability, in addition to separation, calibration, and containment, are everywhere in textbooks, folklore, histories, sciences, practices, rituals, policies, and conversations. When historians speak of benchmarks of human development such as agriculture, civilization, and the city emerging on the banks of rivers, they invoke these lines. When geographers describe a landmass drained by rivers, they draw these lines. When engineers devise embankments, dams, barrages, drains, diversions, and bridges, they work with these lines on the drawing board. When surveyors measure the length of a river, they draw its center line, thereby affirming the lines of its banks. When urban designers envision cities on rivers, they conceive the drawn line as a 'riverfront'. When ecologists speak of a watershed, they see lines gathering from multiple sources like branches of a tree and dispersing like roots into the sea, and when they speak of a riparian zone, they thicken these lines to be an interface between land and river. When scholars translate ancient texts or the spoken word, we dare say, they are already disposed to seeing a terrain marked by lines of flow. When activists, in their drive against displacement by dam projects or against pollution, speak of 'lifelines' to which so many disempowered people are bound, they are referring to the lines through which rivers are seen. And, of course, when people see flood, it is water transgressing these lines.

Indeed, not only are these lines everywhere, their presence is taken for granted as natural. Even flood does not erase their natural status. On the contrary, hydrologists consider flood a "naturally occurring, temporary inundation of normally dry land."[5] When floods have tragic consequences, as they often do, there is much reflection on the nature of the line, its strength, position, height, fixity, temporality, and its management system, but little

CHART of the RIVER GANGES from COLGONG to HURRISONKER.
Exhibiting the State of its Jalvals and Sands during the dry Season of 1796–7.
by B.H. Colebrooke, Esqr.

Heraclitus is well known for his 'river statement': "you could not step twice into the same river; for other waters are ever flowing on to you." The lesson in it, they say, is that change is in the nature of things, although some disagree. Few however question the existence of the line that he asks them to step across, a line dividing stationary land from moving water, *terra firma* from *aqua fluxus*.

if at all on its necessity. In fact, floods have tended to reinforce the line on the ground and in the imagination even as it has reinforced the belief that without their order there will be chaos, a belief best articulated by Niccolò Machiavelli in the 16th century. History, he writes, is "one of those ruinous rivers that, when they become enraged, flood the plains, tear down trees and buildings, taking up earth from one spot and placing it upon another; . . . But although they are of such a nature, it does not follow that when the weather is calm we cannot take precautions with embankments and dikes, so that when they rise up again either the waters will be channeled off or their impetus will not be either so unchecked or so damaging."[6]

There is much to admire in the lines that call out rivers. From their humble foundations in riverbanks, they reach up to hold lofty ideas like civilization and urbanization, but also earthy, taken-for-granted realities such as floods, watersheds, dams, and drains. But is it really chaos that lies beneath the lines of rivers? Or is it a competing belief, namely, that water is everywhere before it is somewhere: it is in rain before it is in rivers; it soaks, saturates, and evaporates before it flows? If so, then the lines of rivers are not universal, but rather products of a particular literacy through which water is read, written, and drawn on the earth's surface, on paper, and in the imagination. Perhaps it is time to ask if this literacy has run its course; and in a time when rivers are overdrawn, polluted, constrained, and the cause of increasing social and political conflict, not to mention floods, we need to take down the towering edifice of imagery, beliefs, policies and practices that have been built for over two millennia on river banks in order to make room for a terrain that can be engaged differently, such as with an appreciation of waters everywhere.

Waters are increasingly everywhere in defiance of being placed somewhere. In flood they cross a line or cannot find the space between lines meant or designed for them.

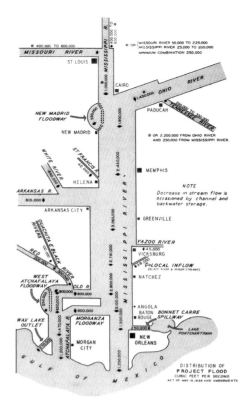

'Project Flood' of the US Army Corps of Engineers keeps the Mississippi in a path. It is an applied science by which the lines of a river are maintained with levees, revetments, riverfronts, and gates which upon occasion release water into wetlands or floodways. It is also a science by which the flows of a river are modified and managed by networks of canals, pipes, and drains.

There was always a suspicion among scholars in an academic tradition reaching back to the ancients that rain, or more broadly, precipitation is the primary if not only source of rivers. Rain, however, just did not seem adequate to the volume of water in rivers or as they saw it, rain was not enough to return water from the ends of rivers in the sea to their beginnings in mountains, for it was widely acknowledged, most famously in the Book of Ecclesiastes of the Bible, that "All streams flow into the sea, yet the sea is never full. To the place the streams come from, there they return again."[7] So a number of these scholars ventured another route through the earth. "Some think," wrote Seneca in the 1st century CE, "that the earth receives back whatever water it has emitted; and for this reason the oceans do not grow larger because they do not assimilate the water which flows into them but immediately returns it to the land. For, the water enters the land by hidden routes—openly it comes to the sea; secretly does it return. Sea water is filtered in transit because it is battered by the many circuitous passages in the earth and sets aside its salinity and impurities. In the many different types of soil it sheds its disagreeable taste and changes into fresh water."[8] How water rose through the earth occupied some great minds including Leonardo da Vinci and Athanasius Kircher. They considered water vaporizing and rising with heat inside the earth, circulating in the earth like blood in a human body, moved up by capillary action or the forces of celestial bodies and tides, and so on.

It took over two millennia for a 'proof' to emerge that could convince scientists of the adequacy of a route through the atmosphere. It was put forth by Pierre Perrault and confirmed soon after by Edme Mariotte in the late 1600s. They made the case that precipitation in the basin of the

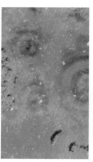

Seine was not only adequate to the flow in it, but that it was six to seven times the amount necessary, the rest going into the earth, consumed by organisms, or returned to the atmosphere. Their "true explanation" was so long coming, writes geologist Frank Dawson Adams because scholars "seeing the great volume of water which rivers bore to the sea, could not believe that the rainfall of the country was sufficient to supply so great a quantity of water. They did not know what vast expanses of the earth's surface were covered by the waters of the ocean, nor did they recognize how great a volume of water was raised from its surface by evaporation."[9]

But even as Perrault and Mariotte were 'proving' the adequacy of rain to rivers, they were also erasing rivers and the 'moment' of their supremacy. After all, precipitation defied not just the point-source and line-course of rivers by bringing in the complexities and temporalities of clouds among other things; it also challenged the land-water divide of the earth surface. It did so with precipitation falling somewhat indiscriminately and unpredictably in a moment when surveyors choose not to practice their art because precipitation confounds, even erases, the lines of separation between land and water and fuzzes the 'things' that they need to see and plot on the ground, such as rivers. Yet little has been done to erase the lines of rivers. On the contrary, they have been extended as if in an attempt to reach every point in a river's basin, making rivers seem more complex without changing the simplistic divided ground on which they are based. Perhaps too much is invested in riverbanks, in reinforcing them and their moment on the ground and in the imagination; or perhaps an alternative moment is yet to be articulated.

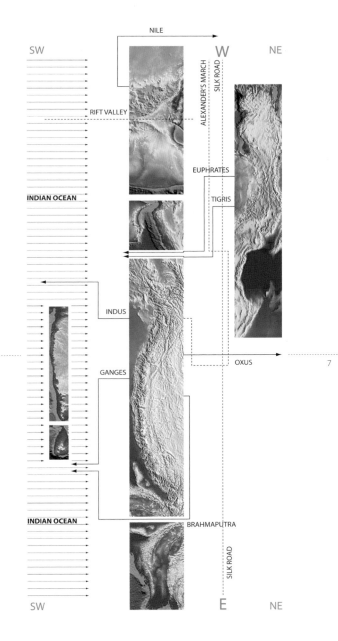

'Monsoon Frontier' is an alignment of high grounds from the Ethiopian mountains to the Chittagong Hills and beyond. It singles out the start of overflows of rain that arrive each year on the wind called the southwest monsoon, which extend from here in emergent and transfiguring, non-linear and field-like ways to reach various seas by a multiplicity of times, constituting grounds such as the Nile, Indus, and Ganga.

On the Deccan Plateau, in the interior of the Indian subcontinent, maps show large expanses of ground without rivers because it is believed that the ground is yet to form perceptible flows. Yet the Deccan Plateau need not be seen as a river landscape at all. It can be seen as a rain terrain where rain is impounded in ancient tanks with the help of bunds—earthen embankments built across swales.

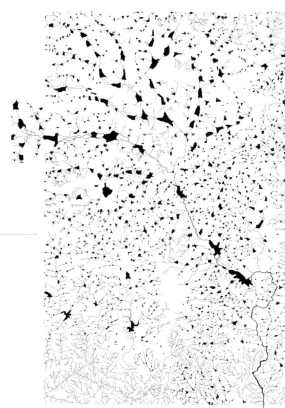

BUNDS: Earthen embankments built across swales

TANKS: Gatherings of rain and earth runoff

Rain does not flow; it rather overflows from one holding to a more extended one like a stain on a blotting paper.

One of many bunds that impound rain and earth runoff on the Deccan Plateau

What is it to construct a ground of design in a moment of rain before it appears as 'water' somewhere confined with lines? In other words, what is it to visualize and appreciate a 'rain terrain' in place of a 'river landscape'?

In a river landscape, rivers flow from a point source or sources to a sea or some other lower ground. If rain falls here, and even if it does so indiscriminately, it is still visualized for design purposes in channels however fine, intricate and extensive these channels be. In a rain terrain, on the other hand, rain does not flow; it overflows after being held where it falls in interstices, pores, fields, depressions, terraces, wells, snow fields, and glaciers, until it exceeds the capacity of that particular holding. It is then held again in a more extended realm, and so on, moving in emergent and transfiguring, non-linear and field-like ways that cannot be confined within lines as flows can. This is particularly the case given that overflows move not just in complex ways across the earth; they also move in complex times. The time of a holding varies from seconds and minutes to centuries and eons, and the pace by which an overflow extends depends on material conditions of the ground, but also on the multiplicity of overflows that rain initiates by falling everywhere. These overflows can overlap, intersect, and bypass in such volumes that at times they could easily appear more like a single flow than multiple overflows.

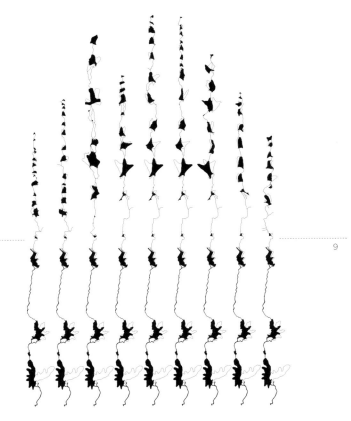

In a river landscape, people live on the banks of rivers; in a rain terrain, people live in overflows of rain. It is the basis of two infrastructures of settlement. Both these infrastructures were visible in 1927 when two grounds—levees and mounds—rose above the rains that gathered in the Lower Mississippi from multiple places across the continent and multiple times. Levees are linear embankments on either side of a flow, reinforcing the divide between water and land, confining the Mississippi to free land for settlement. Mounds on the other hand, are discrete masses of earth built by Native Americans in the centuries before the arrivals of European settlers in America. At first they may appear to confine settlement while letting the Mississippi run free. A closer reading, however, could suggest that they engage a different Mississippi all together; one that does not flood because it is not incarcerated to begin with.

OVERFLOWS: Structure a complex network of series and parallels

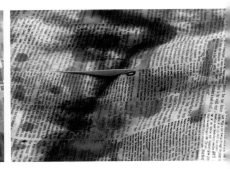

Rains on the west coast of India do not have the time to find the lines that surveyors draw as rivers. They meet the sea more as a layered depth than through channels, a depth marked by cultivations, mangroves, aquifers and backwaters. Maps over the centuries, however, have reduced this depth to a surficial line dividing land from water.

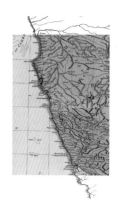

Mumbai is largely seen as an Island City on the west coast of India, drained by rivers and pipes. It is an urban image 'disturbed' by 'informal settlements' that violate lines of urbanity, including the lines of rivers and the coast. The image is also disturbed each year by rains of the southwest monsoon such as those of July 2005, when 3 feet of rain fell in 24 hours causing death and much destruction. To engineers this event posed a problem seen on the basis of probability as rare and solved by improving the carrying capacity of rivers and drains by a calculated amount. In a rain terrain, though, this was not a probable event but a possible one in a place where rain is not a visitor but a resident. Here, rain is held rather than drained. This Mumbai is not a settlement predisposed to lines that divide land from water in plan, but a field of anchors that accommodate fluctuations of the monsoon and sea in section.

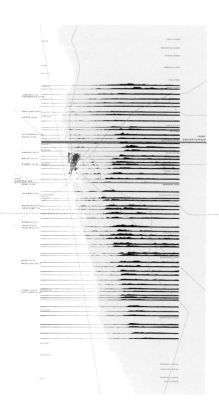

Waters can be everywhere by design as they once were in the Lower Mississippi, Egypt, India, and elsewhere. Here, people built mounds that rose above overflows of rain rather than settlements on the banks of rivers, engaging a ground in section rather than in plan, with an appreciation for horizon rather than lines of separation. Is it possible that what scholars see and students learn as 'ancient river civilizations' are instead 'rain cultures', including Egypt where the Nile gathers, extends, and facilitates overflows of rain that fall elsewhere?

ANURADHA MATHUR / DILIP DA CUNHA_WATERS EVERYWHERE

Another way to see the difference between mounds and levees is that the former assumes a risen Mississippi to be its natural state while the latter takes a fallen Mississippi to be a natural ground. Herodotus saw the first at work in ancient Egypt, a country reached by overflows of rain from far south, particularly from the Ethiopian highlands during the time of the southwest monsoons. In this period, he observes, "the towns, which alone remain above water, look like the islands in the Aegean" and operated as a network that reached "all over the country, instead of merely along the course of the river."[10]

To him, this was the "natural state" of Egypt when overflows constituted rather than flooded a country and the Nile was coterminous with Egypt.[11] A century later Alexander found the same to be the case with the Indus, a name that derives from the Sanskrit word, Sindhu, meaning Ocean. Here, as in Egypt, numerous settlements on constructed high grounds offered him anchors in the construction of an empire that was less a territory and more a network of relations in an open ocean.

Yet today, the Nile and Indus like the Mississippi are appreciated as channels of water rather than oceans of rain. It is a visualization that encourages not just an infrastructure of divisive and defensive embankments, riverfronts, dams, and floodways, but also of 'drains'. Rivers, it is accepted, drain the land and with settlement located on this land, it is not surprising that rivers have become the drains of settlement, some polluted to the extent that the World Wildlife Fund enlists rivers as an endangered species. In a rain terrain that is ocean-like, settlements are not drained; they are rather soaked, calling for an infrastructure that holds their output as it does rain, which is where it falls.

A rain terrain then puts forward another moment of the 'natural state', a moment in which we do not just see nature differently, but see a different nature. It is a moment that actively counters the time of rivers and with it the regime of the drawn line that separates, calibrates, and contains water to a flow and to flood. Today, this moment is an opportune one given not just the problems faced and caused by rivers but also the new appreciation for rain in places where it falls. This appreciation can be the basis of more than 'rainwater harvesting'; it can be the basis of an eye and imagination that 'sees' waters everywhere before they are placed somewhere.

LINDSAY BREMNER
MUDDY LOGICS

THE SUNDARBAN REGION OF WEST BENGAL AND THE DELTA ISLANDS OF SOUTHERN BANGLADESH IS A CONSTANTLY MUTATING ZONE BETWEEN LAND AND SEA, WHERE THE FRESHWATER PLUMES OF THE GANGES, BRAHMAPUTRA, AND MEGHNA RIVERS DEPOSIT THEIR SILT AND INTERACT WITH THE SALINE WATER OF THE BAY OF BENGAL. IT HAS EVOLVED OVER MILLENNIA THROUGH THE NATURAL DEPOSITION OF UPSTREAM SEDIMENTS AND INTERTIDAL SEGREGATION, STABILIZED BY THE ROOTS OF THE LARGEST HALOPHYTIC MANGROVE FOREST IN THE WORLD.[1] NEITHER LIQUID NOR SOLID, THE ORGANIZATION OF THIS FLUID ARCHIPELAGO IS AN ANTI-PATTERN: UNDIFFERENTIATED, OOZY, SQUELCHY, MATERIALIZING AND DEMATERIALIZING IN AN ONGOING PROCESS OF DEPOSITION, ACCUMULATION, STABILIZATION, EROSION, EBB AND FLOW. THIS VERY ANTI-PATTERN PROVIDES A SLUDGY, PROTECTIVE BARRIER TO THE INTENSELY CULTIVATED AND POPULATED LANDS OF KOLKATA, INDIA'S THIRD LARGEST METROPOLIS, AND DHAKA, BANGLADESH'S CAPITAL, BEYOND. AMPHIBIOUS, DISPOSABLE, AND EXPEDIENT, ITS MUDDY LOGICS OFFER STRATEGIES OF BOTH INCORPORATION INTO AND RESISTANCE AGAINST FORCES OF GLOBALIZATION IN TODAY'S WORLD.

FOLDED OCEAN: The Indian Ocean is almost symmetrical about a north south axis running down the length of the Maldives' archipelago. If the ocean is folded about this axis, a number of cities map more or less onto one another. Dubai (United Arab Emirates) folds onto Kolkata (India) along the Tropic of Cancer, Mogadishu (Somalia) onto Singapore along the equator, and Durban (South Africa) onto Perth (Australia) along the Tropic of Capricorn. These cities mark the symbolic geographic extremities of the Ocean. At its central point lies Diego Garcia (British Indian Ocean Territory), which, as Malta is to the Mediterranean, is equidistant from all points. This portrait of the Ocean as figure, not void, de-continentalizes space, de-nationalizes territory and brings the Ocean into view as a hyper-connected global region.

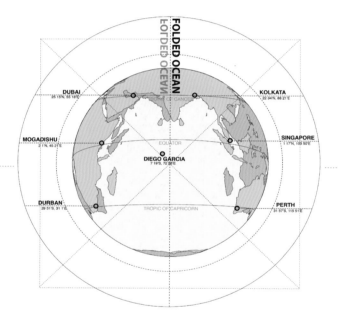

BEACHED

One of the slippery questions for the global shipping industry is how one defines and what one does with waste. Under the Basel Convention of 1992, it is illegal for developed countries to export hazardous waste to developing countries. End of life ships are considered hazardous waste because of the asbestos, oily wastes, polychlorinated biphenyls (PCB's), and toxic paints they contain. Selling ships to be broken without decontaminating them is a form of toxic dumping. What this has meant is that shipbreaking today is conducted via protocols of deception, back room deals, front companies, decoys, and middlemen in networks that span the globe to avoid the cost of compliance with the principle of polluter pays.

Until the late 1970s, shipbreaking was done in the dockyards of Europe, the United States, and Japan. It was a highly mechanized operation. But as environmental standards and health and safety requirements increased, the costs of scrapping began to escalate. As a result, approximately 90 percent of the shipbreaking industry moved, firstly to Korea and Taiwan,[2] and then to India, Bangladesh, China, Pakistan and Turkey,[3] poor nations with seemingly endless supplies of exploitable labor and lax environmental and safety regulations.

The South East Asian industry began at Gadani Beach in Pakistan prior to that country's independence in 1947.[4] It was the largest shipbreaking site in the world until 1983, when it was surpassed by the yards at Alang in Gujarat, India, currently still the largest shipbreaking site in the

world. In Bangladesh, the practice began by accident in 1960, when a twenty thousand ton vessel was beached by a tidal wave at Bhatiari, just north of Chittagong on the Bay of Bengal. The ship could not be refloated and four years later was bought by the Chittagong Steel House and scrapped. In 1971, during the Bangladesh liberation war, a Pakistani ship damaged by bombing was brought to the shore and three years later bought and scrapped by the Karnafully Metal Works.[5] This is considered the beginning of commercial shipbreaking in Bangladesh. Today, twenty ship breaking yards run by sixty eight enterprises occupy a five-mile stretch of the beach.[6] It is the largest facility for large vessels in the world, scrapping some 52 percent of all vessels above two hundred thousand deadweight tons. The large tidal difference of twenty feet provides an ideal intertidal zone for beaching these large ships.[7]

In 1998, the Clinton Administration called for a moratorium on sending United States government ships to the South Asian shipbreaking yards after a report by the *Baltimore Sun* on conditions in Alang, India.[8] In August 2009, under Obama's watch, two ships, the SS Anders (formerly the SS James Anderson) and the SS Bonny (formerly the SS Alex Bonnyman), left the United States, officially destined for Santos in Brazil. In January 2010, one of them surfaced in Pakistan, raising suspicions that they had been sold as scrap, in violation not only of International Conventions, but also of United States law.[9]

By the time ships are rammed into a beach in a ship-breaking yard in South East Asia, they are not ships any longer, nor even waste. They are raw material, unnatural resources, to be mined, dismantled, sold, re-rolled, and redistributed. In Bangladesh, this provides 50 percent of the steel used in its construction industry, as well as the fittings, utensils, sanitary ware, linen, etc. that furnish Bangladeshi homes and businesses.[10] And on the beach just north of Chittagong, a new, provisional post-urban assemblage has taken shape. This has transformed the coastline into a frictional zone where the murkiness of a sea-based economy meets an even more squelchy land-based one characterized by overlapping administrative jurisdictions, military and business collusions, nimble agents, middlemen, decoys, and graft.

Bhatiari is described as the "hidden, green paradise of Chittagong,"[11] owing this reputation to its recreational lake in the forested hills above the Bay of Bengal. It lies in the Sitakunda Upazila, one of the oldest sites of human habitation in Bangladesh, known for its Islamic, Hindu and Buddhist shrines.[12] Local inhabitants have tradition-ally worked in agriculture and fishing and more recently in commerce and the service economy.[13] It also boasts the Bangladesh Military Academy, the Faujdarhat Cadet College, a military sponsored golf and country club, the Chittagong University Campus and a middle-income residential township laid by the Chittagong Housing Au-thority in the late nineteen eighties.[14]

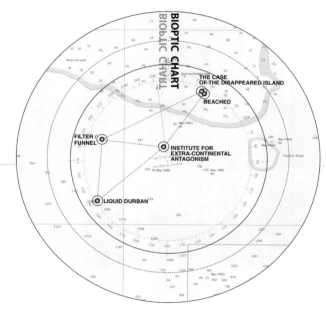

BIOPTIC CHART: This essay is a component of ongoing research into sites in or around the Indian Ocean exhibiting features of rapid change. These are read as clues to global, trans-national or multi-polar realignments and investigated as sites for architectural thought and speculation. As sites are accumulated, they construct a Bioptic Chart of the Ocean; bioptic because it privileges the sample for diagnostic purposes and chart because it serves as an instrument for the navigation of fluid territory.

SS JAMES
SS ALEX BONNYMAN

Between the hills and the sea, into this already charged landscape, ship breaking has injected a new anti-ecology. Tightly guarded, highly concealed tracks lead from the highway to the shipbreaking yards through fenced workers compounds, residual farmlands and stagnant water ponds. Seething ribbons of flotsam, piled high along roads to optimize visibility and floating in waterways, are stacked in yards and left to seep into ground water and fishing areas. Here, the more than one hundred thousand individuals who earn their livelihoods from the scrapping of vessels,[15] mostly recruited from the villages of northern Bangladesh,[16] crowd into makeshift shelters. In more than four hundred nearby steel mills, steel plate is smelted down, reformed, re-rolled, and resold. The highway is clogged with trucks, bicycles, taxis, tuk-tuks, motorbikes, cars and all kinds of makeshift vehicles transporting goods away.

All of this takes place on land which is state owned. Shipbreakers lease their land from the government, subject to an application procedure handled by the Bangladesh Mercantile Marine Department, and administered by the Chittagong Port Authority; leases for adjacent inland areas are dealt with by the Bangladesh Inland Water Transport Authority (BIWTA); environmental matters associated with shipbreaking are under the jurisdiction of the Department of the Environment; import of vessels to Bangladesh for breaking is subjected to yet another governmental authorization procedure, this time from the Department of Commerce—all multiple squelchy, opaque jurisdictions that increase inscrutability and multiply opportunities for gain.[17]

1980 **Odense Denmark**
— Built as commercial cargo ships
— Imported by the USA

1982 **Delaware USA**
— Owned by Wilmington Trust Corp
— Converted for use by the Military
  Sealift Command [MSC]

1985 **Diego Garcia**
— Stationed to support USA military
— Operated by shipping company
  Maersk for 24 years
— MSC charter terminated
— Wilmington Trust Corp sells ships
  to Star Maritime Corp

2009 **Leaves USA destined for Santos, Brazil**
— Purchased by Mr. Mohammed
  Tahir Lakhani
— Sold to Mr. Haji Lokman Hossain
— Reflagged under the
  Caribbean nation of St. Kitts
— Renamed SS Anders and SS Bonny

2010 **Pakistan**
— Resurfaces in South Asian scrapyard

17

The pattern of human settlement that has taken shape confounds accepted typologies or morphologies. It is both a productive landscape and a site of cultural transfer, weaving bits and pieces of ships into the cities, towns, and villages of Bangladesh and beyond. It has reversed the direction of flow of the nineteenth century imperial formations (raw material from the colonies, production in the metropolitan center). Its model is not the factory town of the United Kingdom nor the plantations of the United States, but something very particular to the Indian Ocean itself, drawing on the deep archive of muddy logics through which people have put the ocean and its deposits to work for centuries.

Clues to this condition and the challenges it presents can be found in the architectures of software design, in particular those known as Big Balls of Mud.[18] These are software systems that survive precisely because of their lack of hierarchy or overall structure—"haphazardly structured, sprawling, sloppy, duct-tape and bailing wire, spa-

ghetti code jungles."[19] They often emerge in the software design world from throw away codes, devised expediently in response to market demands or time constraints and never intended for permanent use, but which are then modified as conditions change. They evolve through patch after patch at the hands of multiple maintainers, each of whom tinker about, caring little about the consequences of what he or she is doing or how it might impact on the next. Over time, such processes become Big Balls of Mud: working systems without regulation, which have eroded and accreted unregulated growth and repeated, expedient repair.

It is precisely this lack of differentiation, hierarchy, structure or consequence that makes Big Balls of Mud work. They facilitate economies of speed and rapid change, protecting against market fluctuations and managing risk. Their lack, or rather minimal reliance on overall infrastructure, co-ordination or capital investment, means that they can nimbly adapt to change. They rely on homeostasis and retrospective feedback rather than prediction. They de-emphasize planning and upfront design for feedback and integration.

In the face of the agile inscrutability of such muddy logics, what might design do? Foote and Yoder argue that there are ways to improve the functionality and durability of such systems, given that their inbuilt stickiness tends to become a quagmire.[20] There are ways to cultivate them as they evolve. This is not through "rigid, totalitarian, top-down design,"[21] but through the kind of small, incremental transformations that produced the undifferentiated structure in the first place. This is known in software design as refactoring or making tiny changes to a computer program's source code to improve its functionality. The cure for Big Balls of Mud is "flexible, adaptive feedback driven development"[22] that adapts internal and external forces to one another over time. There is no reason why these cannot incorporate demands for social

and environmental justice as well as supply chains and markets. Key to this however is a measure of enhanced scrutability to enable the identification of patterns, the establishment of frameworks, interfaces, and protocols, the introduction of new components, and, in some cases, the isolation and complete refurbishment of irreparable parts of the system.

This might offer a way forward to the challenges and opportunities presented to activists, designers, environmentalists, and urbanists by the shipbreaking yards of South East Asia. If understood as Big Balls of Mud, their multiple resources (natural, social, political, economic), multiple scales (from the hand held to the global), and multiple ecologies (human and non-human), might be able to be refactored into more resilient and equitable interfaces for today's contingent, open-ended, promiscuous world.

Since 2003, the Bangladesh Environmental Lawyers' Association (BELA), an activist group of lawyers, has been putting this to the test.[23] They have filed a number of petitions in the Bangladesh Supreme Court against shipyard owners and factory inspectors, on grounds that they violate Bangladeshi environmental and labor law.[24] Ship breakers are also in violation of the Basel Convention, to which Bangladesh is a signatory. As a direct consequence of shipbreaking activities, heavy metals (lead, cadmium, arsenic, zinc, and chromium) and a range of other hazardous wastes (PCB's, asbestos and oil) fly around in the air and seep into ground water, causing coastal destruction and long-term damage to people, wildlife, beaches, and the marine environment.[25]

In bringing actions against these conditions to court, BELA exposed the shipbreaking yards as collusions between state and non-state actors, where the state had given itself permission to break its own rules. As a result of their actions, the Bangladesh Supreme Court has issued a number of rulings to the effect that no ships can be broken without pre-cleaning outside Bangladesh, and that shipyard owners should comply with the country's labor laws, failing which they will be closed down.[26] But, despite a high-powered committee being set up to monitor ship breaking in January 2010, it is still business as usual. Shipyard owners have not abided by the rulings and the state has not closed them down. Owners argue that adherence to environmental and labor laws will make the industry unprofitable. Even if profit were the only criteria here, current profitability levels of 16 percent indicate that there is scope for reorganizing the industry without damaging its overall competitiveness.[27] On February 17, 2011, shipbreaking was recognized as an industry by the Bangladesh government for the first time, partly in response to its staggering growth since 2008.[28] This formalized its contribution to Bangladesh's economy, increased scrutability, and presented new possibilities for its restructuring. Whether it will provide a mechanism to finally begin to penetrate its mirky dealings remains to be seen.

This is however going to require of legislators and activists, scientists and intellectuals, urbanists and designers, humans and non-humans, an agility and a vigilance that records, monitors, keeps track of, stirs up, speaks up for, infiltrates, pokes holes in, calls the bluff of, etc. to bring about the changes needed to transform the shipbreaking yards from living hells into, if not living heavens, robust, resilient, civic places. Reliance on modernist institutions and modes of political action is not going to be up to the game. I have a feeling that it will be the catastrophic action of a non-human actor of the kind that initiated shipbreaking in Bangladesh that will cause such havoc as to either bring about the end of shipbreaking on the beaches of Chittagong, or cause it to stop in its tracks and put itself together in new ways. I do not think we, as designers and spatial practitioners, can wait for this to happen. We should imagine and project, into the muddy logics of contemporary shipbreaking, strategic, opportunistic institutions and infrastructures that take the ocean, the atmosphere, the beach and human suffering into its calculations, to redistribute its powers and construct resilient interfaces between land, sea, metal, flesh, worms, crabs, and algae.

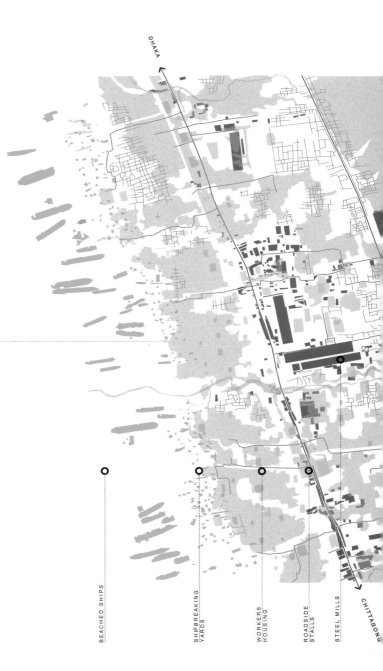

TEDDY CRUZ
THE POLITICAL EQUATOR

IT IS OBVIOUS BY NOW THAT THE CELEBRATED METROPOLITAN
EXPLOSION OF THE LAST YEARS OF ECONOMIC BOOM ALSO PRODUCED, IN TANDEM,
A DRAMATIC PROJECT OF MARGINALIZATION, RESULTING IN THE UNPRECEDENTED
GROWTH OF SLUMS SURROUNDING MAJOR URBAN CENTERS, EXACERBATING THE
SOCIO-ECONOMIC AND DEMOGRAPHIC CONFLICTS OF AN UNEVEN URBANIZATION,
AN URBAN ASYMMETRY WHICH IS AT THE CENTER OF TODAY'S CRISES. NOWHERE IS
THIS ASYMMETRY MORE AMPLIFIED AND PHYSICALLY INSCRIBED THAN IN REGIONAL
JUNCTURES SUCH AS THE SAN DIEGO-TIJUANA BORDER TERRITORY, PRODUCING,
IN TURN, LOCAL ZONES OF CONFLICT. THESE GEOGRAPHIES OF CONFLICT SERVE AS
COMPLEX ENVIRONMENTS FROM WHICH TO RE-CONTEXTUALIZE GLOBALIZATION
BY ENGAGING THE SPECIFICITY OF THE POLITICAL INSCRIBED IN THESE PHYSICAL
TERRITORIES, A RADICALIZATION OF THE LOCAL. THEREFORE, THIS BORDER
REGION HAS BEEN ONE OF THE MOST PRODUCTIVE ZONES FOR MY RESEARCH
IN THE LAST YEARS. IT REVEALS THE CONDITIONS THAT HAVE PRODUCED THE
CURRENT UNIVERSAL INSTITUTIONAL CRISIS, WHILE CONSTRUCTING A PRACTICE
OF INTERVENTION THAT ENGAGES THE SPATIAL, TERRITORIAL AND ENVIRONMENTAL
CONDITIONS ACROSS CRITICAL THRESHOLDS — WHETHER GLOBAL BORDER ZONES
OR THE LOCAL SECTORS OF CONFLICT GENERATED BY DISCRIMINATING POLITICS OF
ZONING AND ECONOMIC DEVELOPMENT.

US-MEXICO WATERSHEDS

SAN DIEGO-TIJUANA WATERSHED

SAN YSIDRO-LAURELES CANYON

DRAIN BORDER CROSSING

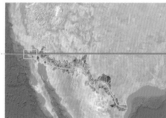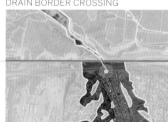

24

The forces of control across the San Diego–Tijuana border, the most trafficked checkpoint in the world, have provoked the small border neighborhoods that surround it to construct alternative urbanisms of alteration and adaptation, generating, in turn, invisible trans-border flows. These flows are physically manifested by the informal land use patterns and economies produced by migrant workers flowing from Tijuana into San Diego, altering the homogeneity of San Diego's neighborhoods. In the opposite direction is the 'infrastructural waste' moving into Tijuana, where the urban waste of San Diego is recycled to construct an insurgent urbanism of emergency across the many slums on its periphery. This double urbanization of retrofit by which the recycling of fragments, resources, and situations from these two cities can trigger different meanings for urban policy, housing, and public infrastructure. While the global city has become the privileged site of economic consumption and display in the last years, these local neighborhoods in the margins remain sites of cultural production.

THE POLITICAL EQUATOR: A point of entry into radical localities, marginal communities, and contentious neighborhoods around the world.

35°

30°

25

Seeking to problematize these local-global correspondences and further engage jurisdictional and environmental conflict as an operational artistic tool, I coined the Political Equator as a practice diagram. It contextualizes my work at the Tijuana–San Diego border in relationship to other global zones of conflict, tracing an imaginary line along the US–Mexico border and extending it across a world atlas. It forms a corridor of global conflict between the 30 and 35 degrees North Parallels. Along this corridor lie some of the world's most contested thresholds. Besides the US–Mexico border, which is the most intensified portal for immigration from Latin America to the United States, there is the Strait of Gibraltar, where waves of migration flow from North Africa into Europe, and the Israeli–Palestinian border that divides the Middle East.

But this global border is ultimately not a 'flat line' but an operative critical threshold that bends, fragments, and

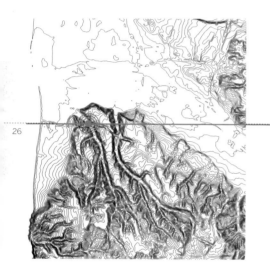

10:40

JUNE 3, 2011

POLITICAL EQUATOR 3: BORDER-DRAIN-CROSSING
Political Equator 3 took place on June 3-4 of 2011. This time, the audience oscillated between two marginal neighborhoods on either side of the San Diego–Tijuana border fence. These communities, which flank the checkpoint and are adjacent to a US protected estuary, now layered with home-land security and militarization, were represented by their local community-based NGO's with whom I collaborate: Casa Familiar in San Ysidro, on the US side, and Alter Terra in Laureles Canyon in Mexico.

10:42

26

stretches in order to reveal other sites of conflict worldwide where invisible trans-hemispheric sociopolitical, economic, and environmental crises are manifested at regional and local scales. The Political Equator has been our point of entry into many of these radical localities where there is a need to imagine new forms of governance and urbanization. There is also the need to argue that the most relevant projects forwarding inclusion and artistic experimentation will not emerge from sites of economic abundance but from sites of scarcity, in the midst of conflicts across geopolitical borders, for natural resources and within marginal communities.

Political Equator Meetings take the form of nomadic urban actions and debates involving the public and communities, oscillating across diverse sites and stations between

Tijuana and San Diego. These conversations on the move, outside institutions, and inside actual sites of conflict, enable the audience to be both witness and participant. The meetings typically unfold around a series of public works, performances, and walks that traverse these conflicting territories and serve as evidenciary platforms to contextualize conversations among diverse publics.

Political Equator Meetings also take the form of an urban-pedagogical research project, producing corridors of knowledge-exchange that link the specialized knowledge of institutions and the political intelligence and activism embedded within communities. This implies opening the conference format as an experimental platform, researching new forms of knowledge, pedagogy, and public participation.

 ARGENTINA

 MEXICO

 U.S.

 COLOMBIA

 BRITAIN

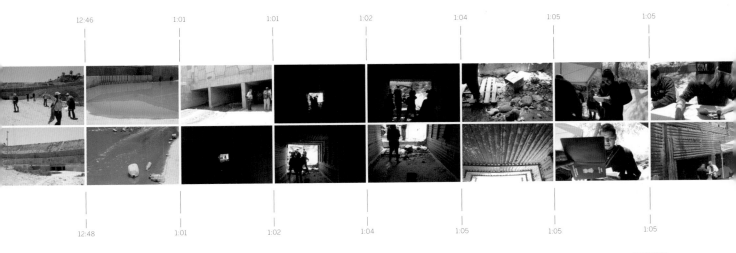

The most emblematic public action during the trajectory of PE3 was an unprecedented public border crossing through an existing drain, recently built by Home Land Security, enabling the participants to slip uninterrupted from San Diego into Tijuana, i.e., from the Tijuana River Estuary, an environmentally sensitive zone on the US side, into Los Laureles Canyon, a slum home to approximately 85,000 people that crashes against the fence on the Mexico side. This drain is a byproduct of a new highway constructed for surveillance that runs parallel to the border wall along a 150 feet wide linear corridor that Home Land Security claimed as its jurisdiction after 9-11. Along this corridor, Border Patrol has been systematically building a series of dirt-dams that truncate the many canyons that are part of the trans-border watershed system.

 AUSTRIA

 INDIA

 GERMANY

 PALESTINE

 ITALY

The public action took place inside this site of exception as we sought to encroach into official institutional protocols and zones. We made the drain a temporary yet official port of entry. This act of crossing resulted from a long process of discussion and negotiation with both Home Land Security and Mexican Immigration who understood this act as an artistic performance even if they perhaps recognized that this crossing would enable the

INFORMAL BORDER-
DRAIN-CROSSING

US / SAN DIEGO

MEXICO / TIJUANA

1:05   1:05   1:07

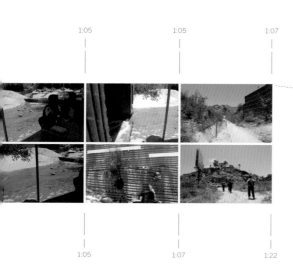

1:05   1:07   1:22

visualization of the collision between estuary, surveillance infrastructure, and informal settlement.

As the participants moved Southbound against the natural flow of wastewater coming from the slum and contaminating the San Diego estuary, they reached the Mexican Immigration officers who had set a provisional tent on the South side of the drain inside Mexican territory, adjacent to the flowing murky water. The juxtaposition of pollution, the stamping of passports inside this liminal zone, and the passage from pristine Estuary to Slum under a culvert amplified the contradictions between national security, environmentalism, and citizenship.

The renewed investment in surveillance infrastructure along the US-Mexico border in the last years has further marginalized the communities adjacent to the border fence even as it has compromised the trans-border watershed systems. By enabling the physical passage across this odd territory, Political Equator 3 not only exposed the dramatic collision between informal urbanization, militarization, and estuary, it also articulated the urgency for strategies of co-existence: Can the Mexican Informal Settlement be the Protector of the Tijuana River Estuary in the US? Can waste and water, which inevitably transgress the border despite the monumental infrastructure we construct, be the starting point of a designed co-existence?

PLASTIC BOTTLES
SODA CANS
TIRES
CIGARETTE CARTONS
STYROFOAM
FIVE GALLON BUCKETS
PLASTIC COMBS
FOOD COOLERS

TIRE EMBANKMENT
CLOTHES LINE
SHELTER
WATER CONTAINER

The need to re-imagine the border through the logic of shared natural and social systems is the foremost challenge for the future of this bi-national region and of many other border regions across the globe. A community is always in dialogue with its immediate social and ecological environment; this is what defines its political nature. But when this relationship is disrupted and a community's productive capacity splintered by the very way in which jurisdictional power is instituted, it is necessary to find a means of recuperating its agency.

NATALY GATTEGNO
AQUEOUS TERRITORIES

WHAT COULD BE SIMPLY TERMED 'WATER' IS MUCH MORE COMPLEX AND SIGNALS MULTIPLE OPPORTUNITIES FOR DESIGN: FOG, ICE, RAIN, GLACIERS, STEAM, VAPOR—TO NAME A FEW—ARE TRIGGERS FOR DESIGN RESPONSES THAT PUSH FORM AND SPACE-MAKING INTO TERRITORIES THAT MAY SEEM UNFAMILIAR. THE PHASE CHANGES OF H_2O BECOME OPPORTUNITIES FOR MULTI-SCALAR APPROACHES. AQUEOUS TERRITORIES ARE VOLATILE, CHANGEABLE, AND EVOLVE OVER TIME IN WAYS THAT NECESSITATE METHODOLOGIES THAT QUESTION THE BOUNDARIES OF CONVENTIONAL DESIGN PROCESSES. THEY ENABLE US TO OPERATE IN FERTILE AND DYNAMIC TERRITORIES THAT ARE FUNDAMENTALLY TRANSFORMATIVE. FAR FROM SIMPLE REACTIVE DESIGN PROCESSES THAT MITIGATE AND FORTIFY AGAINST CHANGE AND TRANSFORMATION, THE WORK PRESENTED HERE EXPLORES THESE ACTIVE TERRITORIES AS FERTILE LANDSCAPES TO TEST ALTERNATIVE METHODS OF DESIGNING AND OPERATING IN OUR VOLATILE ENVIRONMENTS. THESE TERRITORIES ARE CAPABLE OF GENERATING FORM AND GUIDING DESIGN WITH THE ENVIRONMENT AS AN ACTIVE PARTICIPANT IN THE PROCESS.

The projects presented take on multiple forms and scales of 'water': Aurora questions the permanence and embraces the fluidity and elusiveness of ice; the Glaciarium addresses a more intimate and destructive relationship between humans and the polar regions; while Hydramax speculates and develops an urban machine that sees in water and fog productive and vital ingredients for human survival. These projects describe alternative ways of dynamically responding to the material, ephemeral, and productive opportunities of harnessing and containing water at multiple scales. They are characterized by temporality, fluidity, the possibility of open-ended performance, and unknown spatial opportunities and juxtapositions.

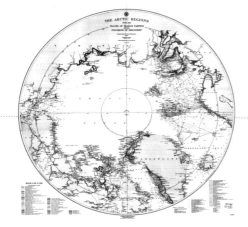

US NAVY, "THE ARCTIC REGIONS WITH THE TRACKS OF SEARCH PARTIES AND THE PROGRESS OF DISCOVERY" [1896]

Terra Incognita grapples with a seemingly simple question: how to represent something that is constantly changing and moving—the Arctic ice shelf. What are the representational opportunities for territories that are in constant flux? In the case of the Arctic ice shelf, the fluctuation is both geographic and material: edges dissipate, solid ground is elusive, and geographical markers gradually shift.

Ancient explorers were the first to contemplate the difficulties of navigating and mapping waters that were changing in both consistency and navigability. In search of the North Pole and the Northeast Passage, they trekked through landscapes that would be solid at one time and viscous at another. Early maps of the Arctic region were creative fictions at best: not only were things exaggerated, but entire regions were invented, marked as 'unknown territory'—terra incognita.

Pytheas, one of the first documented explorers of the polar region, described the limitations of static cartography in his account of his explorations: 'Those places where land properly speaking no longer exists, nor sea nor air, but a mixture of these things... in which it is said that earth and water and all things are in suspension... on which one can neither walk nor sail.'[1]

Terra Incognita is a collection of both historic and contemporary maps of the Arctic. The historic maps describe a process of discovery and speculation about a territory so different than anything previously seen, while the contemporary maps describe a territory that has been harnessed, monitored, measured, and controlled. The Arctic is currently one of the most well documented environments on our planet. Rigged, surveyed, and transmitting, the Arctic is constantly feeding us information, yet it is still plagued by some of the same issues that historic mapmakers confronted: territories are disputed, buoys drift and move with the ice floes, while the precise extents of the receding ice shelf have been the source of public debate.

32

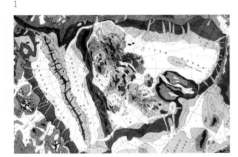

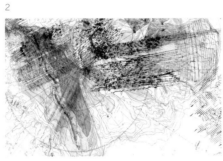

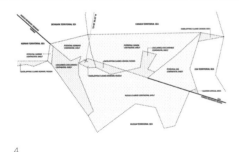

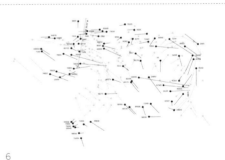

1. GEOLOGICAL DEPOSITS
2. ELECTROMAGNETIC FIELD ANOMALIES
3. SEISMIC EPICENTERS
4. DISPUTED TERRITORIES
5. ICE SHELF BOUNDARY, 1987–2007
6. THREE-DAY ARCTIC BUOY PATH

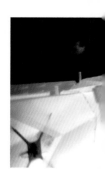

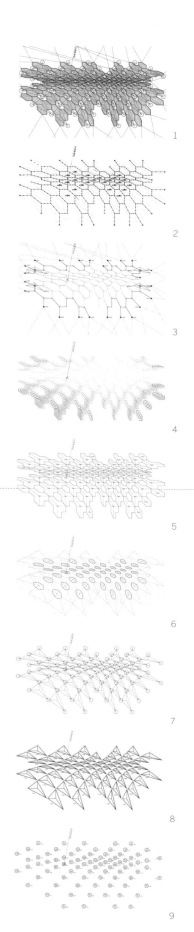

1

2

3

4

5

6

7

8

9

AURORA

Aurora leverages the plethora of information available on the Arctic territory and superimposes that information with the dynamic behavior of multiple users. The surface essentially becomes a lofted piece of ice that has embedded in it bathymetry, salinity, ice age, and ice extent datasets. The elusiveness of these datasets is reinforced by the transparency and fragility of the materials used, as well as the interactive qualities of the model. The surface is brightly lit when left undisturbed, but once triggered by the audience, the embedded LEDs dim and a series of blue cold cathode tubes shimmer in the middle of the surface. Instead of performing for its audience, Aurora retreats when triggered. Though attracted to interact with the model, the audience is ultimately responsible for the degradation of the system.

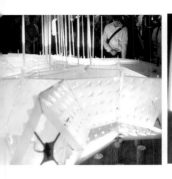
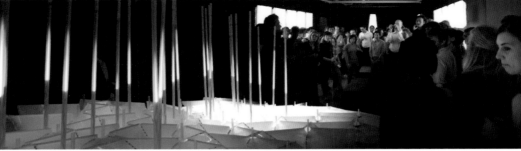

AURORA WAS CONSTRUCTED AS A SERIES OF LAYERS:

1. INAUGURATE: 86 plaster cast buoys were poured in sequence into one of four reusable molds. Each pour had a varying degree of white and black plaster denoting the Arctic Ocean's topography.

2. ARRAY: An array of stainless steel wire towers was soldered to parametric specifications. This highly customized structural system transferred load from the suspended surface above to the cast buoys below.

3. NETWORK: The system of buoys and wire towers interlocked in a way that structurally networked the base.

4. INTERMESH: The surface geometry was the result of a deformed grid yielding a gradient of hexagons. The hexagonal distribution, density, and depth were controlled by a Grasshopper model and adapted to geometries of information from the Arctic region.

5. VARIEGATE: Each hexagon was described by three modules fabricated from PETG plastic. These were laser cut, individually folded, hand sewn, and embedded with a string of LEDs.

6. PERFORATE: Once aggregated, the surface perforations were folded revealing a gradient of porosity: solid in the middle where the surface was densest and deepest; lace like at the edges where the surface was thinnest.

7. SENSE: The surface was networked through a series of embedded edge sensors. These were triggered by the proximity of the visitor and the degree of interaction.

8. ACTUATE: The edge sensors signaled the embedded LEDs and the CRT light field above the surface.

9. SYNTHESIZE: A thickened surface was generated once all the layers were aggregated. The ephemeral effects of the light field shifted one's position from viewer to participant, revealing the consequences of one's individual and collective actions in real time.

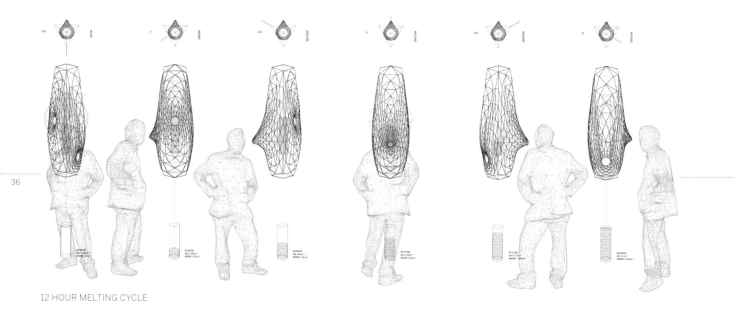

12 HOUR MELTING CYCLE

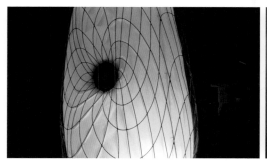

GLACIARIUM

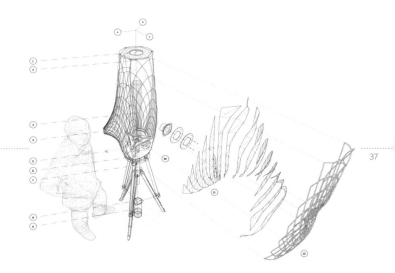

The Glaciarium focuses on an individual's experience of ice melting over time. Taking cues from the ways we currently document, store, and archive ice core samples, the Glaciarium contains a core of ice that melts over time. A much smaller interactive instrument, the Glaciarium engages a smaller group of users' senses through the sight and sound of melting ice. The influence of the individual viewer is linked directly to the materiality and sensation of the project. Increased observation amplifies the internal lighting effects and, depending on the duration of interaction, dramatically accelerates the melting of the ice core, transmitting the sound of melting ice into the space and rendering the environmental degradation visceral and real.

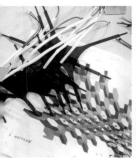

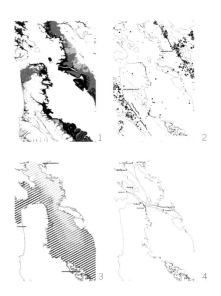

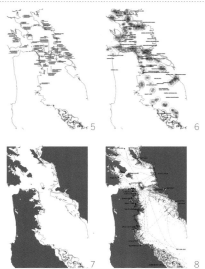

Hydramax speculates on the opportunities of directly harnessing our aqueous environment to develop hybrid spatial and productive strategies. After decades of fortifying its edges against sea level rise and the imminent possibility of liquefaction, San Francisco allows the urban waterfront to become a marshland again. What was once established as a hard and impermeable edge has mutated into a soft and productive territory. The Embarcadero has been eradicated and the primary means of transportation has once again become the water.

A series of radical new machinic structures have emerged at the water's edge serving as infrastructural and ecological hubs connecting the city to the wider Bay Area through water. These fuzzy pier-like constructions have transformed the waterfront into a vibrant network of aquatic parks, community gardens, wildlife refuges, and aquaponic farms. The edge of San Francisco is now an interconnected series of recreation spaces, productive landscapes, and water-based industries.

Hydramax is a synthetic construction that blurs the distinction between building, landscape, infrastructure, and machine. Using thousands of sensors and motorized components, the enormous urban scale robotic structure harvests rainwater and fog, while modulating air flow and solar exposure through intelligent building systems. Citizens move through it, connecting to remote edges of the Bay through a robust ferry network. Fish farms are robotically harvested, while nutrient rich water fertilizes the vegetable farms and parkland embedded within. Fog feathers reach into the sky to collect dew and water is stored in an overhead armature that feeds it back into the system. Parks weave out into the water and back into the city generating productive pubic space. Hydramax is a synthetic urban ecology—an urban metabolic machine that connects, feeds, and sustains its citizens.

EXISTING
1. LIQUEFACTION SUSCEPTIBILITY
2. FAULT LINES AND SEISMIC EPICENTERS
3. SALINITY LEVELS
4. FERRY ROUTES
5. MARITIME TRAFFIC [1.17.13, 15:00 PST]
6. FOG HORNS AND SIGNAL BEACONS

PROPOSED
7. NEW EDGE
8. NEW HYDRAMAX NETWORK EXTENDING ALONG
PERIMETER OF SAN FRANCISCO BAY

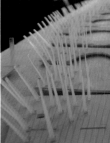

HYDRAMAX

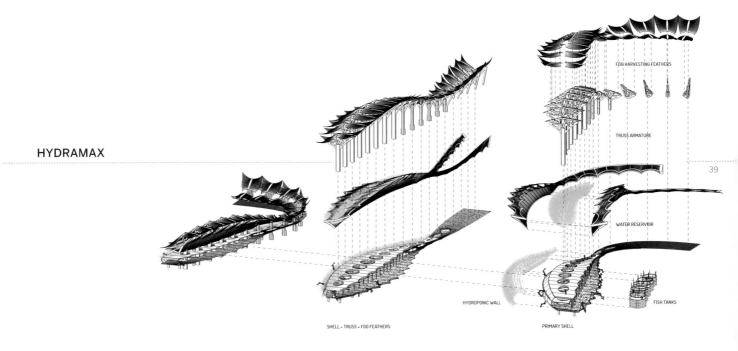

FOG HARVESTING FEATHERS

TRUSS ARMATURE

WATER RESERVOIR

HYDROPONIC WALL

FISH TANKS

SHELL + TRUSS + FOG FEATHERS

PRIMARY SHELL

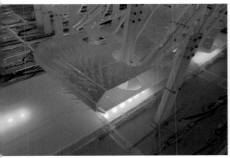
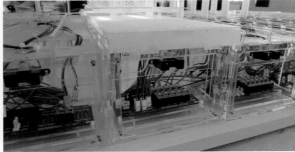

ALISON HIRSCH
IMAGING CHANGE

PROFITING FROM THE FEAR OF NUCLEAR ATTACK, MOST LANDSCAPE ARCHITECTS EXCLUSIVELY SERVICED THE DECENTRALIZED POPULATION WHO HAD SURRENDERED TO THE SUBURBS AFTER THE WAR. DURING THIS PERIOD, LANDSCAPE —AS IDEA, AS REPRESENTATION, AND AS PHYSICAL MATTER—PROVIDED NOT A DYNAMIC MEANS OF CULTURAL EXPRESSION OR A GROUNDING MECHANISM THAT OFFERED STABILITY AMIDST PERPETUAL CHANGE, BUT A PROMISE OF RETREAT. THE TENSIONS AND CONTRADICTIONS OF MODERN LIFE PROMPTED LAWRENCE HALPRIN, WHO REACTED CRITICALLY AGAINST THE NIHILISM AND ESTRANGEMENT HE DEEMED A CONSEQUENCE OF THIS PROCESS OF MODERNIZATION, BUT WHO ALSO RECOGNIZED THE CREATIVE OPPORTUNITIES AND PROVOCATIONS IT PRESENTED. COMPARING HUMAN COMMUNITIES TO ECOSYSTEMS, HALPRIN'S PROGRESSIVE APPROACH TO REPRESENTATION AND DESIGN ASSOCIATED THESE DYNAMIC FORCES WITH THE TRANSFORMATIVE POTENTIAL OF ECOLOGICAL DISTURBANCE. IN THIS FRAMEWORK, CITIES WERE LIKENED TO "BIOLOGICAL SYSTEMS, WHICH HAVE NOT REACHED A PLATEAU OF EQUILIBRIUM OR CLIMAX, BUT WHICH ARE CONSTANTLY IN A PROCESS OF VARIATION...WHERE EACH SMALL CHANGE AFFECTS OTHERS." HALPRIN DEDICATED MUCH OF HIS CAREER TO THE DEVELOPMENT OF NOTATIONAL LANGUAGES THAT VISUALIZED SUCH FLUID COMPLEXITY AND TRANSFORMATION.

DISTURBANCE + DISCLIMAX

Halprin rejected the deterministic or closed predictable behavior of the "biosphere" as adopted by his friend and colleague, Ian McHarg. This model asserts that all ecosystems move toward a balanced state of equilibrium and does not include human activity as part of the natural world but rather in conflict with it. Halprin, who studied natural process in the academy and in the field, obsessively observing his surroundings through repeated sketching, recognized that ecosystems did not necessarily behave in a way that was consistent with the ideal model and predictions of the old paradigm. Rather, he pre-empted a shift in the field of ecology, in which "these systems are no longer seen as closed, self-regulating entities… Disturbance is a frequent, intrinsic characteristic of ecosystems… and species exhibit a wide range of adaptations to disturbance…" according to biologist Robert Cook.[1] Halprin, who welcomed the significant role that chance played in the way the natural world looks and behaves, found the vocabulary of disturbance and "disclimax" applicable to the dramatically shifting urban landscape, and sought to facilitate humans' adaptation to their "whole new set of conditions."

Halprin's visual studies of the Sierra Nevada and the rugged coast of Northern California became aesthetic sources for his urban work. While sketching, he focused not on the scenic or scopic qualities of these landscapes or the compositional codes of drawing, but attempted to re-present processes that shaped the world around him. Experimenting with different modes of mark-mak-

SIERRA NEVADA: Halprin's early experiments entailed studying not the transformations of the city, but their precedent—the "archetypal" processes of growth, entropy and destruction he discovered in the High Sierra and dramatic coast of northern California. With this acceptance of change and celebration of new (as well as timeless) forms of movement, the city, to Halprin, became more than a spatial problem to be fixed in master plans, but a spatio-temporal field of processes and interactions that could be structured to stimulate heightened human creativity and socialization. A reinvestigation of these experiments provides stimulus for more rigorous explorations of methods of visualization that record, generate, and realize productive frameworks for our modern condition.

42

ing combined with words, evoking sounds and actions, and temporal notations, these drawings served as the catalytic foundation for his design process. Through this translatory process, he did not imitate forms he discovered in these dramatic environments, but "transmuted" their expressions into new physical manifestations that invited participation in the city. To Halprin, the introduction of this "experiential equivalency," would stimulate engagement similar to how one might experience nature, or what he calls "wildness."[2] By making nature's processes palpable or by applying the "inherent rightness" of natural form-making to shape spaces in the city, Halprin felt confident that his designs would contain the communicative power to resonate throughout a culturally diverse public and universally invite interaction.

Believing in the binding power of humans' common origins in nature and natural forces of creation, Halprin used this "archetypal" vocabulary of processes such as erosion, deposition, and plant succession to provide a common ground for the fiercely polarized social framework of the 1960s American city. While he underwent Jungian analysis, this search for archetypal or eternal expression would have been inherited from or heightened by his schooling under Bauhaus émigrés at Harvard's Graduate School of Design. Yet rather than seek universal or "immutable" forms of expression for purposes of standardization, Halprin believed their primal resonance would trigger dynamic response without dictating or scripting what that response might be.[3]

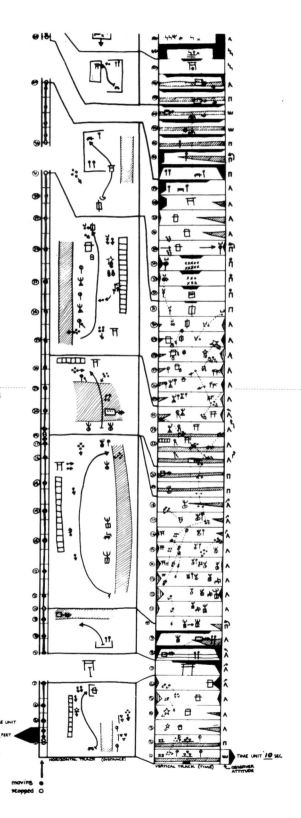

MOTATION: Halprin's graphic scores were drawings intended to embody process and instigate change. In 1965, he proposed a notational system called "Motation" as a supplement to conventional architectural drawings, such as plans and elevations, which he considered too static. In filmic sequence, the frames of "Motation" provide both a horizontal (plan) and vertical (elevation) understanding of spatial relationships and durational measure. By distilling the visual world into a system of symbols, rhythms could be extracted and set in comparison or be used productively to choreograph shifts in the everyday repetitions of life.

Rather than simply provide a descriptive recording device, Halprin developed Motation as a means through which a designer might use movement as a starting point to generate form, explaining, "Since movement and the complex interrelations which it generates are an essential part of the life of a city, urban design should have the choice of starting from movement as the core—the essential element of the plan. Only after programming the movement and graphically expressing it should the environment—an envelope within which movement takes place—be designed. The environment exists for the purpose of movement."[4] The intention was to observe the rituals of everyday life and create a framework for their enhanced performance as well as provide a provocative stage for the instigation of indeterminate and spontaneous events.

CHOREOGRAPHY + KINESTHETICS

While Halprin's early academic studies of the natural sciences inspired his process-driven practice, his dedication to the temporal dimension was exponentially compounded by the artistic symbiosis that existed between him and his wife, avant-garde dancer and choreographer Anna Halprin. It was thus the combination of ecology and dance that motivated his lifelong search for methods of representation (through the media of drawing and building) that propelled open-ended process and change.

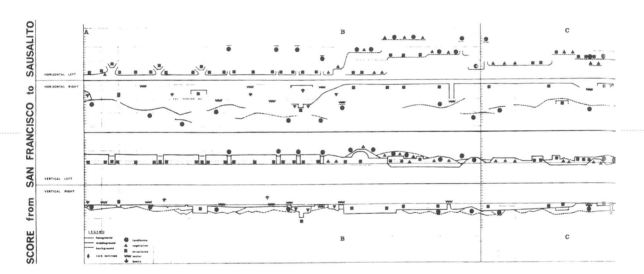

Like "Happenings," emerging from the teachings of musician John Cage in New York, Anna organized interactive events in which environmental situations and loose action guidelines were proposed or "scored," but the ultimate performance was left open-ended and typically involved the audience. From these new art forms, the "open score" became the major tool for stimulating action and transforming the spectator from observer to participant. Lawrence Halprin integrated these emerging performance theories into his creative process, both in drawing—through graphic "scores" that recorded and choreographed movement—and in building and designing spaces as "scores" intended to stimulate open-ended participation and kinesthetic response.

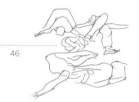

TERRITORIAL IMMEDIACY

Anna Halprin thrived in the territory of immediacy embodied in the landscapes of the west coast. Like Isadora Duncan, who attributed the freedom of her movement to the openness, power, and virgin quality of the California landscape, she recognized the transformative potential of this environment to recapture an "authentic" quality of movement—in response to the rhythms of nature as the source of creativity.

The mountains, flatlands, forests, and coastlines of this dramatic culmination of the western frontier that had been the creative source of inspiration for generations of American writers, poets, painters, and naturalists provided limitless stimulation for the creative mind of the landscape architect. In California, "seas, convulsions, lava, and glaciers had left their record in monuments of stone which seemed to the imagination imminent of release, as if once again there could be a time of seething birth."[5] This geomorphological drama and the liberatory power of an atmosphere of imminent release provoked and propelled the Halprins' creativity.

Anna considered the prereflexive mind-body a state of "supreme authenticity," in which one could communicate without the barriers of cultural conditioning. With a shared interest in Gestalt Therapy to aid in breaking such barriers, Lawrence Halprin used the pre-rational language of "archetypal" forms and expressions to provoke a similar "authenticity" of movement and imaginative engagement. The directness of his sketches—the world as synthesized through the corporeal sensorium and translated onto the page without self-consciousness or preconceived sense of order—parallels Anna's acts of "creative intuition" in direct response to environmental change. While their media were rather different, the former perhaps less filtered than the latter, the process harnessed the same directness of experience, which comes from "nature and man interacting with each other," according to John Dewey, the Halprins' common source of inspiration. Dewey continues, "The artist does his thinking in the very qualitative media he works in, and the terms lie so close to the object that he is producing that they merge directly into it."[7]

Lawrence Halprin's construction of the Dance Deck, in the forest of madrone, oak, and redwood trees on the mountain slope below their house, immersed Anna in the immediacy of elemental forces. She explains, "Since there is ever-changing form and texture and light around you, a certain drive develops toward constant experimentation and change in dance itself. In a sense, one becomes less introverted, less dependent on sheer invention, and more outgoing and receptive to environmental change…"[6]

47

Still Dances with Anna Halprin from the "Sand" and "Driftwood" series, created by Eeo Stubblefield.

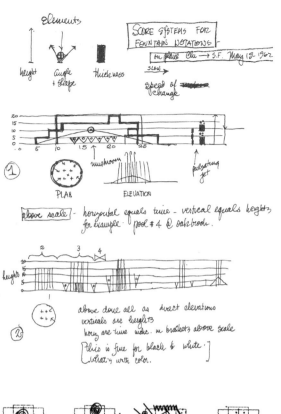

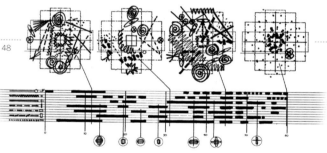

CONFRONTING THE WORLD

While Dewey is setting "the artist" in contrast to the "scientific worker," who is distanced from his/her sources and whose end alienates us further from the natural world, Lawrence Halprin's work and working process contributed to a reconciliation between the instrumentality of the natural sciences and modern technology and the phenomenology of human experience. He responded to the powerful forces of modernization that shaped the city with equally forceful spaces that counteracted alienation from the natural world through the reintroduction of rhythms and a palpable passage of time. While his contemporaries followed the determinism of McHarg's deductive model of scientific analysis, Halprin immersed himself in the sources (objects) of analysis to immediately experience the dynamic forces of change and re-present these shared foundations through a situated negotiation with the immediate conditions of the city in disclimax.

Though Halprin's creative points of origin were open-endedness, process, movement and change, the translation from observation to notation to application in built form ultimately endowed the city with strong material presence that served as a shared framework for creative

"The process of modernization, even as it exploits and torments us, brings our energies and imaginations to life, drives us to grasp and confront the world... and to strive to make it our own."

– Marshall Berman, *All that is Solid Melts into Air: The Experience of Modernity* (1984)[8]

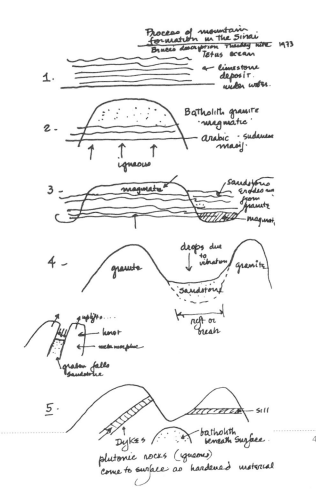

appropriation. His physical contributions were thus quite "solid" and—despite efforts to see them "melt into air" in cities' continued thirst for progress and growth—a few have remained, overgrown and weathered, as palpable reminders of past optimism in our experience of modernity.

Halprin's celebration of concrete—a material appropriately situated in the city—was often dynamically coupled with powerful water elements intended to activate the kinesthetic sense. In other words, he integrated water into his spaces not by recovering pre-existing streambeds or restoring riparian habitats. Rather, he optimized on advanced hydraulic technologies to introduce entirely constructed opportunities for humans to respond to this shared element of the Natural world. Halprin's translation—from record to drawing as ideational act to built work—was a constant negotiation between elemental forces of existence and the processes of modernization that drive us to confront the world and strive to make it our own. His experiments in visualization and his desire to provide both flexibility of appropriation and strong material presence may serve as an example for designers shaping a world whose pace of change only accelerates.

ANNE WHISTON SPIRN
RESTORING WATER

WEST PHILADELPHIA'S MILL CREEK WATERSHED AND NEIGHBORHOOD, WHERE I HAVE WORKED SINCE 1987, IS AN IDEAL PLACE TO STUDY AND ADDRESS CHALLENGES OF ENVIRONMENTAL SUSTAINABILITY, COMMUNITY DEVELOPMENT, AND EDUCATIONAL REFORM. KNOWN LOCALLY AS "THE BOTTOM," THE MILL CREEK NEIGHBORHOOD IS ONE OF MANY SUCH "BLACK BOTTOMS" IN THE US. THEY ARE AT THE BOTTOM, ECONOMICALLY, SOCIALLY, AND TOPOGRAPHICALLY. HERE, HARSH SOCIO-ECONOMIC CONDITIONS AND RACIAL DISCRIMINATION ARE EXACERBATED BY HEALTH AND SAFETY HAZARDS POSED BY A HIGH WATER TABLE AND UNSTABLE GROUND. LANDSCAPE LITERACY HAS BEEN A MEANS FOR RECOGNIZING AND REDRESSING THOSE INJUSTICES THROUGH LANDSCAPE PLANNING AND DESIGN AND COMMUNITY DEVELOPMENT, JUST AS VERBAL LITERACY WAS A CORNERSTONE OF THE AMERICAN CIVIL RIGHTS MOVEMENT OF THE 50S AND 60S. I USE THE WORD LANDSCAPE IN ITS ORIGINAL SENSE IN OLD ENGLISH—THE MUTUAL SHAPING OF PEOPLE AND PLACE— TO ENCOMPASS BOTH THE POPULATION OF A PLACE AND ITS PHYSICAL FEATURES. LITERACY IN LANDSCAPE HAS ENABLED PEOPLE TO READ THE ENVIRONMENTAL, SOCIAL, ECONOMIC, AND POLITICAL STORIES EMBEDDED IN THEIR LOCAL LANDSCAPE AND HAS GIVEN THEM A WAY TO FORMULATE NEW STORIES.

Mill Creek was buried in a sewer in the 1880s and the floodplain filled and built on.

Hills were cut down and valleys filled during the mid-1800s. The current grade above the Mill Creek sewer is now 40 feet or more above the original level of the creek. The old alluvial deposits on the former floodplain buried deep beneath the current surface of the city are a resource for absorbing stormwater and indicate where subsidence may occur.

The single feature of the Mill Creek landscape that has had the most significant, persistent, and devastating effect is the least recognized: the buried floodplain of the creek itself and the hydrological processes that continue to shape it. And yet the strong pattern it creates—the band of open land and deteriorating buildings—is striking once recognized. Today there is ongoing damage from flooding and subsidence, but this situation is not immutable. To those who can read this landscape, it offers opportunities. Landscape literacy provides a way of seeing relationships among actions and phenomena that may seem unconnected, but are in fact closely related.

From the 1930s to the 1960s newspapers reported repeated cave-ins along the Mill Creek sewer. Some cave-ins swallowed whole blocks of homes.

In 1951, residents were evacuated from the 4300 block of Sansom Street. Today the southern half of the block is a parking lot, whose rippled surface shows signs of continuing subsidence.

52 Billions of dollars will be spent in the next decade to overhaul old sewer systems that combine sanitary and storm sewage, which overflow after heavy rains and discharge untreated wastewater directly to rivers—a combined sewer overflow (CSO). The conventional solution to eliminate CSOs is to build underground storage tanks or bigger treatment plants. An alternative is to prevent stormwater from reaching the sewer, to collect and hold it in detention basins that are also parks or plazas, to use it to irrigate gardens and urban farms. Such "green" infrastructure is much less expensive than "gray" infrastructure and provides many other benefits, and vacant blocks in the buried floodplain are ideal locations for such projects. From 1987-1991, my students and I designed such proposals for Mill Creek's watershed and presented them to public officials and neighborhood residents in a plan. Yet the City's 1994 Plan for West Philadelphia ignored the hazards and opportunities posed by Mill Creek, and a large, subsidized housing project for first-time low-income homeowners was built the same year right on the buried floodplain.

Middle-school students in The Mill Creek Project traced their neighborhood's past, deciphered its stories, and described their visions for its future. The tools they used were their own eyes and imagination, the place itself, and historical documents: maps, photographs, letters, and newspapers. The program had four parts: reading landscape, proposing landscape change, building landscape improvements, and documenting these proposals and accomplishments on the Internet.

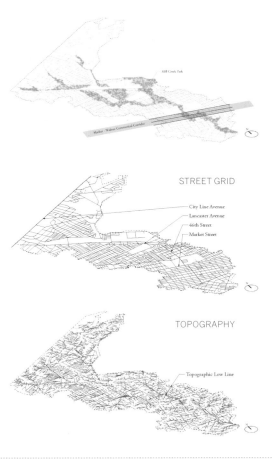

STREET GRID

City Line Avenue
Lancaster Avenue
46th Street
Market Street

TOPOGRAPHY

Topographic Low Line

FLOODPLAIN

Buried Floodplain
Sinks and Depressions

SEWERSHED

Mill Creek Watershed
Mill Creek Sewer

Confronted with skepticism about the existence and dangers of the buried floodplain and disregard for people's health and safety, I began to understand this resistance as a kind of illiteracy—an inability on the part of public officials, and even residents themselves, to read the landscape. In response, my students and I launched The Mill Creek Project, a program on landscape literacy and community development in partnership with community organizations and a middle school, where hundreds of children, 11-13 years old, learned to read and tell the landscape of Mill Creek.

At the beginning of the course, the children described their neighborhood in negative terms and said they would not live there if they had a choice. When my students spoke of designs for change, the children told them, "It won't happen... Someone will wreck it." Two months later, the children expressed newfound pride in their neighborhood and a desire to help "make it a better place." Their teacher reported that their performance in all subjects had improved dramatically. He attributed this to the way that the primary materials challenged and made history real for them and to their growing perception of how their own lives and landscape were related to the larger city, region, and nation.

With help from Penn students, children learned to observe historical documents, to develop a hypothesis, and to test it with evidence. Then they transferred this process to reading the landscape, which is itself a historical document.

Those who are literate can read the larger pattern of drainage and abandonment to which lots belong: a meandering line of open ground on the buried floodplain filled with broken pavement, shrubby thickets, community gardens, and urban renewal projects. One such lot is the tip of a diagonal of vacant land, which cuts across the grid of streets; Mill Creek once flowed across this property. The sole house on another block was once attached to neighboring buildings. The land is unsuitable for homes, but valuable for stormwater detention and other compatible uses. Unfortunately, houses for low-income, first-time home-owners are still being built on vacant land in Mill Creek's buried floodplain.

To those who are illiterate in landscape language, these are merely vacant lots, awaiting new construction.

REDESIGNING SMALL NEIGHBORHOODS

THE URBAN FOREST

A key proposal of the West Philadelphia Landscape Project: A Framework for Action (1991) is to manage the buried floodplain as part of a broad approach to improving regional water quality and as a strategy to secure funds to rebuild the neighborhood and to create jobs. The creek cannot be brought back above ground, for it is now a sewer that carries waste. But a green ribbon of parks, play fields, small farms, and nurseries would recall the creek, protect houses from flooding, provide open space for a variety of uses, and establish a framework for further investment by individuals, institutions, businesses, and public agencies.

54

MILL CREEK PARK

VACANT LAND

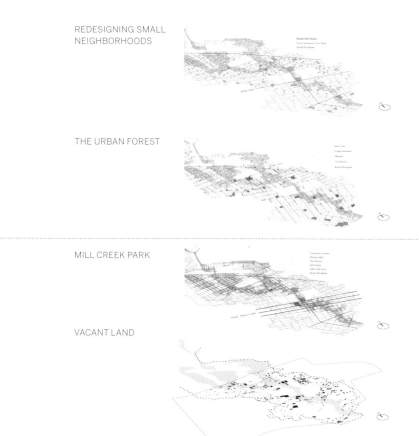

Historical maps in hand, students discovered that one vacant lot in Mill Creek's buried floodplain once contained several blocks of homes and that the buildings were torn down over time, the result of both disinvestment and subsiding ground. Many children had believed that poor conditions of their neighborhood had always existed and could never be changed. Freed from myth, they could imagine alternative futures and ideas for bringing them about.

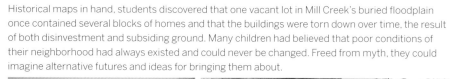

"This garden is a town, we have everything but a penal colony," said Hayward Ford, once president of the Aspen Farms Community Garden, one of many on the former floodplain of Mill Creek. It has a shared infrastructure, like the water supply, irrigation system, and the grid of paths, much like Philadelphia's streets, which divide the gardeners' plots. My students and I have worked with the gardeners since 1988, when they first asked us to design a meeting place. John Widrick's 1988 studio design widened the garden's "Main Street" and provided a framework within which the garden has evolved ever since. Patricia Uribe and Claudia Meyer's 1998 studio design added a pond and outdoor classroom, which was built by middle-school students in West Philadelphia Landscape Project's Mill Creek Program.

From 1996 to 1998, PWD engineers reviewed work produced by students. A field trip in the Mill Creek Watershed in July 1999 led to PWD's decision to seek funding for green infrastructure demonstration projects in Mill Creek. With support from the EPA and HUD, PWD's Office of Watersheds embarked on a series of ambitious projects to reduce combined sewer overflows through green infrastructure. Ten years later, the PWD announced its pioneering Green City, Clean Waters program, which builds on fundamental aspects of WPLP proposals and calls for further innovations.

+ **1987:** WEST PHILADELPHIA'S LANDSCAPE PLAN AND GREENING PROJECT BEGINS

+ **1991:** WPLP PLANNING DOCUMENTS PUBLISHED

+ **1996:** WPLP WEBSITE LAUNCHED. MILL CREEK PROJECT WITH SULZBERGER MIDDLE SCHOOL BEGINS

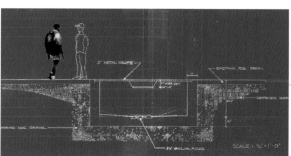

If implemented, Green City, Clean Waters will be a national landmark. If the plan works, it will save the city billions of dollars. But will it work (physically), and can it be done? Since 2010, my students at Massachusetts Institute of Technology have sought answers to these questions. Among their many proposals are one for a new form of parking lot and another, "Mill Creek Speaks," which explores public art as a catalyst for stormwater management and public awareness.

1998: SULZBERGER STUDENTS
PRESENT MILL CREEK PROJECT
TO PENNSYLVANIA LEGISLATURE

1999: PWD ESTABLISHES
OFFICE OF WATERSHEDS

2009: STATE OF PENNSYLVANIA
APPROVES GREEN CITY, CLEAN
WATERS PLAN

I once thought that the worst effect of landscape illiteracy was environmental injustice in the form of physical hazards to health and safety. The Sulzberger students showed me that there is an even greater injustice than inequitable exposure to harsh conditions: the internalization of shame in one's neighborhood. This is a particularly destructive form of injustice. It saps self esteem and can engender a sense of blame and resignation. Without an understanding of how the neighborhood came to be, many believed that the poor conditions were the fault of those who lived there, a product either of incompetence or lack of care. Learning that there were other reasons sparked a sense of relief. Once they had the skill to read their landscape, they came to consider the possibility of alternative futures and brimmed with ideas.

Early in 1996, the WPLP website launched, featuring the digital database, reports, and built projects. Since then, it has been a showcase for ongoing work, including proposals by students in my classes at Penn and MIT, who have analyzed the urban watershed, demonstrated how stormwater could be collected in landscape projects that are also stormwater detention facilities, and proved the feasibility of their proposals through detailed engineering calculations and drawings. Between 1996-2000, the WPLP website received millions of "hits."

57

Verbal literacy—the ability to read and write—is commonly acknowledged as an essential skill for the citizen to participate fully and effectively in a democratic society. Like verbal literacy, landscape literacy is a cultural practice that entails both understanding the world and transforming it. To be literate in landscape is to recognize both the problems in a place and its resources, to understand how they came about, by what means they are sustained, and how they are related. Such literacy should be a prerequisite for urban planning and design. Like literacy, planning and design are cultural practices that can either serve to perpetuate the inequities of existing social structures or to enable and promote change that is not only economically robust and ecologically sustainable, but also beautiful and just.

KONGJIAN YU
COMPLETE WATER

THE DESTRUCTION OF "COMPLETE" WATER STARTS AT AN EARLY AGE.
IN MY CASE, IN THE COUNTRYSIDE, IT BEGAN IN THE FIRST GRADE OF PRIMARY SCHOOL
WITH THE TEACHER'S "SCIENTIFIC DEFINITION" OF WATER: A COLORLESS, TASTELESS,
AND SHAPELESS LIQUID AT ROOM TEMPERATURE. IT LEFT ME AND MY CLASSMATES
CONFUSED AND BEWILDERED. HOW CAN WATER BE COLORLESS? WHAT IS
COLORLESS? THE WHITE SAND CREEK TO THE WEST OF OUR VILLAGE IS WHITE, WHILE
THE BLACK DRAGON LAKE IN THE FOREST SOUTH OF THE VILLAGE IS BLUE. HOW CAN
WATER BE TASTELESS? WE DRINK WATER FROM THE SPRING BY THE CREEK, AND IT IS
SWEET. AND I REMEMBER THE SPRING IN FRONT OF OUR VILLAGE HAS THE FRAGRANCE
OF TURPENTINE OIL AND LOTUS. HOW CAN WATER BE SHAPELESS? OUR LANGUAGE
AND LITERATURE TEACHER HAS TAUGHT US THAT THE CHINESE CHARACTER OF
"WATER" HAS THE SHAPE OF A WINDING RIVER ESCORTED BY RIBBON-LIKE LAKES. AND
WHAT ABOUT THE COLORFUL PEBBLES, DANCING GRASS, AND SWIMMING FISH IN THE
WATER? DON'T THEY HAVE ANYTHING TO DO WITH THE WATER? FINALLY OUR TEACHER
SAID, "YOUR UNDERSTANDING OF WATER IS BASED ON EXPERIENCE, AND IT IS NOT
THE SCIENTIFIC UNDERSTANDING OF WATER." WATER, ONCE FULL OF LIFE, COLOR, AND
MEANING, HAD BECOME CONCLUSIVELY COLORLESS, TASTELESS, SHAPELESS, AND
EMOTIONLESS. I LATER LEARNT THAT THIS WATER IS H_2O, A CHEMICAL MOLECULAR
FORMULA WITH ONE OXYGEN ATOM AND TWO HYDROGEN ATOMS.

This "scientific" water does everything to eliminate "complete" water. In the 1960s and 1970s (and even today), a campaign was launched in the southern region of the Yangtze River to eradicate oncomelania (*Oncomelania hupensis*), the host of blood flukes. Grasses were rooted out along rivers and around ponds, and pesticides were sprayed into the water. It killed not only oncomelania, but also all other aquatic life. Farmers were next forced to standardize their fields, making their land flatter to allow for agricultural machines to be used. River courses were cut off and straightened; meandering streams were converted to hard channels; and ponds once surrounded by flourishing bushes were buried. Gone were springs, fishes, and turtles. The "modernized" irrigation channels, with three facets of their banks being "clear of life", crisscrossed the undulating farmlands, and the ditches that once flowed between plots on the original landscape were replaced by water locks and pumps to control water level. When channels running in front of the villages stopped flowing, the villagers, encouraged by the government, started to pump groundwater. Wells were replaced by pipes before long, and tap-water was supplied to every household. Ponds that had existed in the villages for thousands of years became dumping and discharging pits.

"Complete" water was further eliminated in the 1980s when rivers were used to discharge wastewater, and lakes and ponds became convenient and economical

H   H

O

dumping fields. As a result, water was no longer colorless or tasteless — instead, it was brown, black or the dangerous green (plagued by blue-green algae) with foul odor. If I could return to my childhood, I would once again be puzzled at my science teacher's definition of water. How can water be colorless or odorless? I know its color can be as light as soy bean soup and as dark as black ink, and its odor is so pungent.

This deterioration of H_2O has triggered a rapid development in environmental engineering and pollution control from the 1990s onwards. The aquatic environment in China however has not improved. Indeed, it has deteriorated dramatically. Today, 75 percent of the surface water in China is polluted. It is not that progress has not been made in science and technology. We can measure water quality and analyze it for hundreds of elements. Nor is it because of inadequate government investment. Hundreds of billions of RMB are invested in improving the quality of water of Dianchi Lake (in Kunming, Yunnan Province) alone, and there are more such projects planned for Taihu Lake (in the Yangtze River delta), the Huaihe River and other places across China. Engineers are now improving water quality with technologies such as active carbon, ozone, micrometer and nanometer-sized bubbles, and biological membranes. All these technologies are used to return polluted water to H_2O and not the "complete" water that I knew before my schooling: water full of life, colors, shapes, and aromas.

WHEN INDUSTRIALIZATION MISUNDERSTOOD WATER BY REDUCING IT TO A JUST A CHEMICAL REALITY: A CLEAR COLORLESS ODORLESS TASTELESS LIQUID H_2O,

IT WAS KILLED AS A LIVING SYSTEM

The last three decades of development in China, which has seen a dramatic growth in urban population and cities like Beijing expand 5 to 7 times in pavement area, has delivered "complete" water its final and fatal stroke across scales. Almost all the major rivers in China have been dammed for electricity, all water courses except those in the very remote areas have been channelized with concrete in the name of "flood control," but also for the purpose of reclaiming riparian land for development. As a result, 50 percent of the wetland habitat has disappeared, ground water has dropped by as much as 1 to 2 meters per year in the North China Great Plain, and events of flood and draught have increased dramatically. In addition to the widespread pollution of surface and ground water nationwide, 400 out of 660 cities face water shortages while floods and urban inundation kill more and more people and cause more damage. In the year 2012 alone, 77 people were killed in Beijing, a city known for its lack of water. The response to these problems

GLYPHOSATE   PARAQUAT   ATRAZINE   CHLORPYRIFOS

has been more heavy engineering projects such as the south-north aqueduct that conducts water from south China to Beijing, higher and stronger concrete flood walls surrounding cities and water features, and bigger drainage pipes to flush rain water immediately into the ocean.

When water dies, man dies. That is why I am calling for a return of "complete" water. Instead of H_2O, it is water of a living ecosystem. "Complete" water is not about purity; it is about interconnecting land and organisms, about continuities, about life.

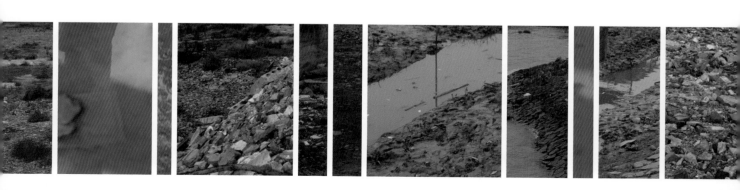

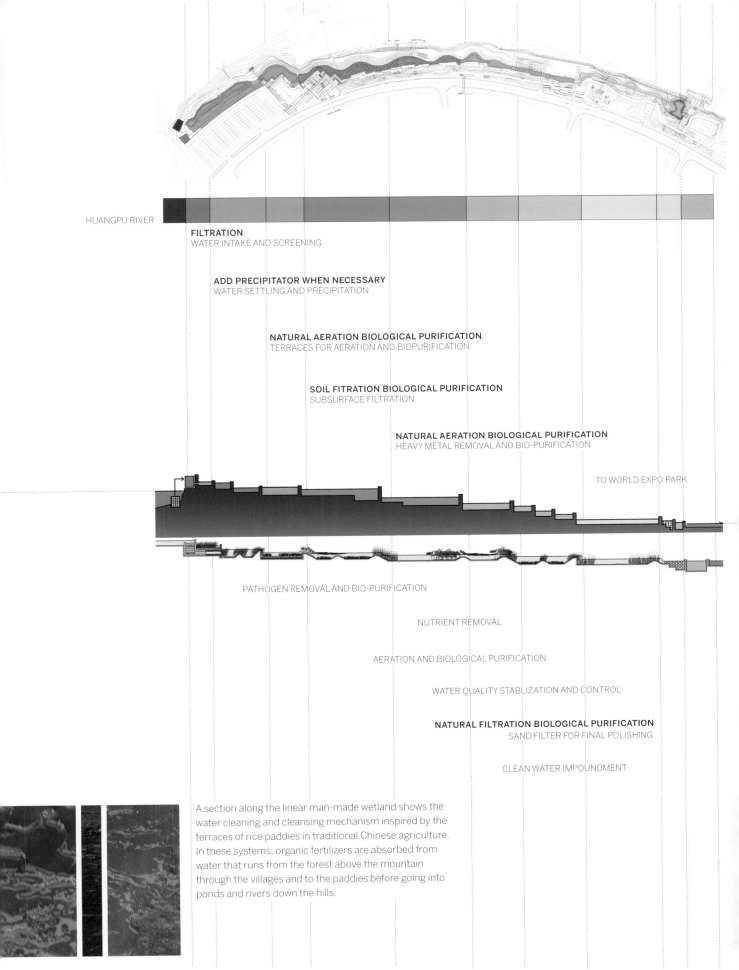

HUANGPU RIVER

FILTRATION
WATER INTAKE AND SCREENING

ADD PRECIPITATOR WHEN NECESSARY
WATER SETTLING AND PRECIPITATION

NATURAL AERATION BIOLOGICAL PURIFICATION
TERRACES FOR AERATION AND BIOPURIFICATION

SOIL FITRATION BIOLOGICAL PURIFICATION
SUBSURFACE FILTRATION

NATURAL AERATION BIOLOGICAL PURIFICATION
HEAVY METAL REMOVAL AND BIO-PURIFICATION

TO WORLD EXPO PARK

PATHOGEN REMOVAL AND BIO-PURIFICATION

NUTRIENT REMOVAL

AERATION AND BIOLOGICAL PURIFICATION

WATER QUALITY STABLIZATION AND CONTROL

NATURAL FILTRATION BIOLOGICAL PURIFICATION
SAND FILTER FOR FINAL POLISHING

CLEAN WATER IMPOUNDMENT

A section along the linear man-made wetland shows the
water cleaning and cleansing mechanism inspired by the
terraces of rice paddies in traditional Chinese agriculture.
In these systems, organic fertilizers are absorbed from
water that runs from the forest above the mountain
through the villages and to the paddies before going into
ponds and rivers down the hills.

CASCADE WALL

1. SLATE GRAY GRANITE TOP, 250X500MM (50MM THICK)
2. PLANTER
3. NON-CLAY BRICK, 120MM
4. 1:3 CEMENT MORTAR 120-150 WIDE BONDED SLATE GRAY SCHIST
5. 1:3 CEMENT MORTAR (INCLUDING 5% WATER REPELLENT), 20MM
6. WATERPROOF MORTAR BONDED RUBBLE RETAINING WALL, LAY 1:0.1 TILTED

7. SLATE GRAY SCHIST, 10MM
8. 1:3 CEMENT MORTAR (INCLUDING 5% WATER REPELLENT), 20MM
9. C30S6 REINFORCED CONCRETE, 120MM
10. C20 REINFORCED CONCRETE CUSHION, 100MM
11. GRAVEL, 300MM
12. PRIME SOIL COMPACTION
13. C15 REINFORCED CONCRETE BASIS, 150MM
14. SEDIMENT PLANTING SOIL, 400MM
15. ROUGH SAND, 400MM
16. GRAVEL, 300MM
17. CLAY COMPACTED IN LAYERS, 600MM

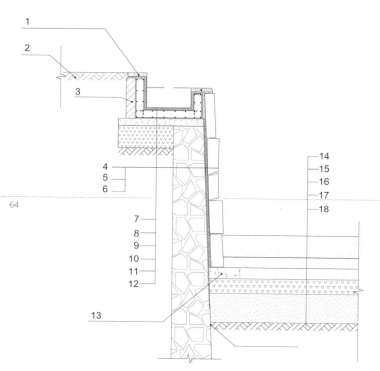

64

HOUTAN PARK

Built on a former industrial site on Shanghai's Huangpu riverfront, Houtan Park's constructed wetlands, re-claimed industrial structures and materials, and urban agriculture are integral components of an overall restor-ative design strategy that treats polluted river water and recovers a degraded waterfront. The narrow 14-hectare site along the Huangpu River was once littered with in-dustrial and construction debris. The river was highly polluted, with a water quality ranking of Lower Grade 5, which is the worst grade on a national scale. It was both unsafe for swimming and recreation and devoid of aquatic life. We identified three design challenges: to transform the landscape into a safe and public space, to improve the site's ability to accommodate a 2.1 me-ter daily tidal fluctuation, and finally, to lay out the site itself, which was continuous for 1.7 kilometers with a width ranging between 30 to 80 meters. After the project was completed, field-testing indicated that 2,400 cubic meters per day of water could be improved from Lower Grade 5 to Grade 3.

We used a variety of regenerative design strategies to transform the site into a living system, which included food production, water management and treatment, and habitat creation. A constructed wetland 5 to 30 meters wide runs the length of the entire site, which reinvigo-rates the waterfront and treats water from the Haungpu. A cascade wall first oxygenates the water; then a series of stepped terraces create a treatment sequence that removes and retains nutrients, reduces suspended sediments, and offers a pleasant experience for visitors. Various wetland plant species were selected to absorb pollutants, including crops such as corn, rice, sunflowers and buckwheat, which form a didactic urban farm. The wetland and agricultural plants change throughout the year: golden blossoms in the spring, sunflowers in the summer, the fragrance of ripened rice in the fall, and green clover in the winter.

HELIANTHUS ANNUUS

ZEA MAYS

SETARIA VIRIDIS

FAGOPYRUM ESCULENTUM

ORYZA SATIVA

NELUMBO NUCIFERA

TRAPA NATANS

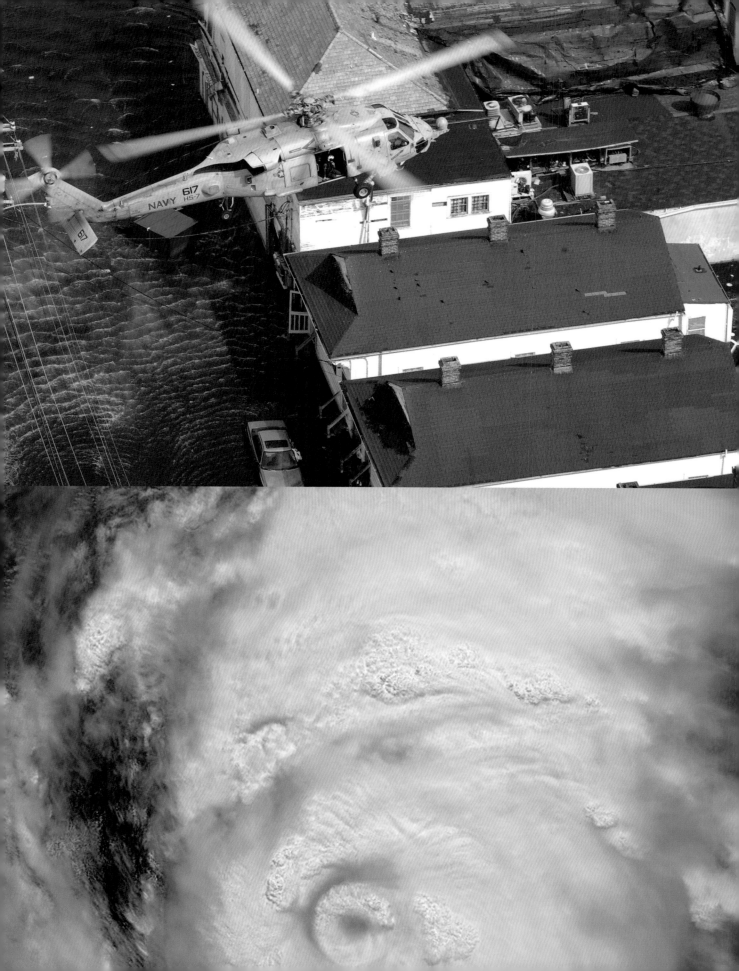

SIMON RICHTER
THE HYDROLOGICAL MOMENT

IF WATER IS EVERYWHERE, IT MUST ALSO BE IN THE HUMANITIES.
WHETHER WE CAN REGISTER HOW THESE WATERS IN TURN SEEP INTO DESIGN REMAINS TO BE SEEN. I WANT TO BEGIN BY EVOKING AN IMAGE OF WHAT I CALL "THE HYDROLOGICAL MOMENT." TO DO SO, I AM GOING TO ENLIST THE HELP OF THE EARLY NINETEENTH-CENTURY GERMAN POET AND SCIENTIST JOHAN WOLFGANG VON GOETHE. OFF AND ON FOR ALMOST SIXTY YEARS, GOETHE WORKED ON AN AMBITIOUS PLAY BASED ON THE EARLY MODERN ALCHEMIST DR. FAUST, WHO, LEGEND HAS IT, MADE A PACT WITH THE DEVIL. ONE OF GOETHE'S UNIQUE INTERVENTIONS WAS TO TURN THE PACT INTO A WAGER. SO CONFIDENT WAS GOETHE'S FAUST THAT MEPHISTOPHELES WOULD FAIL TO SATISFY HIS MEASURELESS DESIRE THAT HE OFFERED HIM A BET: "SHOULD I EVER SAY TO A MOMENT IN TIME, ABIDE, YOU ARE SO BEAUTIFUL, MY DESIRE HAS BEEN COMPLETELY FULFILLED, THEN YOU MAY TAKE ME RIGHT THEN AND THERE. I'LL DIE A HAPPY MAN" (MY PARAPHRASE). IN OTHER WORDS, FAUST BET ON HUMANITY'S CEASELESS STRIVING. FOR THE RECORD, I AM BETTING ON WATER.

New Orleans Behind the Mighty Dike

Decades later and by the end of Goethe's sprawling world drama, a much traveled, wiser, and more experienced Faust undertakes a last grandiose project. In previous negotiations with the Holy Roman Emperor, Faust had acquired a vast tract of wetlands along a coast. Since then, he has built a network of dikes and systematically wrested land from the sea and is now master of a thriving colonial empire. Affected in old age by blindness, he summons his foreman Mephistopheles and orders him to implement his final vision post haste. He hears the clamor of shovels and picks and imagines his project's completion:

There is still a swamp along the mountains—
All my accomplishments it poisons.
To drain this fetid marshland
Would be my last and highest deed.
I would open territory for many millions,
To dwell—not in safety, but in active liberty.
Green are the meadows, fertile;
men and animal herds
Find immediate comfort on the new earth,
Settled against the mighty dike
Erected by a bold and industrious community.
A paradise here within the dike's protective embrace,
While without floods may rage
up to the edge of the dike;
And as waters work to penetrate with force,
Communal action hurries to close the breach.
I am completely committed to this notion,
Wisdom can achieve no higher insight:
`He only earns freedom and existence
Who must daily conquer them anew.
Thus surrounded by danger, childhood, manhood and old age
Here spend their diligent years.
Oh, to see such teeming industry,
To stand on free ground with a free people.
To the moment I might say:
Abide, you are so beautiful!
The trace of my earthly days
Will never be submerged.
In anticipation of such high happiness,
I now enjoy the highest moment.[1]
11559-11586

Goethe

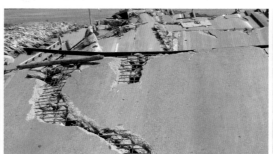

Having uttered the fatal words of the wager in relation to his vision of a Faustian republic living in daily defiance of dammed up waters, Faust dies a happy man. This is Faust's—not Goethe's—highest moment. But let us not confuse it with what I am calling the hydrological moment.

Does it matter that the death of the hero of one of literature's most vaunted texts, whose name inspired the historian Oswald Spengler to call our modern age Faustian[2], is directly linked to a monumental land reclamation project? Most certainly. If Goethe lets Faust's utterance appear to stand like a defiant call to modern technological living, he proceeds to undermine it like the insinuating water that washes against Faust's dikes. Not enough that Faust casts his statement in the subjunctive mood and has already sanctioned the murder of Philemon and Baucis, a rustic couple whose property stood in his way. Remember that Faust has recently been blinded by Care and only *hears* what he takes to be the sounds of progress. Mephistopheles' whispered aside to the audience gives the lie to Faust's defiance: what is being dug is not a trench, but Faust's grave—"Von keinem Graben, doch vom Grab" (11,558). The ground of Faust's vision is his own unacknowledged and impending death. For those reading attentively, Goethe lets on that Faust's vision is wrong and wrong for precisely two related reasons: 1) failure to integrate design with (as opposed to against) the dynamic characteristics of water, and 2) failure to account properly for mortality. Faust's highest moment of happiness is the reverse image of the hydrological moment. What, to take an example close to home, did the sounds of the Army Corps of Engineers re-constructing the levees in New Orleans signify? Or, to travel to the Netherlands and take an opposite example, the sounds of purposeful demolition along an expanded flood plain in Nijmegen?[3]

Mephistopheles

69

Battling the Flood, Louisiana

As Gaston Bachelard points out in *Water and Dreams*, water has an affinity with a particular kind of revery. A river, a shoreline, a wetland: all of these may initially be apprehended in their spatial dimension, but, one might argue in the spirit of Bachelard, a Heraclitean temporality infects each image. "A being dedicated to water is a being in flux. [...] Water always flows, always falls, always ends in horizontal death."[4] Whether the built environments we imagine and hope to realize are conceived in terms of the 100, 1,000, or 10,000 year storm; whether a nation or region fails to plan, plans inadequately, or plans for 200 years; or, as earth scientists are wont to do, we manage to think in geological time and imagine remediating patterns of sedimentation accomplished over hundreds and thousands of years—acknowledged or not, death is the implicit vanishing point of every image and act of imagination.

Victims, Hurricane Katrina, New Orleans

We see horizontal watery death on display in the image collages assembled by Spike Lee in *When the Levees Broke* (2006), his documentary film on the human toll caused by technological failure when Hurricane Katrina struck New Orleans. In the Dutch museum dedicated to the 1953 flood that eventually led to the construction of the Eastern Scheldt Storm Surge Barrier, an art installation projects the names of the 1,835 victims onto a dark shimmering surface—the names and histories of individuals written on water. Such retrospective and commemorative response is important, but let us also remember, as the cultural historian Philippe Aries taught us, that human attitudes toward death have a history.[5] In other words, to fix on death as the vanishing point of human efforts is not necessarily to cast a pall on our collective imaginings, but rather to give them a new chance by inviting the specter of death into our deliberations. Instead of denying death, we may proceed all the more exuberantly.

Battling the Sea, Closing the Urk and Lemmer Dikes

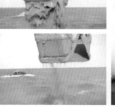

A kind of dystopic exuberance is what we find in Kevin Costner's 1995 film *Water World*. Although the film has obvious flaws, its visualization of a world where dry land is a distant cultural memory and human community a fragile undertaking is bracing. Two primary modes of group adaptation are imagined: the smokers and the atoll. The smokers, led by the "deacon" energetically performed by Dennis Hopper, inhabit the still floating hulk of the Exxon Valdese and practice a quasi-religious, post-apocalyptic doctrine of unlimited growth, manifest destiny, and violent conquest. Their problem is that their floating oil reserves are all but exhausted. The circularly enclosed atoll, by contrast, is governed by an archaically organized principle of sustainability. Population is strictly controlled; even corpses are recycled in a slurry that nourishes the lone ancient tree at the floating atoll's center.

While such atolls were plentiful in times past, they are on the verge of extinction: The less viable the atoll, the more ecological fundamentalism digs in. In the smokers and the atoll we recognize the predominant and opposed paradigms of our current politico-environmental landscape. What the film bleakly suggests is that, under the extreme duress of absolute sea level rise, clinging obdurately to either of these options is not tenable, nor is compromise a panacea. The non-dialectical, third possibility is reviled by smokers and atoll alike: the anonymous mariner, played by Kevin Kostner, whose isotropic gills and webbed feet allow him to thrive amphibiously in the new environment. Perhaps the screenwriters took a leaf from Kurt Vonnegut's novel *Galapagos* (1985), in which the humanoids of a million years hence have returned to the water, have fins in lieu of hands, lead shorter lives, have been relieved by of the burdens of their big brains and are, as Vonnegut repeatedly points out, much happier.

Victims, 1953 flood, Netherlands

Yet he's offered
us another
Holding, on his new-won
land!

Never trust what's built
on water,
On the heights maintain
your stand.
11135-11139

Vonnegut imagines an evolutionary adaptation of the human brain in response to sea level rise and attendant calamities. He is not the first to link consciousness and water. When Sigmund Freud was searching for an instructive analogy to help him describe the work of psychoanalysis, he put it this way: "Where id was, there shall ego be. It is a work of culture—not unlike the draining of the Zuider Zee."[6] His student and apologist Bruno Bettelheim is convinced that the right context for understanding Freud's metaphor is Goethe's Faust. "Since we know that Goethe played a dominant role in Freud's intellectual development, it is not mere speculation that Freud selected the metaphor of the reclamation of land from the sea because it would induce the reader to relate the work of psychoanalysis to Faust, the great poem about the reclamation of the soul."[7] I do not have to point out that Bettelheim and Freud both fail to recognize the hydrological moment. Nor do they gather that the pertinent relation between landscape and consciousness is not one of analogy, but of co-determination. As we see all around us, cultures dedicated to shoring up the defiant Faustian ego at all costs are incapable of responding adequately to the mounting urgencies of global sea level rise. What will be needed, and what Goethe already envisions, is a Post-Faustian, Post-Freudian evolutionary development that opens the terrain of consciousness and individuation for aquatic penetrations both real and metaphorical.

What are the limits of mimesis in design? What kinds of mirrors can design hold up to nature and itself? Can design imagine post-humanity? Can it imagine evolutionary processes that eliminate its capacity to imagine them? Can it imagine a return to water? Can it imagine species extinction under the conditions of global warming? Should it? In what mode might such imaginings be possible?

The culture wars around climate science already pit religion against academic rationality. Framed in this manner, neither side will win—it's the Smokers vs. the Atoll. Design should intervene in a manner that engages both

Freud

72

Zuiderzee Works

sides and prepares both the human ego and the built environment for post-Faustian existence. Here are three suggestions from the humanities:

1. According to Rabbinic tradition, it took Noah a long time to build the ark, anywhere from fifty-two to one-hundred-and-twenty years. Every day was an exercise in prophetic semiosis. Like Noah, design should imagine and create built environments that spell out the future.

2. Theodor Storm's late nineteenth-century novella, *The Rider on the White Horse*, relates the story of a dike master on a Frisian island in northern Germany. His workers honor an age-old tradition of compensatory sacrifice by tossing a stray dog into the pits of the modern dike they are building. The dike master, who is a model of technological progress and scrupulous morality, forbids the barbaric practice. This is, of course, his Faustian undoing. Design should practice and make explicit the ritualized and real sacrifices necessary in the present environment.

3. In a witty aside in his introduction to *Amphibious Living*, Hans Venhuizen suggests that Jesus lived amphibiously. Perhaps it is time to rewrite the parable of the two builders. In Luke 6:47-49 Jesus is reported to say: "Whosoever cometh to me, and heareth my words, and doeth them, I will shew you to whom he is like. He is like a man which built a house, and digged deep, and laid the foundation on a rock. And when the flood arose, the stream beat vehemently upon that house, and could not shake it; for it was founded upon a rock. But he that heareth, and doeth not, is like a man that without a foundation built an house upon the earth: against which the stream did beat vehemently, and immediately it fell, and the ruin of that house was great." We know who built levees in the sand. And we know who has been sinking piles into deep bedrock, even to the extent that sewer systems maintain a stable level while surrounding terrain continues to subside. Both builders seem foolish now. What we need are men and women who build (and bet) on water. It is time to be wise in our foolishness. The hydrological moment requires it.

Oosterscheldekering - Storm Surge Barrier

Faust

73

And yet with all your walls and dams,
You're merely dancing to our tune:
Since you prepare for our Neptune,
The Water-demon, one vast feast.
You'll be lost in every way –
The elements are ours, today,
And ruin comes on running feet.
11539-11543

DOUG JEROLMACK
TUNING SEDIMENT

THE MISSISSIPPI RIVER DELTA IS A LANDSCAPE BUILT BY FLOODS.
IT IS A THICK AND WATERY TERRAIN EVEN THOUGH, FROM ABOVE, IT SEEMS LIKE THE WATER HAS LEFT. TODAY, THE RIVER ONLY COVERS A SMALL FRACTION OF THE DELTA. YET, MOST OF THE REGION IS A HUGE PILE OF SEDIMENT, WHICH BY DEFINITION, IS MATERIAL THAT HAS BEEN TRANSPORTED BY WATER. TO EXPLAIN ALL OF THIS SEDIMENT, WHICH MAY BE KILOMETERS THICK, THE RIVER MUST MOVE. IT IS DIFFICULT FOR PEOPLE TO COMPREHEND THIS IDEA OF DEEP TIME, TO CONSIDER A LANDSCAPE FORMING OVER TENS OF THOUSANDS OF YEARS. THE EXISTING ALIGNMENT OF THE MISSISSIPPI RIVER HOLDS BATON ROUGE, NEW ORLEANS, AND COUNTLESS SMALLER TOWNS. OUR HISTORY IS IDENTIFIED WITH THE RIVER IN ITS CURRENT, FIXED STATE. BUT THIS IS JUST A SNAPSHOT. WATER MOVES ACROSS THE ENTIRE LANDSCAPE OVER THOUSANDS OF YEARS AND IT LEAVES BEHIND A SEDIMENTARY TRACE. EVIDENTLY, THE LANDSCAPE THAT WE SEE IS NOT THE LANDSCAPE AS IT ALWAYS WAS.

DROWNING DELTA: Marshes throughout the Mississippi delta are sinking due to compaction and sea level rise. These marshes play a crucial societal role in the dissipation of storm energy and protection of coastal cities, such as New Orleans. Without adequate sedimentation from hurricanes, floods, or normal fluvial processes, the marshes will literally drown, exposing our coastal settlements to greater risk.

DEFINITION OF A DELTA

Sedimentation, subsidence, and sea level rise are the key variables in a geological definition of a river delta. At the most fundamental level, in order for sedimentation to occur, water must slow down. Basically, the more it slows, the more sediment it deposits. This is possible because the Mississippi River is not flat; it has a gradient, which drives the river's current. In comparison, the ocean is on average a flat surface. So, as the river approaches the ocean, its slope grades to zero and its velocity decreases. As a result, its gradually loses its ability to carry sediment and deposition begins to occur. A delta, by this definition, is essentially the distance over which the river transitions to a zero slope on its course to the ocean and deposits sediment. Today, we know this distance to be approximately 500 km.

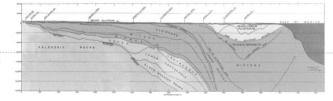

GEOLOGIC CROSS SECTION: Humans are comfortable with landscapes as static quantities, and it is difficult for most to comprehend deep time or a landscape forming over tens of thousands of years. We identify our comparatively short history and ourselves with the Mississippi in its current position. However, 1,500 years ago, the Mississippi River was 200 to 300 km away. If we weren't expending massive amounts of time and energy to hold the river in place right now, it would be 200 to 300 km away again.

Subsidence occurs as sediment deposited by the river settles under its own weight and squeezes water out of its pore spaces. While subsidence drives the delta surface lower relative to the ocean, sea level rise raises the elevation of the ocean relative to the delta. On geologic time scales, the delta achieves a kind of balance where the amount of sediment deposited by the river approximately equals the rate at which land is sinking relative to

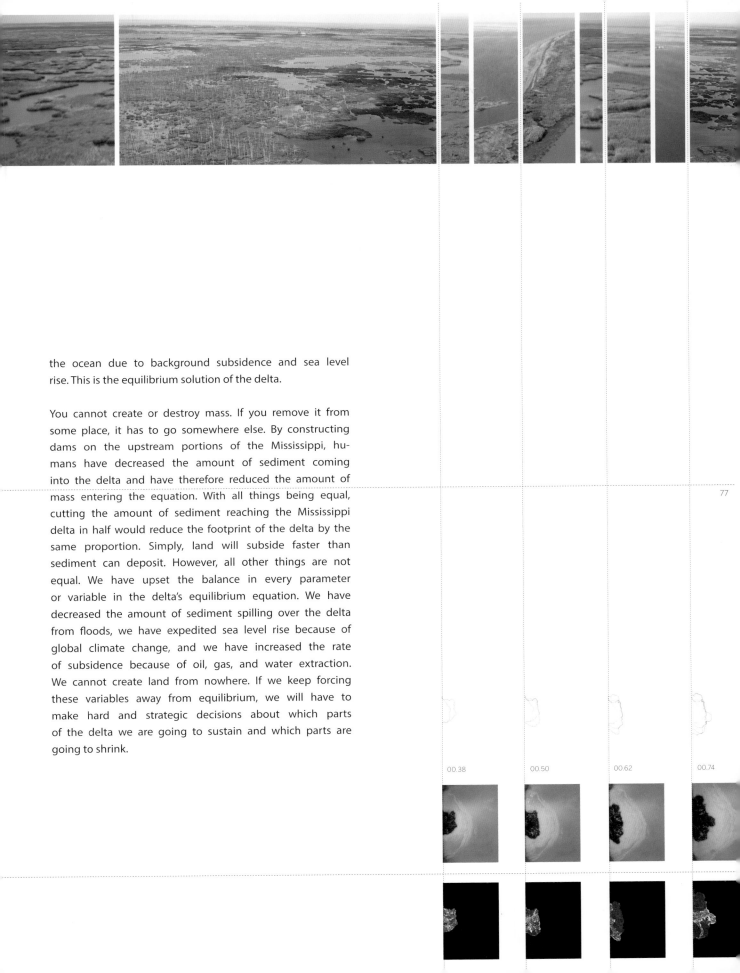

the ocean due to background subsidence and sea level rise. This is the equilibrium solution of the delta.

You cannot create or destroy mass. If you remove it from some place, it has to go somewhere else. By constructing dams on the upstream portions of the Mississippi, humans have decreased the amount of sediment coming into the delta and have therefore reduced the amount of mass entering the equation. With all things being equal, cutting the amount of sediment reaching the Mississippi delta in half would reduce the footprint of the delta by the same proportion. Simply, land will subside faster than sediment can deposit. However, all other things are not equal. We have upset the balance in every parameter or variable in the delta's equilibrium equation. We have decreased the amount of sediment spilling over the delta from floods, we have expedited sea level rise because of global climate change, and we have increased the rate of subsidence because of oil, gas, and water extraction. We cannot create land from nowhere. If we keep forcing these variables away from equilibrium, we will have to make hard and strategic decisions about which parts of the delta we are going to sustain and which parts are going to shrink.

00.38   00.50   00.62   00.74

FIELD MEASUREMENT: After the flood subsided, members from our team went out on a helicopter and collected samples from 40 locations across the shoreline of the delta. They measured how much mud and sand was laid down throughout the region both on the surface and through deep core samples. We also sailed a boat down the Mississippi River, out into the ocean and around the perimeter of the bird foot, scooping up surface water from the Mississippi plume. The boat was able to measure the temperature of the water, its speed, and saltiness. Much of this data was used to calibrate true color satellite MODIS data in order to determine remotely how many grams of sediment were contained per liter of flood or ocean water.

2011 FLOOD

Starting in the late 1800s and completed by the late 1920s, engineers straightjacketed the Mississippi River. Every inch of riverbank within the Delta has been artificially leveed in a comprehensive system, and in this sense, the entire delta has been engineered to stop flooding from occurring. This includes the Atchafalaya River, which branches off the Mississippi River as it enters the delta region. When the 2011 flood came along it was the largest event on record; the two rivers were not nearly able to contain the increased volume of floodwater. As a result, in a kind of doomsday scenario, the Army Corps of Engineers decided to open the Morganza spillway, which connects the Mississippi to the Atchafalaya Basin in order to prevent flooding in the more populous areas of Baton Rogue and New Orleans. When the spillway was opened it flooded a sparsely populated portion of Cajun country that consists of farmland, swamps, and bayous. Despite this, 40,000 people were displaced and their farms and homes were destroyed.

While the floodwater release was catastrophic for the people who lived in the Atchafalaya Basin, as scientists it was interesting to us because the Army Corps of Engineers, for the first time in 80 years, inadvertently simulated a flood that used to be "natural." Before the artificial levees were built, floodwaters would rise and spill out of the channel, inundating broad areas of the delta every spring and compensating for both subsidence and sea level rise. The opening of the Morganza spillway presented the first opportunity in almost a century to

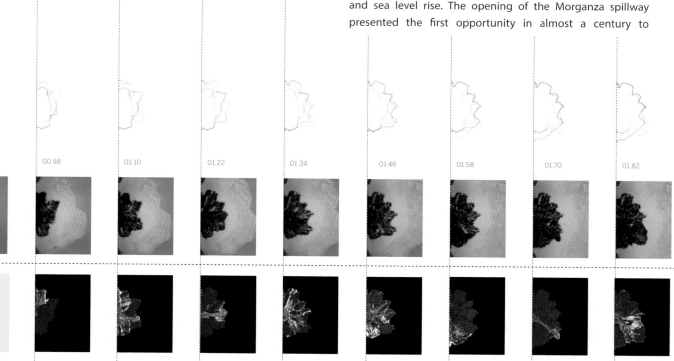

0.86   00.98   01.10   01.22   01.34   01.46   01.58   01.70   01.82

analyze what happens during such a flood. Our hypothesis was that the Mississippi's currents were completely contained within artificial levees and as a result, the river could not deposit sediment on the delta or near-shore marshes. Instead, the river was ejecting all of its sediment into the deep ocean. In comparison, when the Atchafalaya was intentionally allowed to flood, it produced a wide and slow plume of water, which actually deposited a significant amount of sediment over the delta and near shore marshes.

We found that the plume in the Atchafalaya covered an area 100 km wide and deposited sediment of a significant thickness over the entire Basin. However, because the plume was so vast and slow moving, when sediment rich waters reached the ocean, they became trapped in the near shore environment. Over a period of a few months, the ocean waves and tides gently washed the Atchafalaya's sediment-laden water back on the marshes, building them up slowly over time. In contrast, in the Mississippi, which is not allowed to flood, we found that there was not very much deposition, even though this river carries a greater total volume of sediment. Instead, it was concentrated in a very powerful jet, like a fire hose, that was shooting the sediment from the mouth of the Mississippi and into the deep ocean. In the Delta, where centimeters of change that are imperceptible to us mean the difference between being above the ocean and being below it, the dynamics and forces of our impacts on the landscape could not be of more consequence.

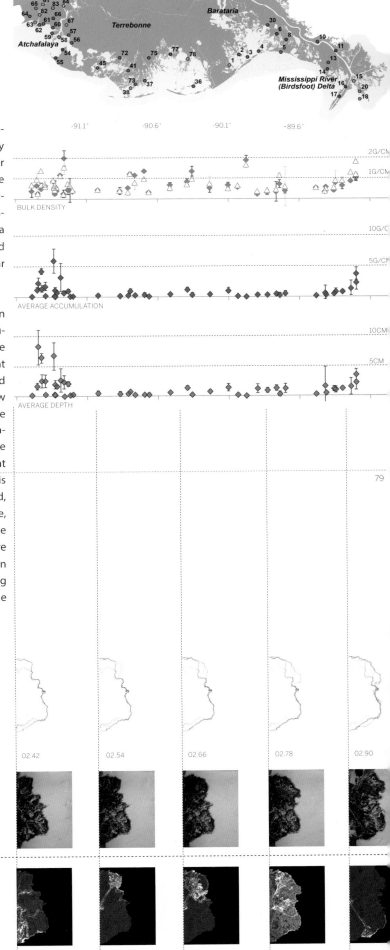

DELTA IN A DAY: The idea with experimental landscape building is that we can speed up time by shrinking spatial scale. Building a delta takes 10,000 years or more, but building a 1 m x 1 m x 5 cm thick pile of sediment can be done in a day. We constructed the bathtub model in 2008, and ran experiments off and on for two years. The model consists of a fiberglass tub bought from an aquaculture supplier, a mechanically turning screw that takes sand from a funnel and allows us to control the sediment feed rate in the basin, and water coming from a tap. Using a camera looking down from above, we tracked the location of the river, the shoreline, and the extent of the delta. We took an image every two minutes during the experiment. In the areas where nothing has happened, you subtract one image from the other and you get nothing. In areas where there wasn't water in one picture and there is water in the next you get a color change. Through image differencing you can literally map the migration of the river channel and the behavior of the delta system.

Bathtub in the Basement

80

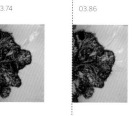

| 02 | 03.14 | 03.26 | 03.38 | 03.50 | 03.62 | 03.74 | 03.86 | 03.98 |

BATHTUB MODEL

The Mississippi delta was constructed over tens of thousands of years. Today, we have only a snapshot of a structure of a system. In the relationship between the river and delta, however, the aspect of the system that is least visible is the dynamics, by which I mean the time-varying elements. I think the challenge of communicating this information more broadly is the challenge of visualizing the interaction between water and sediment in terms of a deep, slow time. This is where connections between disciplines are important. We need to begin coming up with creative ways of visualizing these variables that grip people to see intuitively that this landscape will look different in the future, and that that time in the future is not far away.

Physical experiments to me have a real visceral appeal in this regard; I need to see things change with my eyes in order to have an understanding of how the system works. We had an idea to construct a miniature river delta, to watch how the river makes a channel, and how that channel creates new land. In the laboratory, we built as simple a system as possible, using only a bathtub, a steady flow of water, and sediment. The sediment wasn't even nearly as complicated as it is in the delta; it had a much narrower range of particle sizes, and there were no plants or clay. Every variable was constant, more or less. With the model, we were able to measure the river channel's rate of movement, its average size, and the delta's rate of growth. Yet, even in this very simple system, we observed incredibly spontaneous complexity. For example, eventually, we were able to predict the average

rate at which the river jumped. We found it was about 20 minutes, but sometimes, the river jumped after 10 minutes, and sometimes after 35 minutes. We were also able to determine generally that the river tended to go places where it hadn't gone in a while, because that's where the slope was steepest. We could actually observe and quantify this process. We could watch the sediment grains moving around within the river channel, and we could observe the river channel eroding, shaking around sideways and then just filling up with sediment and, finally, literally jumping out of its channel.

With some very basic physics, we eventually derived a mathematical model to figure out what actually dictates the average amount of time it takes for a river to build out a new lobe (the part of the delta where the river meets the ocean and deposits sediment) and how long it takes to reach a critical slope at which sediment begins to deposit, forcing the river to jump its bank. We examined data from published papers on natural river deltas to see if there was evidence for these processes occurring at the timescales we predicted. The answer was yes. So, we learned that there are characteristic timescales for the processes of delta formation and erosion, and that they are governed by mass conservation. There is a mass balance for the system, overall, which we can measure and understand. Yet, in natural systems, there are things that are predictable and things that simply aren't. We can never predict with certainty, despite our absolute best efforts at control, where the river is going to go, and when it's going to go there. All we have is probability.

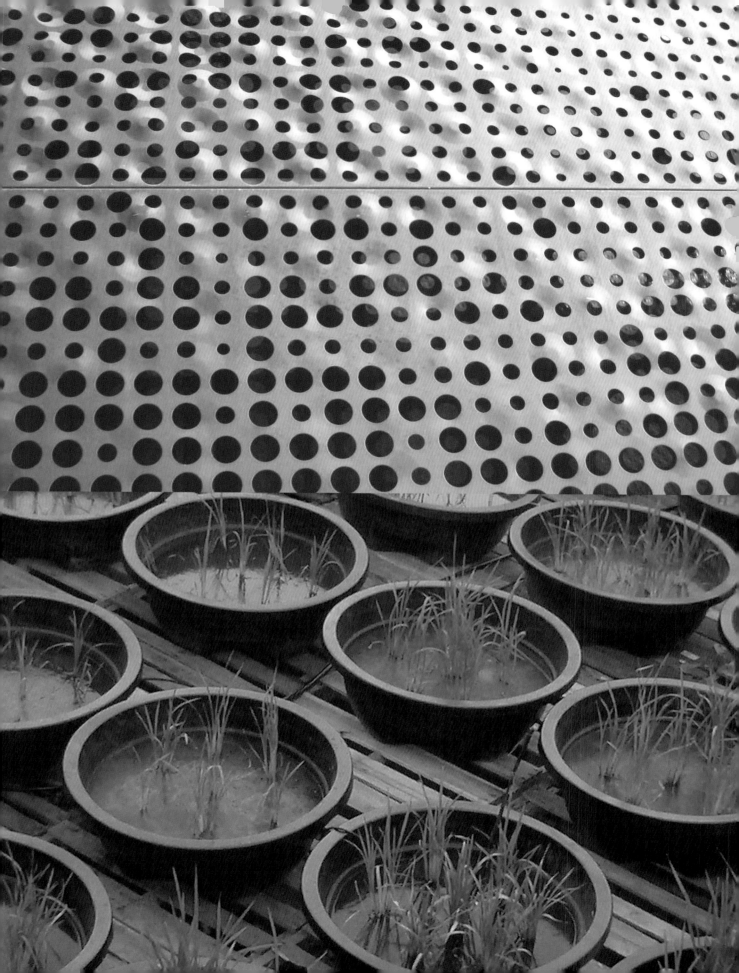

WALTER HOOD
COMMON SENSING

WATER IS EVERYWHERE, YET IT ALSO REMINDS US OF EXACTLY WHERE WE ARE. JUST WHEN YOU FORGET THAT NEW YORK IS AN ISLAND, WASHINGTON, D.C. IS A WETLAND, OR THE SAN FRANCISCO BAY IS AN ESTUARY, WATER BACKS YOU UP. WATER IS CODIFIED AS A REAL ENVIRONMENTAL CONDITION WHEN YOU SEE IT IN THE STREETS, FEEL IT ON YOUR SKIN, OR SMELL IT IN THE AIR. DESIGN FOR WATER SHOULD NOT BE SEEN THROUGH CONVEYORS, CONTAINERS, AND CONDUITS, BUT RATHER AS A MEANS TO HUMANIZE AND ELUCIDATE ITS SENSATIONS IN WAYS THAT ARE PERFORMATIVE AND PROPHETIC. A COMMON SENSE OF WATER ONLY REINFORCES THE MUNDANE ELEMENTS OF SPACE THAT WE NO LONGER NOTICE BECAUSE OF THEIR UBIQUITOUS REPLICATION IN OUR LIVES. COMMON SENSING SUGGESTS BEING IN A PLACE WHERE SENSORIAL STIMULATION OCCURS IN MYRIAD WAYS THROUGH THE ELEMENTS AROUND US. EVENTS CAN SPRING UP THAT CONNECT US AND PROVIDE NEW WAYS TO EXPERIENCE THIS COMMON WATER. IN OUR EVERYDAY LIVES, WE CAN NOURISH THIS SENSING OF WATER AS A WAY TO REMIND, RESPECT, AND REITERATE THIS RELATIONSHIP WITHOUT HAVING TO RECREATE OR RECONSTRUCT ITS NARRATIVE. WHEN WE SENSE, ESPECIALLY WITH WATER, WE CAN FEEL THROUGH SEEING, TASTE BY SMELLING, AND WE CAN SEE BY HEARING. WITH WATER NOTHING IS 1:1.

Port of Wilmington Waterfront Park + Coastlines

IF YOU CAN'T SEE THE OCEAN, IS IT THERE?

THIS NOTION OF COASTLINE DOESN'T EXIST; IT IS JUST A POINT IN TIME. YOU CAN KEEP DRAWING THAT LINE UNTIL YOU'RE BLUE IN THE FACE.

THE COAST NEVER REALLY ENDS.

WILMINGTON WATERFRONT

In Wilmington and San Pedro, CA, a large port and container terminal took away the waterfront and blocked the coastline. Now, a giant park is being built as a buffer between this active industrial area and the neighboring community. We wanted to bring back a vision of the ocean and to challenge the notion of a coast as a static line.

Using local Southern California sandstone as the primary material, we created 18 towers that span a half-mile stretch along West C Street, between King and Neptune avenues. The towers are references to both the eroded San Pedro stone bluffs, which are visible from the site, and the historical coastline as it moved across the landscape. They rise from 1' to 14' and are inclined at different angles to create a spatially diverse experience. The arrangement offers two views of the coast; looking east-west constructs an illusion of a solid bluff while looking northsouth view evokes a rhythmic and varying coastal edge.

Walking through the towers, at certain points you can see the coastline re-emerge; at others it breaks up again.

Spoleto Wandering Coastlines + Water Table

EVER SMELLED A MARSH?

WATER SMELLS, PARTICULARLY SALTY WATER!
   ESTUARIES HAVE A DISTINCT ODOR, BRINY AND EARTHY
   ALL AT ONCE. TIDES ACCUMULATE ON FLAT GROUND AS
   PREVAILING BREEZES BRING DISTANT SMELLS.

PEOPLE LIVING IN THE COASTAL LANDSCAPE OF
SOUTH CAROLINA ARE ENMESHED IN THE SMELL OF WATER.
   YET EVEN AS WE SMELL, IT'S NOT ALWAYS EASY TO
   UNDERSTAND WHAT SURROUNDS US.

   IN MANY PLACES, PEOPLE DISCONNECT FROM THE
   SMELLS, SEPARATING THEMSELVES FROM THEIR SOURCE.

SPOLETO FESTIVAL

For the Spoleto Festival in Charleston, South Carolina we constructed a site-specific installation imitating a plantation rice field using only large polyvinyl tubs, re-cycled wood crating, and steel scaffolding. The design transformed an asphalt schoolyard into an ecological emergence. To invite participation and engagement, we mounted the installation on a platform at table height. This allowed community members to reach into the plants and get close enough to really experience their smell. The Caroline Gold Rice plants, which we grew for six weeks, were meant to evoke the city's historical rice-based agriculture, but also to bring a distinctive water aroma back into the city. Within a month there were croaking frogs and circling blue herons, called to the area by the re-introduced smells. We also initiated an ephemeral form of mapping using blue chairs to mark historical boundaries. These appeared and disappeared throughout the city, encouraging pedestrians to stop and interact with the artists. It was both a demonstration of the inevitable shifting of the lines we draw in addition to an opportunity to discuss possible futures for water in the city.

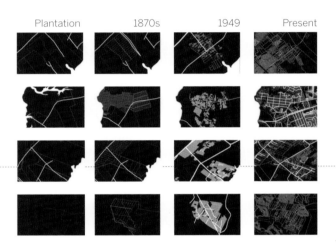

Plantation   1870s   1949   Present

SMELL MAP: Historically, African American communities settled near the water. Now those areas have been reclaimed for suburban developments and for people from the north. By studying historical maps, we can see how the smells of water have been erased from the places we live.

85

YOU CAN HEAR THE FOG.

IN A REDWOOD FOREST, WALKING INTO A CLOUD, LISTENING TO THE DAMP QUIET FOG, YOU CAN HEAR THE DROPLETS OF WATER.

TICK...

TICK...

TICK...

THE SOUND OF RAIN RINGS ON A ROOF; SIZZLES LEAP FROM CAR TIRES AS THEY WHIZ BY.

DE YOUNG MUSEUM

Sometimes you can see things to hear them; you can see something wet or green and actually hear the wind. At the de Young Museum, all the stormwater in the site moves through a central courtyard containing large Australian tree ferns. Through the selection of materials, we attempted to create a dialogue about the ecology of the area, its topography and its history. The space is like a terrarium inside the building, with crushed shale and Appleton green sandstone from a quarry near Manchester, England. We were interested in the stone's variable color hues, which range from green to grey to red, changing as they go from cool and damp to dry and hot. The stones also correspond to the copper paneling of the new de Young, while simultaneously evoking the hilly sand dunes that once existed in the landscape of its construction. The planting for the site was ultimately very simple: the low points were wet, and the high points were dry.

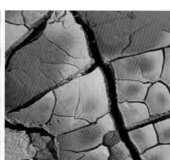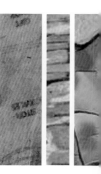

Civil and Human Rights Center, GA

CIVIL AND HUMAN RIGHTS CENTER

In the Civil and Human Rights Center, we proposed a landscape that swells and contracts like clay. The Center

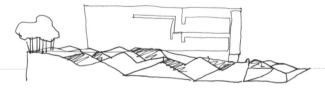

sits in Atlanta's Apalachicola-Chattahoochee Flint River Basin, which is characterized by a rich, red clay soil that shrinks and expands as the region floods and dries. The landscape is organized as a series of fractals, each with its own performance and function. This includes swale fractals, public space fractals, and stormwater retention fractals. As a whole, they are meant to evoke the Georgia clay breaking apart, fusing, and cracking over time based on its relationship with water.

87

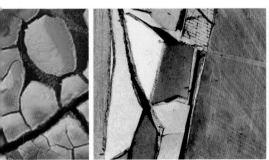

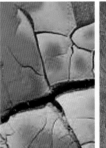

HERRON HILL RESERVOIR

PLACES USED TO GO BY NAMES LIKE SWEETWATER;

YOU COULD JUST TASTE THE PLACE!

IT WOULD BE GOOD TO TASTE SWEETWATER AGAIN.

Working in African American communities, I hear over and over again people say that they remember when the water was sweet. In the Hill District, we have been working on a project called "Greenprint" that attempts to re-connect the community to its landscape and to the greater Pittsburgh area. The Hill's landscape structure is a sampling of Garden City movement planning efforts across America; the Monongahela and Allegheny Rivers bound its thick and verdant edges, while the open center

contains valleys, tributaries, and abandoned stream channels and riparian edges. This gives clarity to the topography of the community, which is located on a set of hills with a rich cultural, artistic, and industrial legacy.

The Herron reservoir sits at the highest elevation in the city and supplies the Hill and the downtown area. Many of the city's preachers used to live around the reservoir, in a community where everyone said the water was sweet. Today, the reservoir is fenced off and surrounded by a bu-colic park. As part of the Greenprint, we are rehabilitating the Alpena Stairway and other access points to improve the connection between the community, the park and the surrounding single-family housing. We are opening up the Reservoir to allow people to have access to the sweet water once again.

LOMBARD STEPS

WYANDOTTE STEPS

ALPENA STEPS

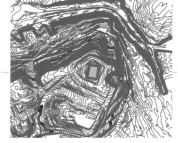

COMMUNITY TOPOGRAPHY: The Herron Reservoir was constructed in 1920 to replace the aging Garfield pumping station and holding tanks. It was built on the highest point in Pittsburgh to take advantage of gravity fed plumbing systems.

BIGELOW STEPS

Alpena Steps to Herron Hill Reservoir

KAZI ASHRAF
WATER AS GROUND

ONCE UPON A PLACE AND TIME, THE CITY OF DHAKA EMERGED DELICATELY FROM AN IRASCIBLE LANDSCAPE CALLED THE BENGAL DELTA. POWERFUL RIVERS CHURN THROUGH THE DELTAIC LANDSCAPE CONSTITUTED BY RAINFALLS, CYCLONES, FLOODS, AND SILTING AND LAND-SHIFTING OF MONUMENTAL PROPORTIONS. IN THIS FLUCTUATING HYDROLOGICAL WORLD, CITIES AND SETTLEMENTS CONTINUED TO BE STRUCTURED BY AN IMPROMPTU ORGANIZATION IN A DYNAMIC MATRIX OF RIVERS, CANALS, WETLANDS, FLOODPLAINS, AGRICULTURAL FIELDS, CHARS (SILTED LANDFORMS), AND HUMAN HABITATION. YET DHAKA AND THE DELTA APPEAR INCREASINGLY AS TWO SEPARATE ENTITIES, ANTITHETICAL AND STRANGER TO EACH OTHER, PARTICULARLY SINCE THE 1960S WHEN A DIFFERENT DEVELOPMENT ETHOS WAS INTRODUCED AND ENCOURAGED. AS PART OF THAT PRACTICE, LANDFILLS, EMBANKMENTS, AND ROADWAYS SUPPORTED THE TECHNOLOGY OF A DRY CULTURE, PITTING THE CITY AGAINST THE DELTA. MANY OF THE CURRENT CRISES OF DHAKA—LACK OF LAND, LACK OF HOUSING, LACK OF CIVIC SPACES—STEM FROM THIS OPPOSITION, AT THE CENTER OF WHICH IS THE INABILITY TO INCORPORATE THE LANGUAGE OF A DYNAMIC AQUATIC LANDSCAPE INTO PLANNING MECHANISMS AND POLICIES. PLANNERS AND POLICY-MAKERS GLORIFY LAND, WHILE WATER IS EXILED TO THE DOMAIN OF POETS, VAGRANTS, AND THE PITIFUL MARGINS OF THE CITY. INDEED, WHAT IS WET IS SEEN AS A SIGN OF BACKWARDNESS AND ARCHAIC PRACTICES.

MEASURES OF WATER

In one of the stories in *Invisible Cities*, Italo Calvino describes how one's perception of a city will depend on how one arrives there, whether by land or by water. It is imperative now that a new design discourse must consider a "water ethos," where water is the measure and instrument of spatial and social organization. A water ethos indicates a fundamental immersion in water with anthropological and sociological significance. A measure of water will have to consider the following:

Water creates a paradox, water is a paradox. There is, often in deltaic places, too much water, and there is often too little water. Water purifies, water needs to be purified. Once water was needed to purify everything, and now water needs to be purified before anything can be done with it. Water disorients and reorients. Water is an agent of transformation, of fluctuations and inversions, and as

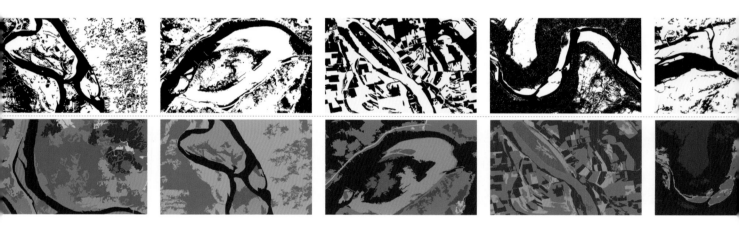

a consequence, generator of ambiguities. Water in the everyday dry domain can disrupt normality, and produce new social and political realities.

Water assures neither terra nor firma. Water challenges taking for granted the fact that land is ground. In a new constitution of ground, we will have to develop new terms of reference, such as the following:

Immersion. Buoyancy. Drift. Level. Depth. Fluidity. Flotation. Ebb. Tide. Rhythm.

THE MATRIX OF THE DELTA

The singular emblem of the Bengal delta is the "char": a land formation induced by the dynamics of soil-shifts and water flows. Water from upland mountains brings pulverized remains to the flat flood-plains in the form of sand, silt, and mud, depositing them in an unpredictable geometry of land-forms and waterways. Here, delicate chars appear one year to disappear in the next, while the more or less stabilized ones among them—it is always more or less—become sites of settlement and habitation.

Borne out of a fluid dynamic, chars pose a conceptual challenge to design imagination. They bear unsettling questions on what is site, what is fixity, and therefore what is architecture. Chars provoke a new thinking in the relation between architecture and landscape, even urging a re-thinking of the copula: *between.* Chars shift the thinking from object to situation, from form to matrix.

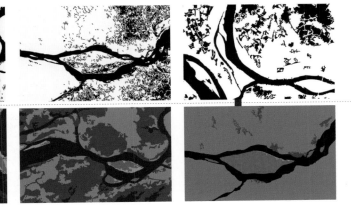

"The bosom of Bengal is draped with rivers and their tributaries, twisted and intertwined like tangled locks, streaked with the white of foamy waves. This verdant land is like a maiden in the embrace of an ancient sage, held to his immense chest, locked in his wet kiss, his dense hair and beard tumbling in sinuous complexity over her youthful body and flowing on beyond." (Advaita Malla Barman, *A River called Titash*)

93

While there are villages focused towards (dry) towns and cities, a vast part of the delta is structured by the char and consequently by shifting and emergent rivers and riverbanks. Advaita Malla Barman, in his epic and auto-biographical tale of life in the delta, *A River called Titash*, imagines the origin of the river Titash: "Once upon a time the restless Meghna, dancing along her way, slipped into a careless moment—her left bank strained and broke. Her current and waves flowed into that breach. The in-flow there created its own course, finding and molding soft alluvium, cutting and twisting through hard ground. After making a broad sweep that held hundreds of villages along the two sides of its course and touched the edges of many forests and flatlands, this pride of the Meghna returned to the lap of the Meghna."

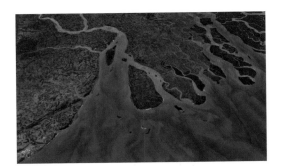

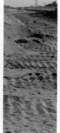

There are then hundreds of stories for hundreds of rivers and their hundreds of twists and turns. Their floods and emergent courses impart to the delta a corrugation of flat plains, ponds, muddy enclaves, and lowlands. Architecture here does not prescribe an enclosed and delineated center, but a string of responses based on dig-and-mound, ghats (riverbank hubs), and elevated machas (impromptu platforms). These assorted spatial typologies then become methods and practices of inhabiting the delta, often as a set of linked systems, but quite often as isolated phenomena.

LIQUID URBANISM

Chars, lowlands, and riverbanks continue to populate popular narratives, from folk culture to modern literature. The vast matrix of the delta, typically "rural," has adopted techniques and practices for dwelling in that landscape. But what of the city? In its positioning as a bastion of dryness, the city has not cooperated with the delta. Can char-thinking offer another kind of urbanism for the delta?

People who dwell in the core of Dhaka city, walk its streets, and live its urban doldrums may not be cognizant of it, but current urban development practices are based, literally, on liquid matter. Present Dhaka is being built, without a pause, from the fluid fabric of its surrounds. In Dhaka's inexorable expansion from its relatively higher grounds into the precious region of floodplains, wetlands, and "lowlands," vast aquatic areas are being furiously filled up by a powerful coterie of developers in an unprecedented scale of urbanistic interventions. Every hour, as part of the operation, barges on various rivers and rivulets ringing and networking Dhaka carry sand and soil from one location to deposit on another—typically, on a "lowland" that is marked for dry development where landfills are eventually parceled off as building lots. In another method, an array of steel pipes, sometimes miles long, pump sand and silt from a river location onto a landfill site. It is precisely at this juncture, where the expansion of the city meets an aquatic matrix, a new kind of city-thinking is needed: liquid urbanism.

Liquid urbanism entails an epistemic shift. The norm in thinking about Dhaka has been to privilege a core. Liquid urbanism suggests that this thinking begins instead from its wet edge, ushering a conception of a city that is integrated with the delta. Here fluid dynamics structures the city, and its infrastructure and hydrological issues serve as starting points and frameworks for future urban planning and design interventions.

A provisional manifesto for such an urbanism may yield the following approaches:

A platform in the delta. The production of platforms will remain a fundamental existential and functional objective in an aquatic terrain. This is poignantly evident during flooding, especially in monumental and turbulent deluges in Bangladesh. The design challenge will

2011

2010

be to work with water and not against it. Innovations in the ideas of dig-and-mound, ghats, and machas can be points of departure for a revised construction of platform architecture.

2009

Fluid dynamics. Form does follow flow in the dynamic of the floodplain where horizontal and vertical movements of water organize and direct architectural and landscape formations. Porosity and perforation become standard conditions in the topography. An organized matrix of mounds and canals may create a new topographical and urban formation as an alternative to the troublesome practice of wide scale landfilling.

2008

An embankment ecology. Following a series of devastating floods in the 1980s, Dhaka is now defined by embankments, a circular barrier and transport infrastructure that physically defines wet and dry. The norms of embankment mean cutting off wetlands and agricultural lands from conventionally prescribed developments, and posing unresolved questions for urban expansion. Instead of a sharp delineation, the embankment may be conceived as a fractured formation. It can be undulating or porous, multi-leveled or layered. The critical thing is to allow the passage of water. What that means is a redefinition of the embankment as an edge. It can be, instead of a barrier, developed into an integral landscape with boulevards, terraces, drainage systems, and water reservoirs. Controlled fractures and openings may allow flow of water from both sides in response to wetlands, reservoirs, retention ponds, and agricultural parks.

95

2007

2006

2005

2004

Over the past decade the pace of land-filling in the floodplains northeast of Dhaka are clearly visible from satellite imagery. The city's need for housing has outweighed the less immediate risk associated with disturbing the hydrologic dynamics of the delta. White blotches of transported sand create escarpments that delineate the encroaching edge of this development.

Embankment is a barrier, how do we deconstruct it? The given embankment can be reconfigured from a ribbon into a matrix. Instead of a single large embankment along the river or another waterscape, a field of small embankments can be created to develop a matrix of spaces and functions throughout a certain area. The idea behind the size, direction, and location of such mini-embankments is to intertwine the built and natural environments, as well as to control and retain water for agriculture, water table recharge, and everyday human needs. The embankments also act as dynamic circulation paths. Producing these embankments will also help to restore the natural dynamics of the river and create recreational landscapes and gardens. On a more ambitious level, the embankment may be conceived as the basis for a city.

Elevated System. With the intention of bringing "the city into the flood-plain and the flood-plain into the city," a network of cautious and careful development—streets, walkways, housing, and public places—that are mostly elevated either on stilts or non-continuous earth mound over agricultural fields, gardens, and parks, each at different elevations and responding to different levels of flooding may be proposed. The porosity at the lower level will assure an unimpeded flow of water at different seasons.

Where there is water, floatation is not far away.

In a terrain of constant water, floating decks and buildings are an inevitable response. People in the delta have developed responses through boat-houses, floating markets, floating vegetable gardens, and other buoyant devices. Islam Khan, the Mughal governor of Dhaka in the 17th century, is known to have lived on a barge. Floating gardens and markets still continue in practice. Floating schools and hospitals are becoming known as part of various NGO operations. There are many areas in and around Dhaka that still retain a watery landscape, a vestige of an earlier wetland or agricultural condition as leftovers from the embankment intervention. Certain selected areas could be developed as 'demonstration villages' to show how a community could live more effectively on water, utilizing its ecological resources and potentials. The settlement could be designed as floating or partially floating on water through innovative vernacular architecture amidst purposeful and productive bamboo groves, orchards, and fish farms. A large segment of adjoining riverbanks could be planned for agriculture (rice-fields) in which the people of the settlement could be engaged. The reason to build such a community in and around the city itself is to make a strong rhetorical and visual example: that paddy-fields can be an economic enterprise, a civic, public space, and part of the city's landscape. Water becomes a common denominator for agriculture and urbanism.

Re-configuring Embankment

Planning (cities and townships) around land and water, and not land versus water, seems to be a natural recourse in the delta. As the Dhaka based architect Saif Ul Haque notes: "Water could provide inexpensive transport solution for the city, it could serve as reservoirs for containing monsoon rains, it could provide for valuable protein for the city dwellers by fish farming, and it could help in keeping the underground water table stable by way of percolation and other methods."

97

PETER HUTTON
TRAVELING BY WATER

ONE NIGHT MANY YEARS AGO, I WAS ON THE FOREPEAK OF A SHIP STANDING LOOKOUT AS IT CROSSED THE INDIAN OCEAN. MY JOB AS A DECKHAND WAS TO REPORT LIGHTS ON THE HORIZON TO THE MATE ON THE BRIDGE BY RINGING A BELL. IT WAS A VERY WARM, MOON-LIT NIGHT AS WE PLOWED ACROSS THE OCEAN HEADED TOWARDS THE PERSIAN GULF. I NOTICED IT SUDDENLY GETTING DARKER; THE MOON VANISHED BEHIND THE CLOUDS. THE SEAS WERE BECOMING MORE TURBULENT, AND I REALIZED THAT IT WAS ALSO GETTING COLDER. I WATCHED AS IT BECAME DARKER AND DARKER, AND COLDER AND COLDER; ALL TRACES OF LIGHT WERE VANISHING. IT WAS AS IF I WAS SAILING INTO AN INK WELL. I WAS AMAZED BECAUSE I HAD THIS REALIZATION THAT WHAT I HAD KNOWN AS DARKNESS WAS STILL EVOLVING, I HAD NOT REALIZED THAT THERE WERE SO MANY DEGREES OF DARKNESS IN THE WORLD.

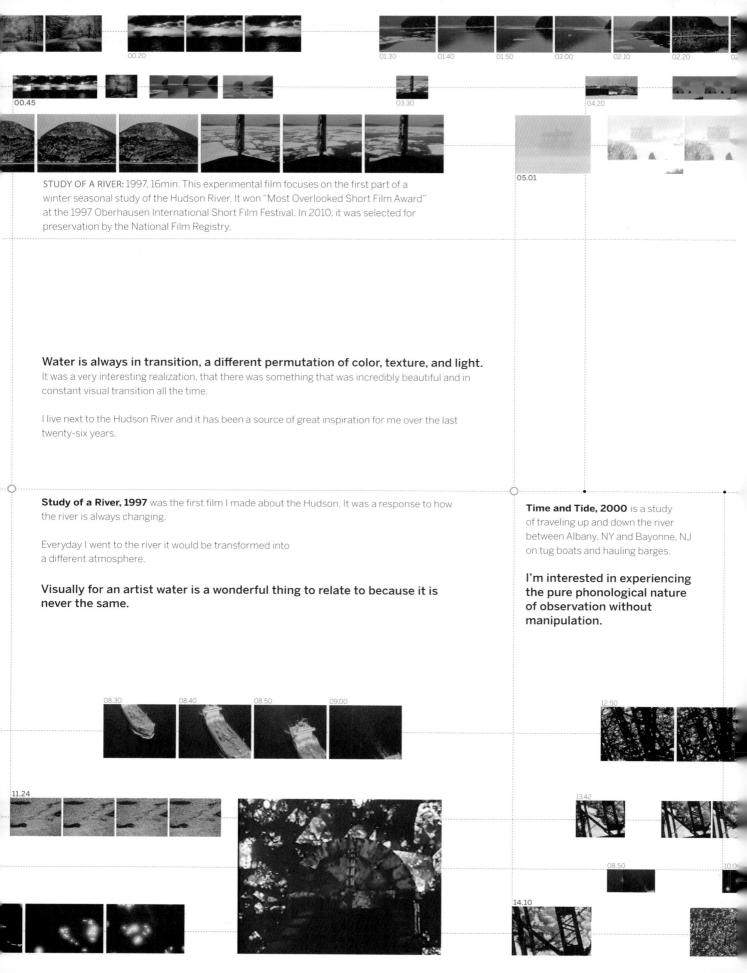

00.20   01.30   01.40   01.50   02.00   02.10   02.20

00.45   03.30   04.20

05.01

STUDY OF A RIVER: 1997, 16min. This experimental film focuses on the first part of a winter seasonal study of the Hudson River. It won "Most Overlooked Short Film Award" at the 1997 Oberhausen International Short Film Festival. In 2010, it was selected for preservation by the National Film Registry.

Water is always in transition, a different permutation of color, texture, and light.
It was a very interesting realization, that there was something that was incredibly beautiful and in constant visual transition all the time.

I live next to the Hudson River and it has been a source of great inspiration for me over the last twenty-six years.

Study of a River, 1997 was the first film I made about the Hudson. It was a response to how the river is always changing.

Everyday I went to the river it would be transformed into a different atmosphere.

Visually for an artist water is a wonderful thing to relate to because it is never the same.

Time and Tide, 2000 is a study of traveling up and down the river between Albany, NY and Bayonne, NJ on tug boats and hauling barges.

I'm interested in experiencing the pure phonological nature of observation without manipulation.

08.30   08.40   08.50   09.00

12.50

11.24

13.42

08.50   10.0

14.10

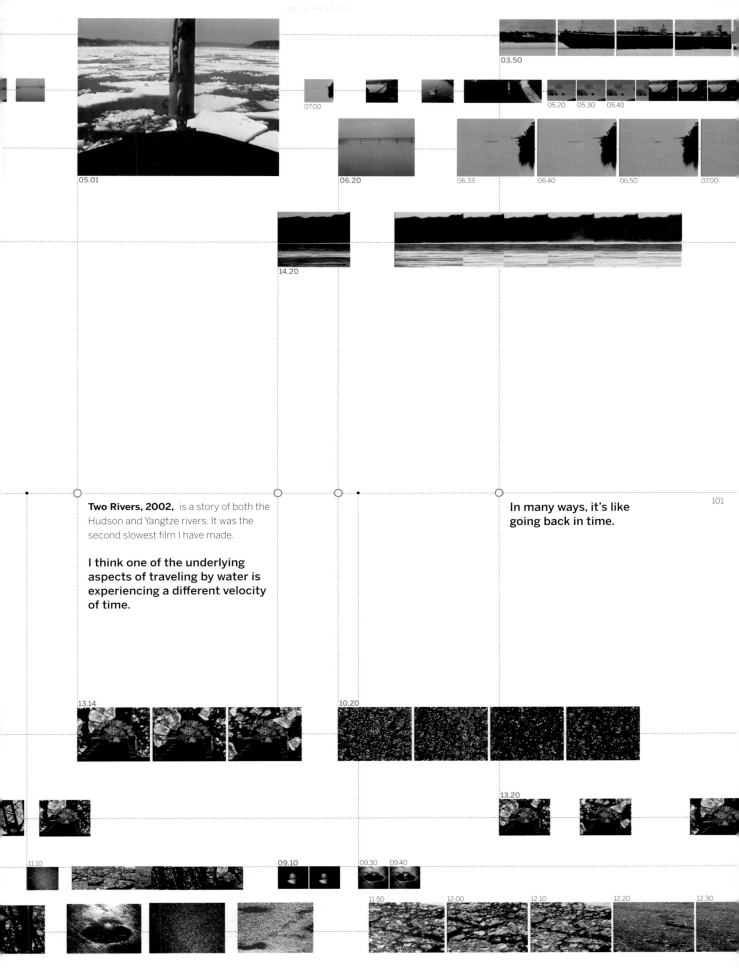

03.50

07.00

05.20 05.30 05.40

05.01

06.20

06.33 06.40 06.50 07.00

14.20

Two Rivers, 2002, is a story of both the
Hudson and Yangtze rivers. It was the
second slowest film I have made.

**I think one of the underlying
aspects of traveling by water is
experiencing a different velocity
of time.**

In many ways, it's like
going back in time.

13.14

10.20

13.20

11.10

09.10

09.30 09.40

11.50 12.00 12.10 12.20 12.30

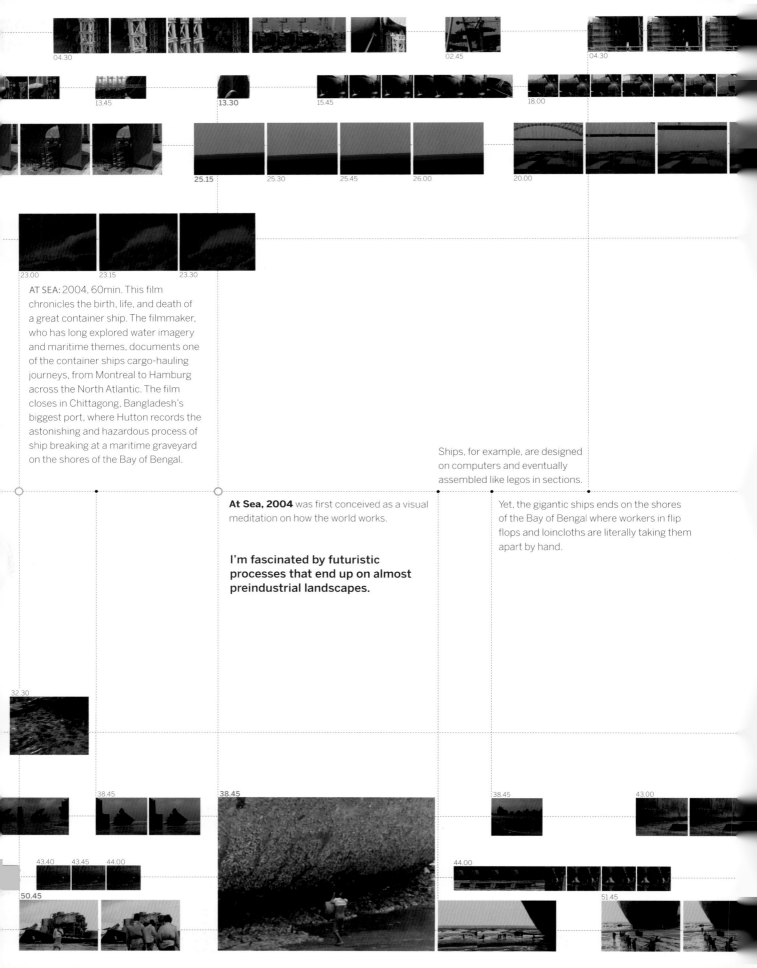

04.30   02.45   04.30

13.45   13.30   15.45   18.00

25.15   25.30   25.45   26.00   20.00

23.00   23.15   23.30

AT SEA: 2004, 60min. This film
chronicles the birth, life, and death of
a great container ship. The filmmaker,
who has long explored water imagery
and maritime themes, documents one
of the container ships cargo-hauling
journeys, from Montreal to Hamburg
across the North Atlantic. The film
closes in Chittagong, Bangladesh's
biggest port, where Hutton records the
astonishing and hazardous process of
ship breaking at a maritime graveyard
on the shores of the Bay of Bengal.

Ships, for example, are designed
on computers and eventually
assembled like legos in sections.

At Sea, 2004 was first conceived as a visual
meditation on how the world works.

Yet, the gigantic ships ends on the shores
of the Bay of Bengal where workers in flip
flops and loincloths are literally taking them
apart by hand.

**I'm fascinated by futuristic
processes that end up on almost
preindustrial landscapes.**

32.30

38.45   38.45   43.00

43.40   43.45   44.00   44.00

50.45   51.45

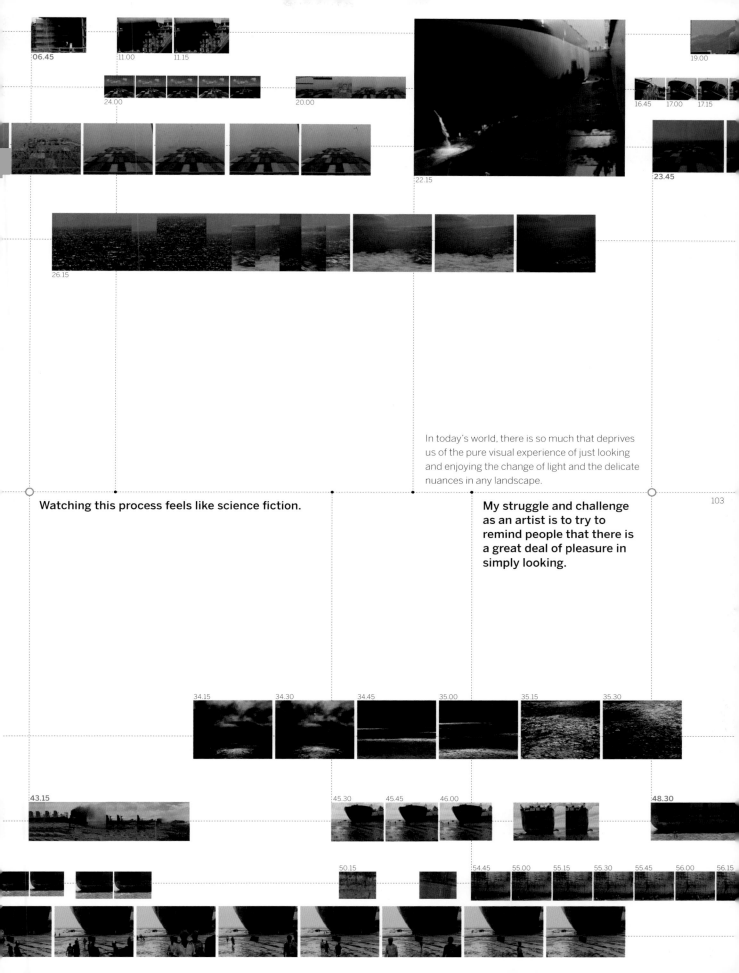

06.45

11.00 11.15

19.00

24.00

20.00

16.45 17.00 17.15

22.15

23.45

26.15

In today's world, there is so much that deprives us of the pure visual experience of just looking and enjoying the change of light and the delicate nuances in any landscape.

Watching this process feels like science fiction.

My struggle and challenge as an artist is to try to remind people that there is a great deal of pleasure in simply looking.

34.15 34.30 34.45 35.00 35.15 35.30

43.15 45.30 45.45 46.00 48.30

50.15 54.45 55.00 55.15 55.30 55.45 56.00 56.15

ELIZABETH MOSSOP
MISSISSIPPI DELTA PROJECT

ISSUES OF WATER AND RIVERS AND DELTAS EPITOMIZE

THE DISJUNCTURE BETWEEN NATURAL SYSTEMS AND THE HUMAN SYSTEMS OF ADMINISTRATION, PROPERTY, AND POLITICAL STRUCTURES. WITH ITS GENERALLY STRONG DISTASTE FOR PLANNING, THE US HAS BEEN SLOW BOTH TO ALIGN PLANNING OR ADMINISTRATIVE BOUNDARIES WITH THE NATURAL BOUNDARIES OF WATERSHEDS, AND TO CREATE MULTIFUNCTIONAL MANAGEMENT AGENCIES (WITH SOME NOTABLE HISTORICAL ANOMALIES SUCH AS THE TENNESSEE VALLEY AUTHORITY). QUESTIONS OF FLOODING, LAND LOSS, AND STORM PROTECTION IN THE MISSISSIPPI DELTA ARE PLAGUED BY AN INABILITY TO EVEN CONCEPTUALIZE THE ISSUES IN A SYNTHETIC WAY. THE MOST DIFFICULT TASK SEEMS TO BE HOW TO BRING TOGETHER A DISCUSSION OF THE FORMS AND PROCESSES OF HUMAN INHABITATION AND ACTIVITY, AND THE BROADER QUESTIONS OF ECOLOGICAL SUSTAINABILITY, WITH THE SCIENCE AND ENGINEERING OF RIVER MANAGEMENT AND COASTAL PROTECTION. IN THIS CONTEXT, THE ACADEMY CAN PLAY AN IMPORTANT ROLE IN TRYING TO CONTRIBUTE TO PUBLIC DISCOURSE BY DEVELOPING INFORMED SPECULATION THAT IS GROUNDED IN BOTH ACCURATE DATA AND A REAL UNDERSTANDING OF THE LOCAL POLITICAL AND CULTURAL CONTEXT.

Louisiana State University's Coastal Sustainability Studio (CSS) brings together scientists, designers, and engineers to collaborate on specific projects with the aim of developing techniques for reducing environmental vulnerability and enhancing community resilience along the Louisiana coast. This drives a project approach that incorporates political and economic realities as well as research-based investigation into possible scenarios, thus placing the work in an interstitial zone between academic speculation and the politically sanctioned proposals of the various levels of government. The CSS is also unique within the regional context because of its central involvement of designers and planners and the cross-disciplinary methods that are applied to projects at all scales.

The confinement of the Mississippi River by flood protection levees interrupted the annual cycles of flooding across the river's floodplain, and the deposition of the silt that provided both the raw material for agriculture, and continued to build new land in the delta. The resulting withdrawal of this delta-building sediment, combined with the impacts of the oil industry and catastrophic storms, has resulted in the dramatically escalating land loss we see here. Current projections of continued land loss combined with sea level rise over the next 100 years dramatically changes the picture for the existing communities of south Louisiana and forces a major rethinking of options for the future. Without massive land-building efforts, the coastal region will disappear within a relatively short time.

So at the regional scale it is necessary to return the Mississippi River to its role as delta builder. The primary action proposed is a series of five spillway diversions constructed at strategic locations along the gulf, at the endpoints of the five historic basins of the delta. Each diversion would be designed as a hybrid between soft and hard infrastructure, strategically placed with regard to ecological, economic, and settlement patterns. The spillway gates would be periodically opened when the Mississippi is high, providing a steady pulse of sediment that over the century will build up, maintain, and protect large expanses of land.

In order to test this strategy, it is necessary to also zoom in and explore how these issues operate at the metropolitan and neighborhood scales. The project's area of focus is the Central Wetlands Unit, the Lower Ninth Ward and Saint Bernard Parish on the eastern border of the city with Lake Borgne. It is an area of great vulnerability to storms, particularly because of its location in relation to major industrial shipping infrastructure. Our work here is informed by a long-standing interaction with the community and a specific consultation process over the course of the project. The L9 Centre for Sustainable Engagement and Development is our partner in this work and has collaborated with us to focus the four main project goals: a balanced regenerative ecosystem, intelligent storm protection, a productive innovative economy, and a dynamic and sustainable community.

For these goals to be achieved, the neighborhood as we know it will have to evolve—to become better integrated with natural systems and flexible to changing water levels. Its architecture will have to become nimble, and increased open space will be needed to absorb seasonal floodwaters. Much of the Lower Ninth Ward, for example, was formerly wetlands, and will need to be re-imagined as a flexible urban/protective/middle zone once again.

9TH WARD: Looking at historical maps of the Lower Ninth Ward illustrates what has happened over time to the protective buffer of wetlands that used to exist between the settlement and the bayou. Prior to Hurricane Katrina in 2005, this landscape demonstrated an idiosyncratic settlement pattern encompassing both the colonial urbanism of New Orleans and the post WWII suburban expansion.

1878 1945 1952

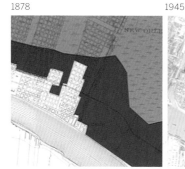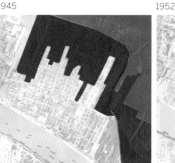

DISAPPEARING DELTA: The Mississippi Delta is a landscape shaped by the underlying conditions of the river system and the imposition of the engineering control system. The dominance of the latter has resulted in a rapid rate of land subsidence throughout the delta region.

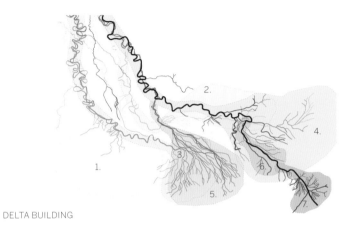

DELTA SYSTEM		STAGES
1.	SALE CYPREMORT	4600 BCE
2.	COCODRIE	4600-3500 BCE
3.	TECHE	3500-2800 BCE
4.	ST BERNARD	2800-1000 BCE
5.	LAFOURCHE	1000-300 BCE
6.	PLAQUEMINE	750-500 BCE
7.	BALIZE	550 BCE

DELTA BUILDING

SEDIMENT SPILLWAYS

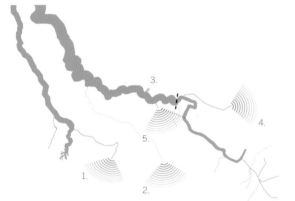

SPILLWAY DIVERSION		CAPACITY
1.	TERREBONNE	100,000 CFS
2.	BAYOU LAFOURCHE	100,000 CFS
3.	BONNET CARRE	250,000 CFS
4.	MRGO/BAYOU LA LOUTRE	100,000 CFS
5.	DAVIS POND	100,000 CFS

2004   **2005**   2006   2007   2008

Landscape of the Lower 9th Ward

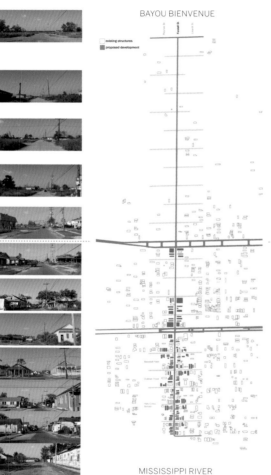

BAYOU BIENVENUE

existing structures
proposed development

FLORIDA AVE.

LAW ST.

N. DORGENOIS ST.

N. ROCHEBLAVE ST.

N. TONTI ST.

N. MIRO ST.

N. GALVEZ ST.

N. JOHNSON ST.

N. PRIEUR ST.

N. ROMAN ST.

N. DERBIGNY ST.

CLAIRBORNE AVE.

N. ROBERTSON ST.

VILLERE ST.

URQUHAR ST.

MARAIS ST.

ST. CLAUDE AVE

N. RAMPART ST.

BURGUNDY ST.

DAUPHINE ST.

ROYAL ST.

CHARTRES ST.

DOUGLAS ST.

MISSISSIPPI RIVER

It cannot be overstated how politically contentious post-storm proposals to change the form of New Orleans urban development have been. With little faith in any level of government to act in the interest of all citizens, it has been impossible to consider alternatives to a restoration of the pre-storm status quo. So it needs to be stated very clearly that this work is aimed specifically at empowering the local community to take an effective role in shaping the discussion of these issues. A key driver has been the need for primarily incremental solutions that can be flexible at the scale of individual properties and also the assumption of a viable land tenure system. The proposals have come about through an extensive process of engagement and discussion and are a testament to new understandings of the urban conditions six years on from the storm. There is a broad understanding that new solutions are required for these neighborhoods although it is far from clear how this change will be achieved.

Much of the neighborhood is now open land with emergent vegetation, in some areas there are new houses and in others there has been significant restoration and reoccupation. There has been a succession since the storm, of flooding, debris, clearing, and regeneration and there remains a transition from more to less density, between the river and the bayou. The bayou is largely open water with the ghost of the cypress swamp still visible, edged by a sea wall built in the 60s after Hurricane Betsy that protects the neighborhood. Unfortunately, the wall com-

pletely disconnects the neighborhood from its tradition-
ally close relationship with the bayou (where residents
once trapped and fished in the extensive wetland environment), making an artificial delineation between water
and land.

So rather than preparing yet another New Orleans master plan, we identified key topics of speculation through
consultation, research, and analysis. And from this developed a series of themes for our investigation: housing
and neighborhoods, productive landscapes, recreation,
industry and jobs, and wetland restoration. Each area of
focus was analyzed through precedent research, community and site investigation, and design speculation
and then developed into a series of single-issue scenarios. The individual scenarios were then evaluated against
a series of environmental performance criteria, including
carbon footprint, sea level rise, storm and flood defense,
investment, and potential return.

We have further combined a series of these scenarios
into a complete vision of the place intended to animate a
possible long-term future for the neighborhood within a
re-generated coastal environment. This is a snapshot of
selected scenarios, rather than a comprehensive or exclusive plan. It is a key means of communication with our
stakeholders to illustrate how different scenarios could
make a new neighborhood.

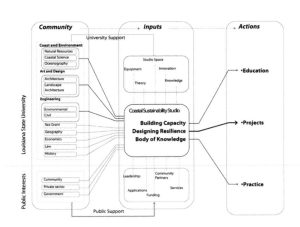

INVOLVING COMMUNITY:
Proposals are aimed specifically
at community engagement and
empowerment. They reflect a new
understanding of urban conditions
after the storm, and the role of
local community members in
shaping new solutions for their
neighborhoods.

SNAPSHOT PROPOSALS: The northern part of the Lower Ninth Ward (and the extension into Saint Bernard Parish) is uniquely located on the edge of water and settlement. This position and its relationship with the Central Wetlands Unit offers a number of opportunities for both enriching the Lower Ninth Ward as a vibrant community and protecting it from future hurricanes and storm surge.

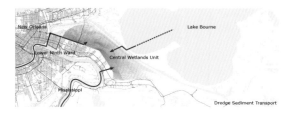

Dredge Sediment Transport

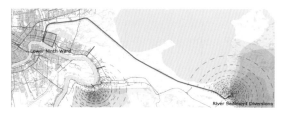

River Sediment Diversions

Cypress Tree Reforestation

Municipal Wastewater Assimilation

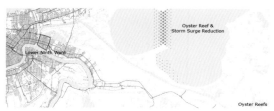

Oyster Reefs

The vision is driven by the concept of a robust wetland zone that supports the needs of a thriving and resilient natural environment alongside a growing and sustained human settlement. The northern part of the Lower Ninth Ward is transformed to take greater advantage of its location on the edge of water and settlement. Dense housing and community buildings are concentrated in infrastructural corridors reaching to the wetland where schools and institutions utilize the unique qualities of the location. Large open spaces between these neighborhood concentrations return productivity to the land-

URBAN RECREATION   LOCAL PARKS + STREETSCAPE   WETLAND PARK

scape through community and large-scale agriculture and increase the resilient capacity of the neighborhood environment by dramatically increasing open space areas for stormwater retention.

Claiborne Avenue is important as the line that separates the neighborhood roughly between above and below sea level. Traditionally, it separated the urban from the rural parts of the neighborhood. Claiborne Avenue once again takes on the role of threshold between different types of dwelling. To the south the neighborhood is densified while to the north the neighborhood is developed along infrastructural corridors along Tennessee, Caffin, and Tupelo streets that historically extended into the wetlands at the north of the neighborhood. New housing and commercial space along the main corridors are elevated to withstand flooding. The space in between becomes farmland and open space for recreation and stormwater retention. The

farmer's market would become an important hub in the neighborhood that links the productive landscape of the Lower Ninth Ward to the urban consumers of New Orleans and the region beyond.

Returning the massive amounts of vacant land in the northern parts of the Lower Ninth Ward to productive and resilient use was a major focus of the project. A combination of backyard farming, community gardening, large-scale commercial farming, and aquaculture are possible ways to utilize land that has too great a flood

would be reforested as cypress swamps. All of these offer a substantial range of economic development possibilities based in tourism and recreation.

The development of this project has allowed the illustration of some key ideas in relation to techniques for exploring resilience at the intersection of water systems and urban development. The complexity of current issues related to the settlement of the Mississippi Delta requires this broad disciplinary collaboration that can bring together the three poles: research and data, planning

SUSTAINABLE CLUSTERING  INFILL DENSIFICATION  HOUSING + NEIGHBORHOODS  PRODUCTIVE LANDSCAPES  EDIBLE PUBLIC SPACES  PRIVATE FARMING

risk for rebuilding. Galvez Street becomes a focus of agricultural activity and contains both small farm cottages to the south and larger commercial farming operations to the north.

The lowest and emptiest part of the neighborhood becomes public open space. The low point in the northwest corner becomes a wetland park with significant water storage and cleansing in the landscape, taking pressure off the overstretched pumping and drainage infrastructure. A regional park provides sports and recreation facilities much needed by the city and there is the opportunity to take advantage of the bayou's proximity for educational and tourist facilities. Subsidence has created roughly four hundred acres of open water at the western end of Bayou Bienvenue, which is a great potential recreational amenity for fishing, birding, kayaking, canoeing, sailing, and crabbing, while the rest of the Central Wetlands Unit

and design, and cultural issues. We also have to be able to zoom in and out from regional, to metropolitan, to neighborhood to site strategies as the means of testing the validity of both broad-scale strategies and understanding the implications of physical design decisions. Using design scenarios as the basis for the development of future visions provides a flexibility missing from many master-planning processes, as well as being a useful means of communicating to communities the possibilities of how different strategies combine in an integrated plan. The process has also reinforced the overriding importance of appropriate methods of communication. Strategic thinking, development alternatives, and physical proposals have to be translated into models and images that will have resonance with key stakeholders and communicate ideas effectively.

ILA BERMAN
INUNDATION TO SCARCITY

NATURE IS CONTINUOUS, WHEREAS CULTURE IS INHERENTLY DISCRETE. IN CULTURAL ARTIFACTS, THE CONTINUOUS MATERIAL AND EXPERIENTIAL FIELD DEEMED INTRINSIC TO THE NATURAL WORLD, IS DIVIDED INTO DISCRETE SIGNIFIERS, FIGURES, AND FORMS—TO RENDER VALUE TO MATTER, AND ATTRIBUTE TO IT A FRAMEWORK FOR HUMAN INTELLIGIBILITY, PERCEPTION, AND USE. THIS DIVISION IS THE MEANS BY WHICH WE INSTRUMENTALIZE THE REAL, AND TRANSFORM NATURAL MATTER INTO USEFUL AND MEANINGFUL CULTURAL ARTIFACTS. IF IT IS THE "LIFE" AROUND US THAT WE ARE SEEMINGLY DESTROYING IN THIS PROCESS, PERHAPS THIS RESULT IS INTRINSIC TO THE CONCEPTUAL SYSTEM WE ARE OPERATING WITHIN, SO THAT IN ORDER TO REVIVIFY OUR ARTIFICIALLY-PRODUCED ENVIRONS, WE MIGHT NEED TO ENTIRELY INVERT OUR DESIGN THINKING: TO REREAD ARCHITECTURAL AND URBAN CONDITIONS THROUGH NATURE'S MATERIAL CONTINUITIES AND ENVIRONMENTAL COMPLEXITIES RATHER THAN THE REVERSE. IT IS IMPERATIVE THAT WE IMAGINE A FUTURE INTEGRATION OF CULTURAL AND NATURAL SYSTEMS, RATHER THAN THEIR SEPARATION AND OPPOSITION, AND ALSO UNDERSTAND THIS INTEGRATION THROUGH A TEMPORAL MODEL THAT RECOGNIZES TIME AS A MATERIAL REALITY WHOSE INTENSITIES AND DYNAMIC RHYTHMS EXCEED THE LIMITED FRAMEWORK OF PROGRAMMATIC INTERVALS THAT WE IMPOSE UPON THEM.

Los Angeles Water Supply Infrastructure

In relation to the way in which our cities confront their fluid environments, this might mean conceptualizing the city's boundary conditions—where land meets water, or water meets land—in far less precise terms through subtle gradient changes in thickness or depth, or the increased articulation, layering, or permeability of our urban edges, surfaces, and grounds. This might also entail generating a new culture-nature continuum that moves toward soft dynamic infrastructures, fluid and adaptive spatial strategies, and productive programmatic and material mixtures such as the insertion of desert landscapes and wetlands in place of lawns and asphalt back into the core of the city. These insertions could reduce consumption, expand rather than reduce groundwater storage, enhance local urban water capture, filtration, and recycling for the digestion and regeneration of our own cultural effluents, and create strategies for local flood mitigation that would recalibrate the relationship between, and blur rather than differentiate, natural and cultural domains. It will only be at the point when we reinsert ourselves back into the complexity of this fluid material dynamic, rather than assuming that we can delimit and control it, that our own process of cultural regeneration will begin.

ENGINEERED MEGA-INFRASTRUCTURES

Water inundation and scarcity are two extreme conditions recently amplified in our cultural consciousness.
They threaten the enormous investments that we have
made in our contemporary cities and limit conditions
that have been the drivers of the immense works of
modern engineering. They are currently also the markers
of crisis that make us question previous intentions and
ideologies, while provoking us to re-conceptualize the
ground upon which we are operating.

During the 20th century, we witnessed the dominance of
two parallel yet seemingly inverted trajectories of urban
and infrastructural development in the United States
as a response to either the overabundance or scarcity
of water. Along the southeastern coast of Louisiana in a
wet terrain threatened by intense deluges, flooding, and
sea level rise, we converted soggy marshland into solid
ground, while in the southwestern territories of California in a region vulnerable to drought, we transformed a
brown arid landscape into a green oasis, both as an in-
stantiation of our ability to colonize water and generate
artificial landscapes resulting from the magnitude of its
control and redistribution.

New Orleans Flood Control Infrastructure

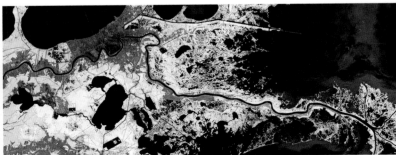

INUNDATION

The common historic emergence of urban centers located directly adjacent to water—a result of the life-sustaining potential that such sites have held for food, water, transport, trade, and tourism—has rendered even more serious the expected catastrophic impact of imminent sea level rise and extreme weather resulting from global climate and atmospheric changes. As is evident from the many recent architectural exhibitions, symposia, and competitions on the subject, our deep-seated anxieties associated with losing the artificial ground that we have so painstakingly built and being submerged below a liquid landscape, have been heightened by our awareness of the devastation brought about by recent hurricanes, tsunamis, and floods in Europe, Asia, and America.

116

In the aftermath of these events, we have also come to realize that our static levee flood-control systems, intent on constraining and neutralizing the environmental fluctuations impacting our cities, have been partially responsible for unintentionally amplifying urban and ecological risks. New Orleans's instability, for example, results from the multiple fluctuating phenomena that were responsible for its genesis, and which continue to impinge upon it. The city was originally built upon unstable ground— the persistent deposition of silt and sediment carried across an entire continent by the fluid movements of the Mississippi River. Notwithstanding the fragility of this ground, and the entire region's susceptibility to extreme atmospheric and hydrological forces, the city's vulnerability is also the result of antithetical forces—those highly orchestrated artificial systems that, in an effort to stabilize this domain, have unintentionally exacerbated its instability. As engineered hydraulic conduits and artificial levees have replaced the complex fluviomorphology of natural river floodplains in the Mississippi delta, the increased speed and directionality of the river's flow, and the decrease in the lateral spread of alluvial sedimentation required to replenish and rebuild these deltas, has

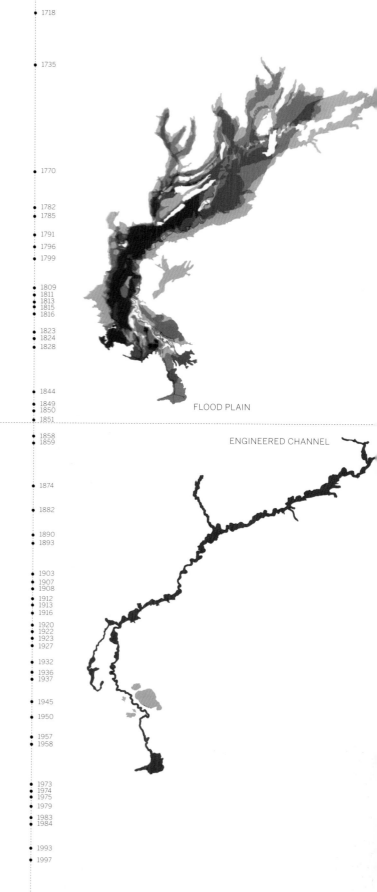

MAJOR FLOODS

1718

1735

1770

1782
1785

1791
1796
1799

1809
1811
1813
1815
1816

1823
1824
1828

1844

1849
1850
1851

1858
1859

1874

1882

1890
1893

1903
1907
1908
1912
1913
1916
1920
1922
1923
1927

1932
1936
1937

1945

1950

1957
1958

1973
1974
1975
1979
1983
1984

1993
1997

FLOOD PLAIN

ENGINEERED CHANNEL

AMPLIFIED RISK: Lateral urban expansion into unstable and low-lying territories has exposed new settlement to increased risk. The impact of Hurricane Katrina was particularly devasating, with an estimated $81 billion in damages and over 1,500 lost lives.

diminished the natural regenerative potential of the territory surrounding, and upon which, the city was built, leading to the deterioration of fragile ecosystems and contributing to the acceleration of coastal erosion.

It is the forceful and dynamic lateral shifting of the Mississippi River across an enormous continental terrain that over 5,000 years enabled the redistribution and deposition of soil and the layering of delta lobes that produced the ground upon which the coastal urban territories of the gulf depend. Large volumes of alluvial deposition are required to generate land, and yet in this territory, as a direct result of the infrastructural and urban boundaries we have produced, land is being eroded more rapidly than it can be regenerated. By substantially diminishing the fluid and material functions of the river through our infrastructural interventions, we have not only reduced our own capacity for coastal regeneration, but have also amplified the risk of flooding and intensified the instability of this domain.

These problems have been further exacerbated by urban sprawl and extensive territorial consumption. The city's metropolitan footprint has doubled in the last 40 years in spite of substantial decreases in its core urban population. This low-rise lateral extension of the city, in combination with the pumping of marshland to facilitate uncontrolled suburban expansion has lead to the over-in-

habitation of low-lying regions whose ground continues to compact and significantly subside, resulting in territories threatened by a dramatically amplified risk of future flooding. This risk is increased as the territorial buffer zones between the Gulf of Mexico and the city rapidly diminish due to the acceleration of coastal erosion, the mitigation of which is delayed by local settlement patterns. The widespread fragmentation of property ownership in these buffer areas directly impedes coastal regeneration strategies dependent upon levee perforation as a method to artificially create new delta lobes through the productive redeployment of shifting sediment.

Our failures within this context are interpretive and conceptual as much as they are real. Our representations of the river as a fixed and contained figure, rather than a dynamic fluid material force; our desire to conceptually separate form from material, and land from water, rather than understanding that at the edge these conditions always operate only as mixtures—fluid soil and soggy, floating land; and our need to establish a functionalized hierarchy of the one river over its many ramified tributaries, not only stop us from understanding how a line branches to become a surface and that this principle within nature is the strategy that enables water to become land, but also prevents us from comprehending the real complexity of the river's function in relation to multiple temporal, spatial, scalar, and material distributions.

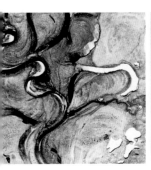

SCARCITY

The enormous scope of the engineering of the Missis-sippi River, and the transformation of the largest flood plain in America into an efficiently controlled conduit, in addition to the extensive levee and pumping systems that enabled the construction and expansion of New Or-leans's dry terrain, is perhaps only equaled in scale on this continent by the immensity and complexity of water infrastructure that sustains the California economy and supports its coastal urban populations. There are over 1,400 reservoirs in California, more than 1,000 miles of canals, aqueducts, and water conveyance systems and it seems that every significant river within the state has been dammed at least once. Although California is hydro-logically cut off from states to the east, its rivers are sea-sonally swollen by the Sierra snowpack, and it has some of the largest reservoirs in the country. All of these rivers and reservoirs, however, satisfy only two-thirds of the state's growing water demand—a figure decreasing with coastal population growth and the projected reduction of water resources resulting from the impact of global warming. The rest of the water comes from groundwater, and as we've learned from the historic transformation of what is now commonly referred to as the "dustbowl" in the Midwest, water being pumped out of the ground from aquifers that is not replenished—referred to as ground-water overdraft—is as nonrenewable as oil.

The megacity of Los Angeles, spanning 4,800 square miles and supporting a growing population of 18 million inhabitants, is located in a coastal desert, that according to the California Department of Water Resources has a regional environmental capacity to support at most, 1/2 million inhabitants on its own water. The city's sprawling urban growth, in concert with its desire to transform this desert into an artificial urban oasis, is both the cause and result of one of the largest water diversion and convey-ance strategies in US history, the resulting desiccation of its neighboring territories, and a series of political "water wars" that continue to this day.

By the end of the 19th century, Los Angeles's 170,000 in-habitants had already run out of water. The city's mayor and the superintendent of the newly-created LA Depart-ment of Water and Power (LADWP), devised a strategy to construct a gravity-fed aqueduct to convey water from Owen's Lake, located in a valley fed by the runoff of the Sierra Nevada mountains to a reservoir in Los Angeles, 223 miles away. In addition to building the aqueduct, the strategy for procuring the water included purchasing both the lands and water rights in the Owen's Valley by ensuring that federal support for irrigation was denied to local farmers, and lobbying to create the Inyo Na-tional Forest to protect it from development so that the watershed feeding the river would be entirely controlled by the city.

In 1913, the completed aqueduct could deliver 10 times the quantity of water available from local resources, and by 1924, had diverted and extracted so much water that it transformed Owen's Lake into a brine pool. Although the local valley farmers and ranchers protested by dyna-miting part of the system, by 1928 Los Angeles owned 90 percent of the land and water rights in the distant valley. Over the next 40 years, the city's enormous growth—en-abled by its imported water—repeatedly exhausted its resources, each time leading to the expansion of its artifi-cially colonized urban watershed, which included drilling thousands of groundwater wells and extending the initial aqueduct 350 miles north to the Mono Lake Basin. These water diversions resulted in substantially depleting the groundwater aquifer, desiccating Owen's Lake and turn-ing it into a toxic dust storm region, transforming the once lush vegetation of the valley into a desert dunescape, and ravaging the Mono lake wildlife ecosystem. After mul-tiple lawsuits and the second of a series of water wars spawned by the environmental movement of the 1970s, that, for the first time in history, enabled the residents to fight against the annexation of ground water and the death of their land by providing legal leverage through the California Environmental Quality Act (CEQA), Los Angeles was ordered by the California Supreme Court to mitigate its environmental damages. Although the law suits were only settled in the mid-1990s, the valley has never environmentally recovered.

LOS ANGELES AQUEDUCT: The megacity of Los Angeles has grown in tandem with its vast and complicated water supply network. The original LA Aqueduct was lengthened by 350 miles to meet an ever-increasing demand. Today, it draws water from a number of reservoirs on its route from Mono Lake.

MAJOR INFRASTRUCTURE

- 1929   MOKELUMNE AQUEDUCT
- 1930   LOS ANGELES AQUEDUCT
- 1934   HETCH HETCHY AQUEDUCT
- 1939   COLORADO RIVER AQUEDUCT
- 1940   COACHELLA CANAL
- 1942   ALL AMERICAN CANAL
- 1945   MADERA CANAL
- 1948   CONTRA COSTA CANAL
- 1951   FRIANT-KERNAL CANAL
- 1959   CORNING CANAL
- 1963   CALIFORNIA AQUEDUCT
- 1965   SOUTH BAY AQUEDUCT
- 1967   SAN LUIS CANAL
- 1970   FOLSOM SOUTH CANAL
- 1971   SAN DIEGO AQUEDUCTS
- 1975   CROSS VALLEY CANAL
- 1990   NORTH BAY AQUEDUCT
- 1997   COASTAL BRANCH AQUEDUCT
- 2003   EAST BRANCH AQUEDUCT

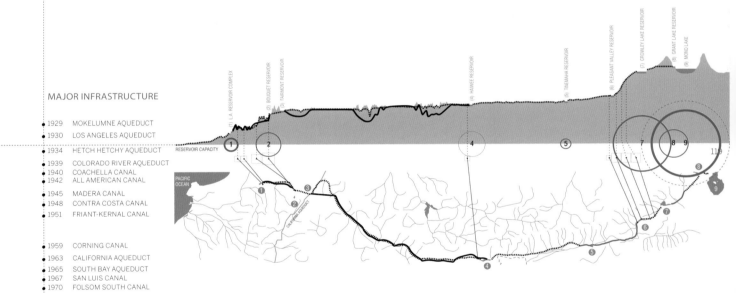

RESERVOIR CAPACITY

(1) L.A. RESERVOIR COMPLEX
(2) BOUQUET RESERVOIR
(3) FAIRMONT RESERVOIR
(4) HAIWEE RESERVOIR
(5) TINEMAHA RESERVOIR
(6) PLEASANT VALLEY RESERVOIR
(7) CROWLEY LAKE RESERVOIR
(8) GRANT LAKE RESERVOIR
(9) MONO LAKE

PACIFIC OCEAN

CONSTRUCTION AND CONFLICT

1913 **Los Angeles Aqueduct Completed**
— 223 miles in length
— Built by Los Angeles Department
   of Water and Power
— Directed by William Mulholland

1924 **Water Wars**
— Owens Lake becomes
   dessicated and alkaline
— Farmers sabotage portions of the
   aqueduct 15 times in three years

1927 **St. Francis Dam Failure**
— 12.4 billion gallons discharged
— 600 dead

1928 **City of Los Angeles Controls 90%**
of Owens' Valley Property Rights
— Local farming economy collapses

1941 **Lake Mono Extension**
— 350 miles of additional
   water infrastructure

1982 **Ecosystem Destruction**
— Lake Mono volume decreases
   by half; alkalinity doubles
— Negit Island landbridge forms

1994 **California Supreme Court**
— LADWP required to raise
   Lake Mono by 20'

These municipally-owned waterways were only a small part of what was to later become one of the largest and most complex water infrastructural networks in existence. It was expanded by the Federal Central Valley (1935) and State Water Projects (1960), which were created to provide a major north-south transfer of water from the Sacramento-San Joaquin Delta, which includes the California Aqueduct that supplies additional water to Los Angeles. California receives only 44 percent of the precipitation of the eastern states. Since only 1/3 of this total amount occurs within the lower 2/3 of the state, and less than 2 percent of this occurs on the southern coast that supports 50 percent of the state's population, water scarcity and distribution is responsible for the historic struggle between the North and South, and between urban, agricultural, and environmental advocates.

Despite the fact that only a small percentage of total water use is urban, the larger effects of amplified urbanization supported by industry and agriculture, and enabled by water diversion and overconsumption, have depleted aquifers without recharging them because of the imperviousness of urban surfaces; polluted ground, surface, and seawater because of lack of local water recycling for urban and agricultural use; led to the loss of biodiversity by short-circuiting and transforming the flows of necessary environmental cycles; and amplified the climatic and environmental extremes, whose unpredictable fluctuations we had initially set out to neutralize and constrain. By insisting on the clear legibility of our infrastructural systems, while simultaneously assuming the limitlessness of the environments we have exploited, we have largely disregarded the vast impacts of these systems on a broader and more nuanced ecology. We have also diminished our own capacity for resilience by ignoring the complex and multi-faceted functions intrinsic to nature's material dynamic that have been thoroughly instrumentalized to unilaterally support unbridled cultural production and capitalist growth within a very limited (and highly biased) definition of urban and environmental stability.

Water may only make up 1/10th of 1 percent of the earth's mass but our existence is of course entirely dependent

on it. 97 percent of the world's water is in the ocean, and of the remaining 3 percent, 2.2 percent is locked in the polar ice caps, the melting of which, due to global warming, will not only lead to sea level rise, and the potential flooding of all coastal and low-lying cities, but also to a loss of the largest percentage of our fresh water resources on the planet—two impacts that will no doubt catastrophically amplify the extremes of water inundation and scarcity. Of the remaining water, another .3 percent is too deep underground to recover and use, leaving only .5 percent of the world's water as freshwater to support human and other life forms. Water on this planet, like oil, is considered to be a limited resource—believed to be the same in quantity although certainly not in constitution or distribution as it was five billion years ago.

Although the inadequate protection from environmental threats and uneven distribution of resources has brought water into the domain of intense global political negotiation, the greater struggle is between the artificial cultural urban landscapes that we have produced and the devastated natural environments upon which these depend. Just as our increased desire for ground unintentionally led to the erosion and intensified flooding of our southern coast, our desire for more water in the west has produced a greater potential drought in the future of our coastal deserts, as we face our inability to support the massive aging infrastructures we created, and to alleviate their destructive impact on the natural ecosystems they displaced. Waterscape development is responsible for California's distinction as one of the globe's extinction epicenters of the twentieth century, since our mono-functional instrumentalization of water wholly ignored its importance for the survival of all other species and life forms beyond our own. In this system far from equilibrium, the gap between the precipice upon which we are perched, and a viable ecological future will not come as a set of simple solutions from science, politics, economics or design. It will only emerge when we are able to invert the culture-nature continuum, and come to understand the irreducible difference between the conceptual, representational, and functional limits that we impose upon the terrain of water and the unlimited fluid material matrix that is intrinsic to its true nature.

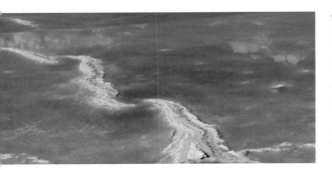

OWENS LAKE: Once a massive terminal water body, Owens Lake is now a largely dessicated salt flat. High winds frequently cause massive and toxic dust storms that affect air quality throughout the region. The LADWP has been forced to pump enormous quantities of water back into the lake in an attempt to control the dust.

CHRISTIAN WERTHMANN
POLLUTION + PROPAGANDA

IT IS A FAMILIAR STORY — CITIES GROW NEAR RIVERS AND PAVE EVERYTHING IN THEIR WAY; ENGINEERS CHANNELIZE WATER BODIES IN THE NAME OF FLOOD CONTROL; AND SETTLEMENT UNFOLDS ACROSS THE LANDSCAPE ENTIRELY UNCHECKED. IN SÃO PAULO, THIS CONQUEST OCCURRED ON A RUTHLESSLY MASSIVE SCALE, STEAMROLLING OVER 2,000 KM^2 OF AN UNDULATING PLATEAU IN THE HEADWATERS OF THE TIETE RIVER. THIS REGION WAS ONCE HOME TO AN INCREDIBLY RICH AND BIO-DIVERSE ECOSYSTEM KNOWN AS MATA ATLÂNTICA, OR ATLANTIC RAINFOREST. NOW, IT IS AN UNRECOGNIZABLE PULP, CRISSCROSSED BY SUTURES IN THE FORM OF ROADS, BRIDGES, CANALS, AND PIPELINES WHICH SEEM TENUOUSLY TO STITCH THE NATION TOGETHER. HERE, AS IN MANY OTHER LARGE CITIES, THE OLD CLICHÉ HOLDS TRUE—WHEN SINS ARE COMMITTED FOR THE SAKE OF ECONOMIC PROSPERITY, NATURE STRIKES BACK WITH A VENGEANCE. THE IMPERMEABILIZATION OF THE RIVER AND ITS TRIBUTARIES RESULTS IN A POLLUTED RUN-OFF THAT REGULARLY EXCEEDS THE CAPACITY OF EVEN THE CITY'S BEST-ENGINEERED CHANNELS. AND, AS IN SO MANY OTHER CITIES, RAW SEWAGE, INDUSTRIAL EFFLUENTS, AND OTHER GROSSLY POLLUTED WATERS, FLOW DIRECTLY INTO SÃO PAULO'S RIVERS. IN THIS CONTEXT, AND IN A MILIEU OF MISGUIDED BLAME AND PROPAGANDA, POLLUTION AND POVERTY, WHAT DOES IT TAKE TO CHART A WAY FORWARD?

+ **1987:** NELSON AND CIMPRAMAR REAL ESTATE CO.
SELL 5 X 25 M PLOTS TO LOW INCOME RESIDENTS

SÃO PAULO

São Paulo is in a midlife crisis. Its expansion from a city of one million in 1929 to a metropolis of over 20 million today occurred with a remarkable speed that has resulted in maladies ubiquitous to rapidly urbanizing areas around the world: serious traffic congestion, air and water pollution, heavy flooding, social inequality, lack of public space and urban fragmentation (roughly four million live outside the formal housing market). The push for industrialization was coupled with massive rural-to-urban migration that constituted an unstoppable force which has been unfolding over the last 100 years. This migration will most likely continue into the foreseeable future, and leave in its wake large low-income populations, subsisting in vast urban corridors, vexed with massive environmental problems. However, urban growth has begun to slow down. In this period of relative calm, São Paulo looks at what it has become and does not like it very much. Provoked both by self-examination and a vocal and aggressive environmental movement, one that is far fiercer than in many post-industrialized countries, São Paulo is now confronted with many of the negative consequences of ignoring the reciprocal relationship between people and environment. In São Paulo, there is no landscape in the common sense, just an undulating terrain covered in a sea of buildings. According to one frustrated Brazilian, "Rio has the beach, we do not have anything."

A PLACE IN HEAVEN

124

TIETE WATERSHED
160,000 INHABITANTS

+ **1995:** SABESP INSTALLS
WATER FOR $350 MILLION

+ **1995:** PHONE LINES
INSTALLED

CANTINHO DO CÉU

Cantinho do Céu ("a place in heaven") is a neighborhood of roughly 30,000 in the south of São Paulo's metropolitan area. The community is located on a peninsula jutting right into the Billings Reservoir, the region's largest body of water. Until the 1950s, the Reservoir's watershed was pristine, un-urbanized, and completely surrounded by Atlantic rainforest. However, as São Paulo grew quickly towards the south, much of the 560 km^2 watershed was decimated by the agriculture and unbridled urbanization necessary to accommodate an influx of around 160,000 informal residents. Regulations made it illegal for government entities to improve conditions in new informal settlements, which, on paper, were not supposed to exist in watersheds protected by law (the law has been modified in the meantime). As result, Cantinho, as well as many other favelas in the Tiete watershed, was left without basic civic infrastructures, including drinking water, sewage, telephone lines, electricity, street names, and reliable mail service.

In São Paolo, there was, and still is, a line of thought that any official acknowledgement of these towns, as indicated through the provision of services, would set a bad precedent and would only encourage further illegal settlement activity. One has to understand that the informal urbanization of the protected Billings Reservoir was considered a major government failure.

As a result, and given their special prominence in a very visible location at the water's edge, the community of Cantinho do Céu was publicly accused of destroying the water quality of the Reservoir with their untreated sewage and surface runoff. Indeed, despite having the highest theoretical yield capacity of São Paulo's reservoirs, in 2009 Billings provided only 9 percent of the city's water needs due to serious eutrophication. To make up for the shortfall in capacity, the city was actively looking to build new and costly reservoirs farther to the north. In light of this serious environmental problem, which currently affects the whole metropolitan region, the informal settlement turned into the poster child for the overall Reservoir's deterioration, or as one government official put it, "losing the Reservoir." When visiting the neighborhood in 2009, one could not be faulted for making the intuitive link between the miserable water quality of the reservoir and the cobbled together community. The visual evidence was clear; it was easy to see and smell the waste of Cantinho's households entering the lake.

In 2008, the São Paulo Housing Agency (SEHAB) began an upgrading project in Cantinho do Céu as part of a larger initiative to improve settlements throughout the watershed. In Cantinho, SEHAB was wedged between conflicting interests. As a housing agency, its core mission was to improve conditions for all of São Paulo's residents,

125

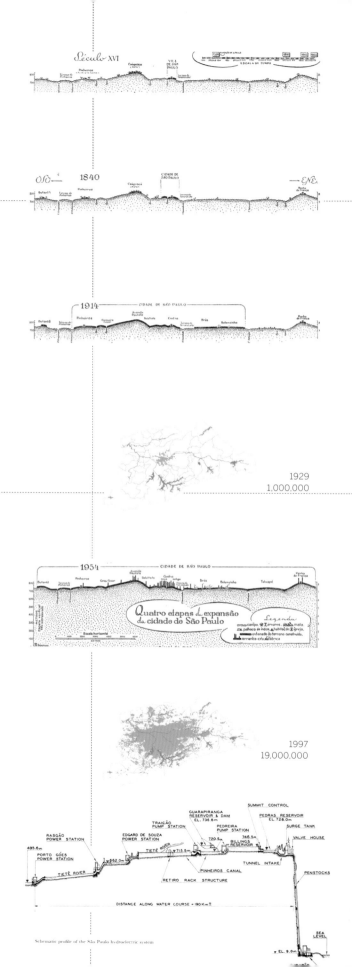

residents, but as a public agency, it also had to respect the official environmental protections governing the Billings watershed. To complicate the matter further, if SEHAB were to listen to the demands of São Paulo's environmental agency, the whole of Cantinho would be razed, its residents resettled elsewhere, and the entire area would be re-vegetated with Atlantic rainforest.

Ultimately, a political compromise was worked out between the two agencies by enforcing the minimal requirements of the law through the establishment of a 50 meter vegetated buffer, or "eyelash forest", between any urbanization and the shoreline. In addition, the compromise stipulated that a new park should be established at one of the fingers of the peninsula. The buffer zone and park would necessitate the removal of 2,000 houses and the resettlement of up to 6,000 residents, approximately 20% of the existing population. Based on previous experiences of forceful resettlement initiatives, SEHAB was still skeptical. Even under the fairest, most respectful, and most participatory processing methods, the resettlement of residents by government had proven to be a conflict-prone undertaking.

It was at this point of tension that a collaboration with the Harvard Graduate School of Design was struck, and I started to work with a team of landscape architecture students and local experts on the question of whether a healthy coexistence between a biologically intact reservoir and the nearby residents could be achieved. Through design, we sought to develop not master plans, but small catalytic tactics that could initiate chains of reaction of improvement in an informal urban settlement characterized by diametric opposition.

126

1929
1,000,000

1997
19,000,000

Schematic profile of the São Paulo hydroelectric system

BILLINGS RESERVOIR

After studying Cantinho in detail, our team turned to a closer examination of the Billings Reservoir. The reservoir was built in the 1920s, not to store drinking water, but for the generation of hydroelectric power. Contrary to conventional logic, where waterpower is harnessed at the point where the river is damned, São Paulo's geography, and unique location on an escarpment 720 m above the Atlantic Ocean, makes possible an entirely unique form of power generation. At its closest, the Billings reservoir is less than 20 km as the crow flies from the Atlantic Ocean, yet the rivers of São Paulo shun the quick and easy route to the sea. Instead, they follow a tortuous and epic course into the interior of the continent, finally discharging into the ocean some 2500 km later through Argentina's Rio de la Plata (the world's second largest river basin in area, only after the Amazon).

The ingenuity of the Billings reservoir was to generate electricity by taking advantage not of the meager 26 m drop provided by its dam, but of the considerably greater plummet between São Paulo and the sea. The energy output of the reservoir was substantially heightened in the 1950s by redirecting water from the major Tietê River into the Pinheiros River canal, pumping it uphill into the Billings reservoir. This was done using a system of regulating dams and strategically located pumping stations, which essentially reversed the direction of flow of the Pinheiros River during operation.

An extraordinary engineering feat, this allowed a power plant located far below the city to generate an astonishing 880 megawatts of electricity. The construction of Billings reservoir according to some claims, made the extraordinary rise of Brazil's largest city physically possible.

Only later as the city's growth exploded, fueled by seemingly limitless energy, did the downsides of the scheme become apparent. The reversal of the river and continuous pumping brought not only water to the reservoir, but also all of the "formal" city's polluted runoff and untreated sewage. Industrial effluent from manufacturing facilities located along the Tietê and Pinheiros rivers contributed additional toxic sediments, which were laced with PCBs and heavy metals.

In 1989, water quality monitoring was implemented for Billings, and a three-year deadline was set for a cessation of all pumping activities. Due to that limitation, the power plant began running at only a quarter of its total capacity and currently supplies only 8 percent of the city's power. While the metropolitan area could have lived with this reduced capacity, São Paulo had become dependent on the pumping scheme not only for energy supply, but also as a gigantic flood control mechanism necessary to make up for the urbanization and loss of the region's natural flood plains and rivers. As a result of an emergency decree, the pumps on the Pinheiros River are started up after heavy rains, sucking massive amounts of heavily polluted floodwater (up to 200 m³/s) upstream, out of the city, and directly into the Billings Reservoir. And far from being a rarely used emergency measure, the pumps run with an average frequency of two to three times per week in the rainy season from November to March.

+ **1998**: INDIVIDUAL DWELLINGS
CONNECTED TO ELECTRICITY

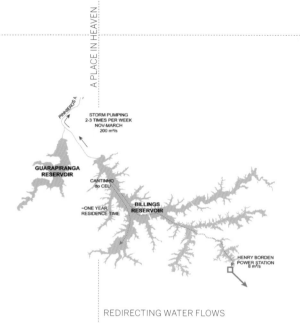

REDIRECTING WATER FLOWS

SÃO PAULO SEWERSHED

128

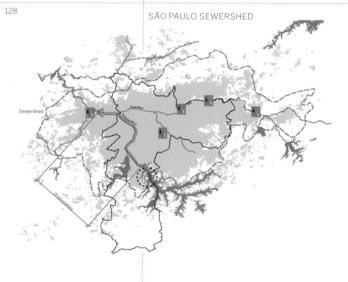

POLLUTION AND PROPAGANDA

Through my team's research, it became clear that the biggest culprit in the deterioration of the Billings Reservoir's water quality was not the comparatively small amounts of effluent contributed by the informal settlement, but by the polluted floodwaters stemming from the so-called "formal" urbanization outside of its watershed. The polluted run-off from Cantinho is certainly harmful, but it is far from the primary reason for Billings' deterioration. In fact, even when settlement of Cantinho first began, the reservoir was already polluted such that its waters were undrinkable.

It is clear that if São Paulo does not gain control over its flooding problem through alternative approaches to stormwater management, the Reservoir's water quality will never improve. These facts are known by all the experts, but when it comes to solving problems inside the heavily built-up fabric of the 2,000 km² metropolis, the endeavor becomes bigger and more complicated than a 2,000 family relocation plan. Absolution requires a sacrifice; and it seems that São Paulo had found its scapegoat.

In the end, one could claim that Cantinho attracted the wrath of environmental sentiment simply by being too close to the water. The water in the reservoir was undrinkable before the first of Cantinho's settlers even

2009: FAVELA "UPGRADING"
BEGINS

2011: CONSTRUCTION OF
CANTINHO DE CÉU PARK

arrived. The tragic consequence is that Cantinho has to live now with a double stigma. The first is the settlement's non-formal status, having been conceived outside of the legal framework. The second is that it seems to pollute what could otherwise be a nice lake for São Paulo's citizens. The fact that most of Cantinho's residents bought their property, albeit under initially false pretenses, and that São Paulo proper is polluting the reservoir to a much larger degree, has moved to the background of the discussion. Under these circumstances, the mandated 50 m "eyelash forest" that will make Cantinho invisible from the water, could be interpreted more as a cosmetic cover-up than an ecological necessity, an empty propaganda piece.

THE WAY FORWARD

In the case of Catinho, culpability itself is highly complex and politically augmented. Focusing on the tangled failures of the past is a reactionary approach that is ultimately futile, harmful, and antithetical to progress through design or strategy. In the massively restructured terrain of megacities such as São Paolo, the restoration of an original condition is neither possible nor desirable. While it may be painful and unsettling to recognize the loss of pristine rain forest or the pollution of a reservoir, the way forward requires a pragmatic and undogmatic approach, in addition to a deep suspicion of popular belief.

In the end, our team of experts and students were able to show that a socially and ecologically healthy co-existence between settlement and water in Cantinho is technically possible without removing all the residents from the water's edge. We suggest that redirection of the funds allocated to relocation of residents, could instead be used for the improvement of drainage patterns, the creation of stormwater treatment wetlands and the establishment of local sewage treatment plants which could also serve as new public spaces. These research proposals influenced the designers of record for the project ultimately proposed by SEHAB. While it is not yet complete, SEHAB has constructed a new beach and a public lakeside promenade in one part of the community. Most of Cantinho's households are now connected to a sewage system and have paved roads and other amenities. Even though the infrastructure design is more conventional than what we had hoped for, the recreational aspect of the project is very successful. The Reservoir's waters are still not swimmable and the storm pumping continues. It is reported that many residents from nearby favelas come to Cantinho on the weekend to visit the beach. Once marginal, and to some degree still incorrectly censured, Catinho now must cope with a new issue of urbanization: parking.

129

MARION WEISS
CULTURAL WATERMARKS

PERHAPS IT IS FAIR TO SAY THAT THE FUNDAMENTAL SIGNATURES OF CULTURAL ENDEAVORS ARE THE INFRASTRUCTURES THAT WE CREATE; INFRASTRUCTURES THAT ALLOW OURSELVES THE FICTION OF CONTROL. WE DESIGN INFRASTRUCTURES THAT CONNECT US WITH HEROIC QUANTITIES OF CONCRETE AND STEEL, AND WE SUBMERGE URBAN WATERS INTO COMBINED SEWAGE AND STORM WATER NETWORKS TO ELIMINATE ITS PROBLEMATIC PRESENCE. WE MANAGE WATER AS IF IT RESPECTS THE PROPERTY LINES THAT WE HAVE CREATED, AND AS DESIGNERS FROM ALL DISCIPLINES, WE RESPOND TO PROPERTY LINES CREATED BY EXTERNAL ADMINISTRATIVE AND ECONOMIC AGENCIES BECAUSE WE ARE INVITED TO THE TABLE BY THOSE THAT SHAPE AND AFFIRM THOSE LIMITS. SO WHAT ABOUT WATER? TOO OFTEN, IN OUR EFFORT TO CONTROL IT, ECONOMIC EXPEDIENCY AND TECHNICAL EFFICIENCY HAVE BEEN THE EXCLUSIVE CRITERIA TO DEFINE THE INFRASTRUCTURE THAT ENGAGES IT. BUT WATER CARRIES LITTLE RESPECT FOR BOUNDARIES. WATER IS VOLATILE / FRAGILE / VIOLENT / SERENE / ELUSIVE / UBIQUITOUS / NOURISHING / DEVASTATING AND FUNDAMENTAL TO LIFE. BECAUSE IT IS ALL AROUND US, WE CAN SAY IT IS GLOBAL. BECAUSE WE DEPEND ON IT EVERY DAY, AS INDIVIDUALS, WE CAN SAY IT IS THE ESSENCE OF LOCAL. BUT TO LEVERAGE ITS TRUEST VALUE, WE MUST DESIGN MORE MULTIVALENT, SUPPLE, RESILIENT STRATEGIES TO COLLECT, CLEANSE, DISTRIBUTE, CULTIVATE, AND ULTIMATELY ENJOY THE FUNDAMENTAL NATURE AND LUXURY OF WATER... AND MAYBE, WE MUST DESIGN WITH WATER AS IF OUR LIVES DEPENDED ON IT.

MUSEUM OF THE EARTH

The Museum of the Earth houses one of the nation's largest paleontological collections and demonstrates the intrinsic relationships between geological events and biological evolution. Shifted and carved by a receding ice sheet twenty thousand years ago, the site is marked by a gradual, forty-foot slope. The design capitalizes on this rich condition, making vivid the dynamic interrelationship between biology and geology that is central to the museum's mission. We were intrigued with the idea that if this building were indeed going to be a museum of the earth, it had to do a little more than merely clad the exhibition inside: it had to somehow reveal the more powerful forces that were once at work at the site.

Approached from the south, a series of ten-foot sculpted landforms and linear water terraces organize the site and museum into a coherent whole: a sequential section became a device that could meter the drop in grade and create distinct precincts for parking. These precisely graded parking areas divert water into stone-lined, terraced bio swales with gravel filters and prehistoric grasses such as equisetum, which cleanse the groundwater of chemicals and pollutants. Channeled between the two wings of the museum, water makes its way downhill where it collects in a glacial garden. Water fills the garden until it overflows into a new detention habitat at the lower end of the site where a new wetland ecosystem is now flourishing. At this detention basin, the water is further cleansed and released into Lake Cayuga.

10 YEAR STORM
7,616 C.F. OF WATER

50 YEAR STORM
12,912 C.F. OF WATER

100 YEAR STORM
15,221 C.F. OF WATER

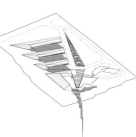

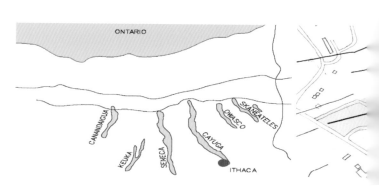

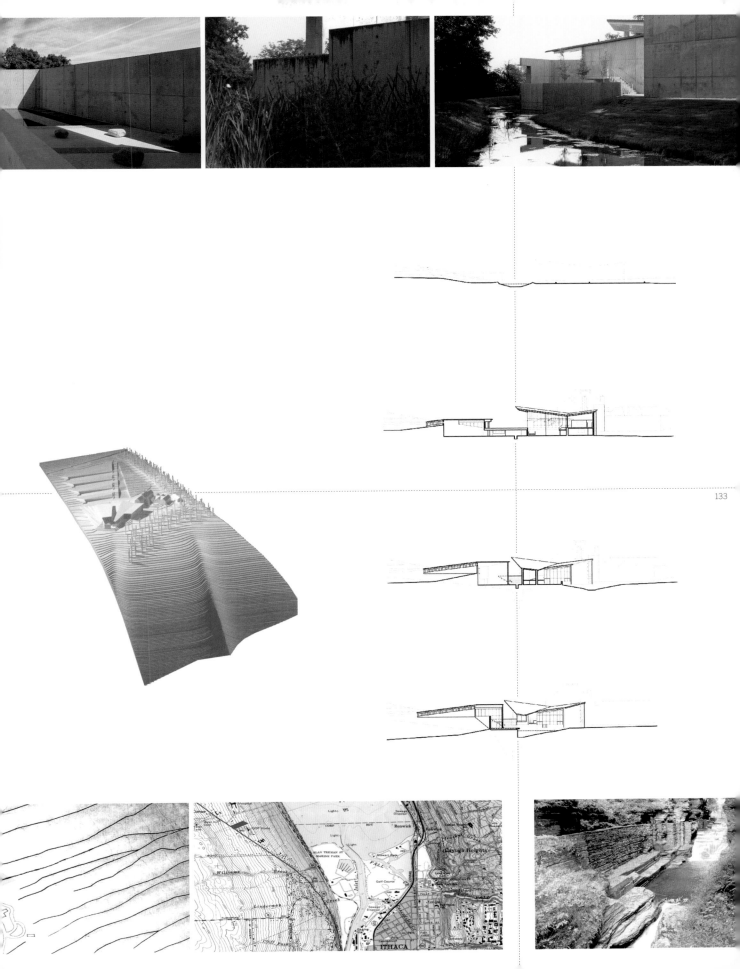

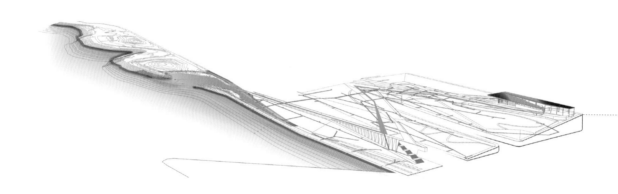

OLYMPIC SCULPTURE PARK

The Olympic Sculpture Park, overlooking Elliott Bay in the Puget Sound, is located at an 8.5 acre former industrial site sliced into three parcels by train tracks and a four-lane arterial road. The park unfolds as a continuous Z-shaped landscape that wanders from the city to the bay, alternatively revealing and concealing the train and roadways below. The design, a continuous constructed landscape for art, transforms the city's connection to the water by rising over the existing infrastructure to connect the urban core to a revitalized waterfront.

A century ago this site was broken down by hydrological power, and this enhanced earthwork re-establishes the original topography of the site to connect city and water. The hybrid landform provides a new pedestrian infrastructure layered over the existing site, capitalizing on a forty-foot grade change from the top of the hill to the water's edge. Layers of surface and subsurface systems together create a resilient and flexible framework for water management, environmental remediation, power, and teledata across the site. The landform and plantings collaborate to direct, collect, and cleanse storm water as it travels down the site and is ultimately released into Elliott Bay. At the water's edge, a newly created beach allows free movement, long denied, between downtown Seattle and the waterfront. A crumbling, hard-edged concrete sea wall was taken down and replaced by a shoreline garden and a series of tidal terraces—a restored ecosystem that accommodates juvenile salmon and saltwater vegetation. Five years after the opening, this thriving urban habitat is now the subject of an ongoing ecological study.

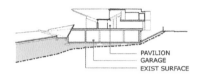

PAVILION
GARAGE
EXIST SURFACE

NEW FILL/SOIL CAP

ELLIOTT AVE
ELLIOTT BRIDGE
BSNF BRIDGE

BSNF RR
SEAWALL
SALMONOID
BEACH HABITAT

STRUCTURE MSE

135

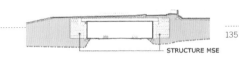

ENGINEERED
SOIL CAP

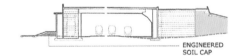

BATTERED MSE
VERTICAL MSE

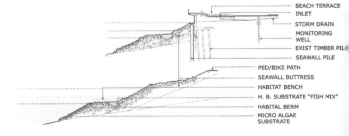

BEACH TERRACE
INLET
STORM DRAIN
MONITORING
WELL
EXIST TIMBER PILE
SEAWALL PILE
PED/BIKE PATH
SEAWALL BUTTRESS
HABITAT BENCH
H. B. SUBSTRATE "FISH MIX"
HABITAL BERM
MICRO ALGAE
SUBSTRATE

MCCANN RESIDENCE

Tuxedo Park, New York, the site of the McCann Residence, is an illustrious setting around three glacial lakes. Developed in 1885 as a country resort, Tuxedo Park is distinguished by a number of estates designed by prominent architects at the turn of the century. Dense forests, dramatic rock outcroppings, and pronounced topography characterize this rugged timberland landscape in the Catskill Mountains. The house is designed to embrace this historic setting and express its distinctive landscape through the interconnectivity of the home and picturesque landscape. The house embeds itself into the hill as an ascending route that is open to panoramic views of the lake and hills beyond. The lower levels emerge from the dramatic stone of the site, and the uppermost level is expressed as a glass pavilion to frame vistas to Tuxedo Lake in the distance.

The deeply sloping site is host to significant runoff as water descends into Tuxedo Lake. A series of new stone retaining walls meter the topography of the site, define program areas, shape outdoor terraces, and decelerate water runoff into the lake below. The descending terraced gardens created by the retaining walls are planted with a mix of ferns, mosses, mountain laurel, ash, and oak trees to prevent erosion.

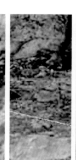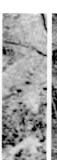

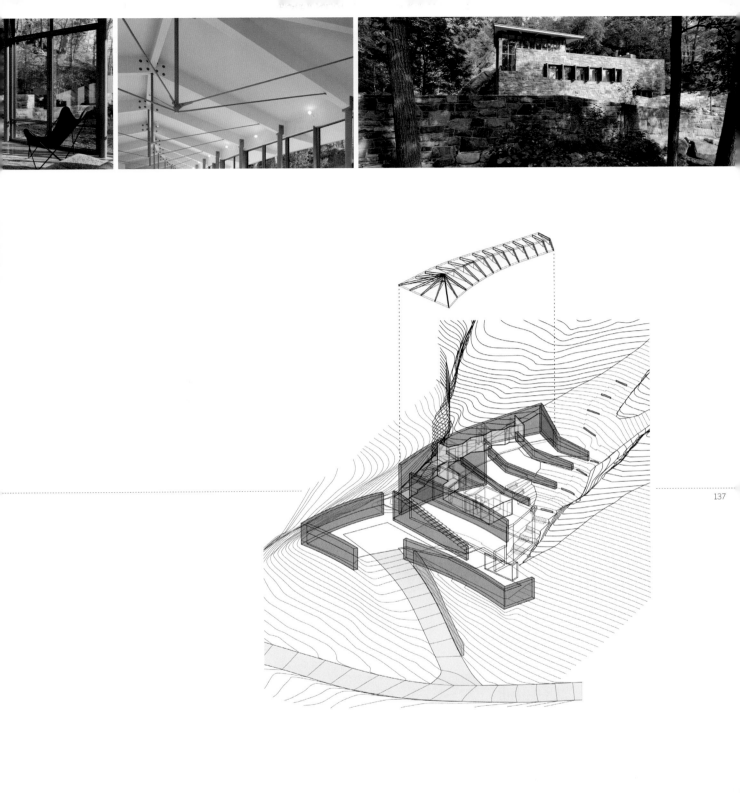

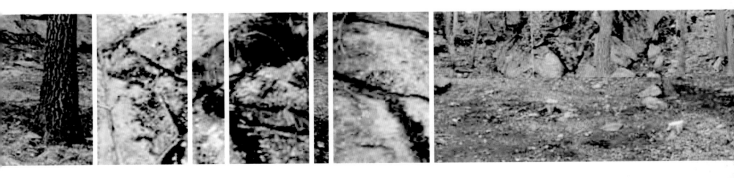

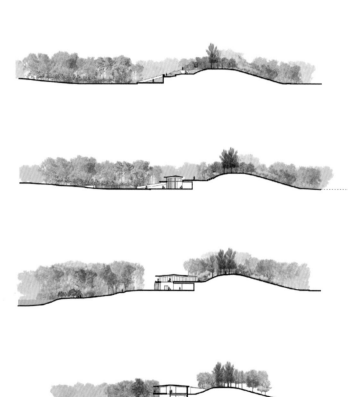

BROOKLYN BOTANIC GARDEN

The new Brooklyn Botanic Garden Visitor Center provides a legible point of arrival and orientation at the interface between garden and city. The building is conceived as an inhabitable topography at the threshold between the city and the constructed landscapes of the 52-acre garden. Like the gardens themselves, the building is experienced cinematically and is never seen in its entirety. The serpentine form of the Visitor Center is generated by the garden's existing pathways. A chameleon-like structure, the visitor center transitions from an architectural presence at the street into a structured landscape in the botanic garden. On either side of the building, a series of bio-infiltration basins capture storm water and runoff from a neighboring parking lot. Approximately 190,000 gallons of water per year is filtered and transferred to the Japanese Garden pond, eliminating the use of treated city water. The water is eventually released into a bioswale where it is further cleansed while descending across the site. The new Visitor Center, literally small in size in comparison to the Botanic Garden, is a key component of the Garden's site-scale water management program.

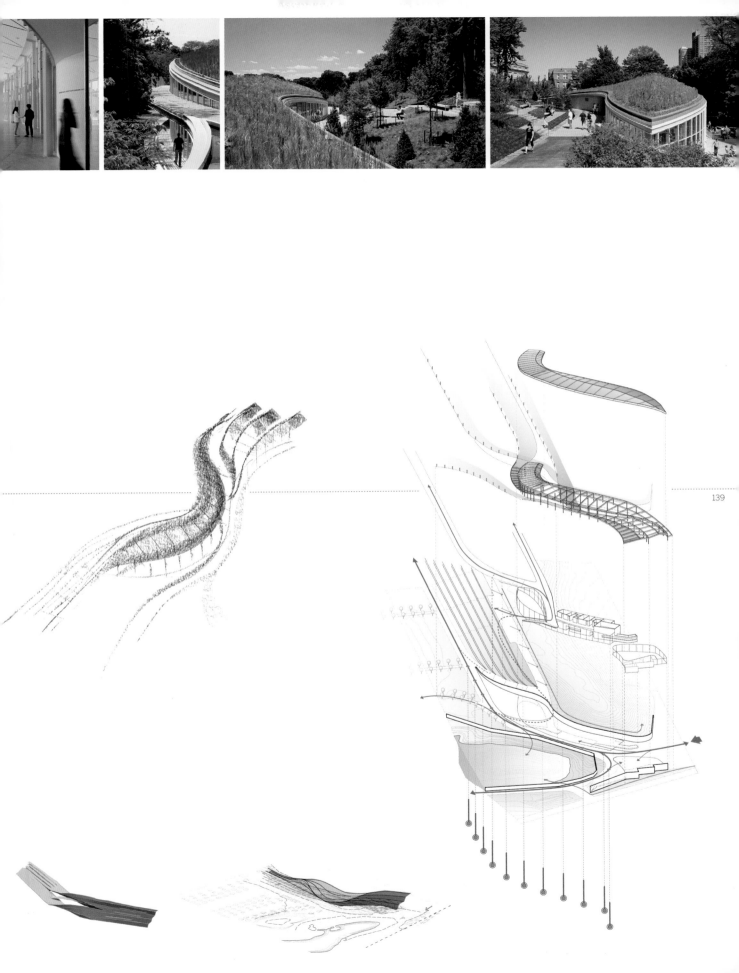

WILLIAM BRAHAM
WASTE, WORK, AND WORTH

FOR MOST OF HUMAN HISTORY, PEOPLE COULD BE DIVIDED

INTO TWO CLASSES: THOSE WHO CARRIED THEIR DAILY WATER, AND AN ELITE WHO HAD SOMEONE ELSE CARRY IT FOR THEM. WATER IS QUITE HEAVY; IT WEIGHS APPROXIMATELY 8 POUNDS PER GALLON AND MOVING IT TAKES WORK. AS A RESULT, IT IS LITTLE SURPRISE THAT PEOPLE WHO HAVE TO CARRY WATER USE ONLY A FEW GALLONS A DAY FOR DRINKING, COOKING, BATHING, AND CLEANING. WHEN WATER CAN BE SUPPLIED WITHOUT HUMAN WORK, THE AMOUNT OF WATER USED EACH DAY INCREASES DRAMATICALLY. IN ROME, AT THE TIME OF THE EMPIRE, WATER WAS DELIVERED TO NEIGHBORHOOD FOUNTAINS, APARTMENT BUILDINGS, AND THE RESIDENCES OF THE WEALTHY, SO AFFLUENT CITIZENS USED UP TO THE LUXURIOUS VOLUME OF 150 GALLONS PER DAY. THE CORRELATION BETWEEN WORK AND WATER EXEMPLIFIES THE CLASSIC PARABLE OF TECHNOLOGICAL INNOVATION, IN WHICH HUMAN LABOR IS REPLACED BY MECHANICAL (OR HYDRAULIC) INGENUITY AND THE AMOUNTS OF WORK (OR WATER) THAT CAN BE DELIVERED ARE DRAMATICALLY INCREASED.

Fairmount Waterworks

With abundance, however, comes waste. In 1842, Charles Dickens visited the Philadelphia Waterworks, part of the first modern water supply system, and expressed his surprise at the waste:

Philadelphia is most bountifully provided with fresh water, which is showered and jerked about, and turned on, and poured off, everywhere... The river is dammed at this point, and forced by its own power into certain high tanks or reservoirs, whence the whole city, to the top stories of the houses, is supplied at a very trifling expense.[1]

The Waterworks was built thirty years prior to Dickens's visit and had rapidly become a model for

metropolitan water systems across the country and around the world. As the model spread, so too did increases in water use, largely due to the installation of pressured and piped supply systems. Much of that flow was lost in the leaky systems of distribution as they were extended into households and business, but since the supply was rarely metered until the twentieth century, the population was free to explore uses of water that had been unimagined by even the wealthy bathers of previous generations.

WASTE

As water consumption exceeded the capacity of local ecosystems to simultaneously provide fresh water and absorb waste, water intakes were extended and distribution systems made more efficient. However, consumption continued to increase as Philadelphians began to experiment in new ways with a readily available water supply. In a report of 1900, it was noted, "the average daily consumption in Philadelphia has risen from 36 gallons per capita in 1860, to 215 gallons in 1897."[2] As a result, municipal engineers began seeking the installation of meters to help moderate rates of use. These dramatic increases in consumption can seem quite abstract in the engineering reports, so it is important to recognize the dramatic changes in personal habits that were accompanied by the hundreds of gallons that began flowing through households. At its most fundamental, this cultural change involved a transformed concept of cleanliness, both of the water and of those that used it.

In the final chapter of *Mechanization Takes Command*, Siegfried Giedion examined this change through the history of the modern bathtub, contrasting it with the public bathing habits of the ancient world and locating the shift to private cleansing in the political and corporeal anxieties of the early modern period. It can be hard to imagine a regime of cleanliness so different from our own, in which daily bathing prevails. The change in concept and degree didn't happen all at once (or everywhere at the same rate), but as we consider the subject of water use in the twenty-first century, it is imperative to understand the moist evolution of habits, habitats, and inhabitants that are involved in the new technologies of water use. An infrastructural alignment and a public health regulation illustrate this evolution.

The installation of the first water supply systems typically preceded the construction of sewage systems,

Bathing

> "The concise lines of this white bathtub will perhaps bear witness to later periods for the outlook of ours as much as the amphora for the outlook of fifth century Greece. It is a luxury article, which the combinations of refined metallurgical and technical skills transformed into a democratic utensil. In its own way, this double-shell tub, which on the other side of the atlantic still smacks of luxury, numbers among the symbols of our time."
> Siegfried Giedion, *Mechanization Takes Command*

Bathroom

sometimes by decades. Dirty water was simply dumped into existing yards, privies, and drains until they over-flowed, causing a host of problems and demanding an investment in sewage piping and closed sewers. This ultimately ushered in the armature of modern plumbing, which uses one set of pipes for clean water and another for dirty. The real acceleration in water use began once the two systems were aligned, when the drain for dirty water was located below the faucet delivering clean water. Public health officials quickly learned about the dangers of letting the systems connect, with one person's dirty water siphoning back into another person's supply pipes, and so legislated a minimum "air gap" between the bottom of a faucet and the top of a bathtub or sink. The diagram of the alignment between faucet and drain, with its hygienic gap and simple backflow prevention mechanism, describes the realization of a powerful new technology for maximizing the conversion of clean water into dirty. You don't have to touch water; all you have to do is turn on the tap.

Giedion posed the question of bathing as a choice between cleansing and leisurely regeneration, and hoped that a recovery of the more public forms of bathing might help redeem industrialized culture. However, he also recognized the power of the new technologies of the bathroom, and their luxurious appeal. To Giedion, the smooth white tub signaled much more than the fruit of advanced metallurgy; it symbolized the luxury of hot and cold running water itself ("on every floor" as hotels used to advertise). The term luxury is quite precise in this situation, meaning the willful and visible expenditure of wealth, in the form of an unnecessary expenditure of some of that massive hydraulic power. Arguably, the first gallon or so a day is a biological necessity, but the rest is a luxury to which we have become accustomed.

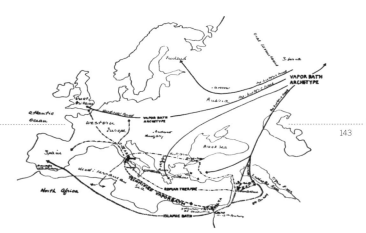

143

MIGRATION & EVOLUTION OF BATHING IN EUROPE: "The manner in which a civilization integrates bathing within its life, as well as the type of bathing it prefers, yields searching insights into the inner nature of the period." Siegfried Giedion, *Mechanization Takes Command*

WORK

The water delivered through modern pipes is luxurious in two ways. First is freedom from the mostly physical work of lifting and conveying all that water. This entails, on the part of most municipal water systems, the moving of water that is already fresh, drawing it from lakes, rivers, and underground aquifers, filtering it for particulates, and then pumping it through the massive water supply infrastructure under pressure. The typical cost of the water supply, whether paid through taxes or individual meters, covers the work of building and operating that hydraulic enterprise, which increasingly includes some amount of chemical purification. This brings us to the second luxury, the "freshness" of water. The largely biochemical work of distilling and cleaning water adds value that becomes starkly apparent in regions where water re-use is necessary. In such cases, freshness can be achieved by distilling, boiling, and condensing water using large sources of heat, or by osmotic filtration under very high pressure, using electrically powered pumps. The amount of electricity used to power the osmotic process for cleaning dirty water can be up to ten times greater than that used in facilities which start with fresh water sources. This makes evident some of the work already performed by the biosphere to make the fresh water in lakes and rivers.

Water filtration methods can also be applied to sewage, in a process called "toilet-to-tap," which according to a county official in San Diego, is "one of the most expensive kinds of water you can create."[3] While he was referring to the economic cost, that expense also reflects the tremendous amount of work that natural waterways provide up until their biological processes are overwhelmed. Toilet-to-tap is really just the final step of water recycling implemented to reduce the burden on local ecosystems that began when American legislators enacted the Clean Water Act of 1948. Along with the revisions of 1972, this legislation made the common practice of dumping raw sewage illegal and required effluent to meet secondary treatment standards, mostly through the elimination of biodegradable organics. Most of that treatment work is performed in sewage treatment facilities by microbes similar to those found in natural waterways, which consume the organic material as food, converting it to carbon dioxide, water, and heat. They biologically neutralize wastewater before it is returned to waterways, where some of it is simply extracted again for the water supply system. A common urban saying is that the river water of major cities is "drunk seven times between the source and the sea."

POTABLE WATER COMPONENT COSTS: 30 MGD

DISINFECTION	$120
WASTEWATER REUSE	$250
COAGULATION & FILTRATION	$540
LIME SOFTENING	$410
MEMBRANE SOFTENING	$590
REVERSE OSMOSIS	$601

WORTH

In spite of all the work that goes into water treatment, anxieties about cleanliness and the last step from sewage to drinking water are profound. San Diego ultimately decided to pump its osmotically filtered sewage water into local aquifers, where it actually became somewhat less pure before it was subsequently withdrawn again for consumption. However "laundering" water in this way more adequately satisfies public superstition about cleanliness. This is a fascinating perception, in which we trust the natural processes of the hydrologic cycle to deliver cleanliness, while counting their services as "free," but we distrust the engineered services for which we have to pay. Pristine nature versus imperfect people perhaps, but the distinction highlights the difference between common sense perceptions and the economic exchange value of natural resources. As long as the human uses of a river are within the capacity of the waterway to clean itself, the exchange value more or less reflects the work of obtaining and delivering it. But once the renewal capacity is exceeded, as consumption grows past those limits, the real price of purifying and delivering the water becomes evident, as costlier forms of work and greater quantities of energy are required to reproduce the natural supply. Municipal engineers can purify seawater and recycle sewage to augment or even replace fresh water supplies, but it requires tremendous amounts of work to do so. In other words, the luxury of abundant fresh water is purchased with work, whether through the "free" work of the biosphere or the paid work of the technosphere.

As ecological economists have demonstrated, monetary costs undervalue the contribution of the biosphere until its capacities are exceeded. An alternate approach for evaluating environmental work (and worth) is bio-physical accounting. In the method developed by H. T. Odum, every form of energy transformation is tracked to provide a common evaluation of the many different kinds of work and resources required to deliver fresh water. Ultimately all the work performed in the biosphere can be traced

6.58 E+11	MUNICIPAL LAKE
2.56 E+13	INDIVIDUAL: FILTERED
9.76 E+13	INDIVIDUAL: BOILED
1.13 E+14	INDIVIDUAL: SOLAR DISTILLER
1.56 E+12	BOTTLED WATER

SOLAR EMBODIED ENERGY (SEJ/M³)

146

back to the sun, whether as part of the hydrologic cycle, the human conversion of fossil fuels to work, or the production of food to support human labor. Putting these many different contributions in the common terms of solar embodied energy (solaremjoules, sej) enabled Andres Buenfil to quantify the total cost of the different delivery mechanisms for fresh water in Florida.[4] The clean water delivered to a lake involves about 250 million sej per cubic meter of water. Not surprisingly, the least expensive fresh water supply was a municipal system drawing fresh water from a lake, which required about one trillion sej per cubic meter. Using an osmotic filtration system with brackish water doubled that cost, while a system purifying seawater was over seven times as expensive. This largely confirms the conventional engineering ranking, but reinforces the contribution of ecosystem services and the value of maintaining the health of existing watersheds. Of course the most expensive method of delivering fresh water is in plastic bottles, which requires over 150 times as much total work and energy as the municipal supply from a lake, even when the water had been drawn from the same fresh water source. It turns out to be much, much more expensive to drive water in a diesel-powered delivery truck than to pump it through pipes.

Life unavoidably generates waste, and the ubiquitous plastic bottle of water stands as a symbol of the particularly wealthy life-style of the early twenty-first century. It is a wealth obtained by extracting work from a biosphere reaching the limits of its capacity to provide more fresh water and absorb more wastes. However, there is a more human lesson to be taken from this brief history. Clean water isn't valuable because it is scarce, it becomes scarce because it is so useful. Water is a powerful agent of chemical transformation and of heat and mass transfer, which is integral to most biological activities and many social and symbolic ones as well. We simply use water to the point of scarcity, and that is what makes its abundant use so luxurious.

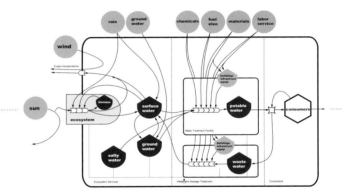

ENERGY SYSTEMS: Potable tap water for consumers is the result of a complicated matrix of energetic and material inputs stemming from industrial and ecological systems.

ANNA HERINGER
HANDMADE IN THE DELTA

EVERYTHING THAT I BUILD ENDS SOMEWHERE BACK IN THE GROUND, IN THE ATMOSPHERE, OR AS WATER. EVERY MATERIAL CHANGES AND IS TRANSFORMED, BY TIME AND BY ITS INTERACTION WITH WATER. SO, WHENEVER I BEGIN A PROJECT, I ALWAYS HAVE THIS TRANSFORMATION IN MIND. OUR EARTH IS VERY MUCH SHAPED BY WATER. FOR INSTANCE, THE ATLAS MOUNTAINS IN MOROCCO ARE CONSTANTLY ERODING; THEIR MATERIALS ARE BEING CARRIED BY WATER DOWN INTO PLAINS AND VALLEYS. THIS FOR ME IS A VERY IMPORTANT THING. WE ALWAYS THINK WE SHOULD MAKE STRUCTURES THAT LAST FOR ETERNITY. BUT WHEN THE ATLAS MOUNTAINS ARE ERODING, OR THE ALPS, OR THE HIMALAYAS, HOW CAN WE THINK THAT OUR BUILDINGS WILL NOT SHARE THE SAME FATE? HOW CAN WE THINK THAT OUR BUILDINGS WILL NOT, OR SHOULD NOT, BE ERODED BY WATER IN TIME? IN WATER, EVERY THING THAT WE USE, EVERY MATERIAL, ENDS UP SOMEWHERE.

I work with mud. In this substance, you have two inseparable, elemental materials: water and earth. These are available almost anywhere on the planet. In Bangladesh, water is plentiful and the quality of earth is excellent. When combined to make mud, it has fantastic material characteristics. Mud regulates humidity perfectly, absorbs sounds and smells; it is environmentally friendly; and it has aesthetic value—you can make it formally dynamic or straight, very rough or very refined, it can have a variety of colors and textures.

In mud, water is always present; it cannot be removed or isolated. Normally, we don't see the energy that is in our building materials; it is absolutely embodied. I wonder why we don't just take the raw material as a lot of people still do in Bangladesh? Why do we try to improve technologies? Why don't we respect water and the earth just as they are, combine them with our hands, and use our skills and our craftsmanship?

The mixing machine was powered by water buffalo. We couldn't use cows because they are actually not that good at mixing; they are too intelligent and always step in their previous holes. With human labor, the animals mix the straw and mud and water. The mixture is cured overnight, and then it is put on the building's foundation. This was the most important improvement for creating more durable buildings. The material is placed by hand on top of the foundation and then cut with a spade at an angle. That is practically all we needed.

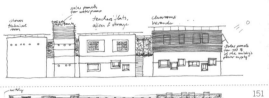

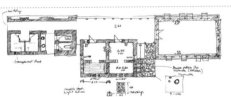

151

Whenever I leave Dhaka to go to the north, I pass through brickfields. It is always incredible for me to see mud, a raw material that can be used to build any kind of structure, being waterproofed and ruined. Building in the correct way absolutely does not require this. I am trying to promote earthen architecture all around the world again because I think we shouldn't be afraid of water erosion. I think we have to learn how to build with erosion and to incorporate it back into our architecture.

I make earth architecture. When I lived in the village of Rudrapur, in Bangladesh, I found the mud houses there to be extremely beautiful, but they have the disadvantage of low durability. Often, the people are afraid because they think they are not living in safe conditions. The village elites build in brick, concrete, and corrugated iron sheets, as do the governmental and non-governmental organizations. These materials are considered more durable. Despite this, most Bangladeshi's use loam, bamboo, or other local products to make their houses. In Rudrapur, the hierarchy of materials is very clear.

I think you only see something as precious when you develop it and become invested. This is crucial, because the traditional earth and water structures are extremely durable, something we don't normally expect, as long as they are in use and maintained. All you need to re-do your building is to add water and human labor. You can then construct new walls upon the old ones. If the building is no longer in use, then with the addition of water, it can easily go back to the ground. When you don't need the structures any longer, you can take them down without making any waste. Water is used to make the mud for the buildings, but through erosion, it also carries the mud away.

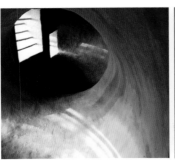

The school's philosophy is learning with joy. So we tried to make different spaces where students would be comfortable, such as the 'caves room.'

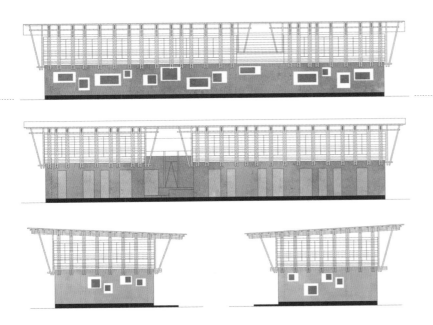

Plan and elevations, METI - Handmade School in Rudrapur, Bangladesh

In many ways, earth is so different from cement. It provides such a wonderful tactile experience; with cement, you cannot have that.

DAVID LEATHERBARROW
HORIZON OF ALL HORIZONS

FOR ARCHITECTS WATER IS THE MOST FUNDAMENTAL AND
AT THE SAME TIME THE MOST DESTRUCTIVE OF THE WORLD'S BASIC ELEMENTS.[1]
WITHOUT WATER, ALBERTI SAID, ALL THAT GROWS AND MULTIPLIES ON THE EARTH
WOULD COME TO NOTHING. YET, WATER IS ALSO THE BUILDING'S GREATEST ENEMY, A
FOE THAT IS EVENTUALLY VICTORIOUS IN EVERY SINGLE CASE. AS FOR GEOMETRY AND
FORM, WATER IS THEIR SWORN ENEMY, HAVING NONE OF ITS OWN. INCOMPARABLY
PASSIVE, WATER IS SURPRISINGLY AGGRESSIVE. ALTHOUGH IT WILLINGLY CONFORMS
TO ANY SHAPE IT IS OFFERED, IT RELENTLESSLY PURSUES ITS OWN LEVEL, LEVELING
EVERYTHING IN ITS PATH.[2] IN ITS BLIND ATTRACTION FOR GRAVITY, IT FORCES ITSELF
OUTWARD, FIRST MARKING THEN ABSORBING EVERYTHING IT MEETS. ITS DISSOLVINGS
FEED AN INSATIABLE APPETITE. EVERYONE KNOWS THAT WHEN IT GETS HEATED
IT BEHAVES LIKE AIR—HIDING ITSELF, BLOWING, AND SOMETIMES REFRESHING;
YET FOG, "SHAPELESS SILENCE" ACCORDING TO W.H. AUDEN,[3] DISASSEMBLES
THINGS, IF ONLY TO RENEW OUR INTEREST IN THEM. BEFORE WATER VAPORIZES,
WHILE IT STILL ADHERES TO SOLID SURFACES, IT IS ALTERNATELY NOURISHING
AND INVASIVE, INTEGRATING THINGS ACCORDING TO ITS OWN LEVEL, BUT THEREBY
DESTROYING THEIR INDIVIDUALITY. TOO MUCH OF IT MAKES A MESS OF THINGS, TOO
LITTLE HARDENS THEM. THE SHORE BETWEEN THE SEA AND SAND IS WHERE MANY
SETTLEMENTS HAVE THEIR BEGINNING—ALMOST ALL GREAT CITIES ARE RIVER, LAKE,
OR OCEAN CITIES—DESPITE THE FACT THAT WATERY EDGES TEND TO FLUCTUATE.[4]

Le Corbusier, Villa Savoye, Poissy,
1928-31, aerial view, sketch

BUILDING AS BOAT

In what follows I will try to show that continual change is okay in the art of building; more largely, that alteration is an essential dimension of architecture when it accepts water as a dimension of its milieu. Considering the tasks and aims of creative design, I will also propose a thesis of co-operation that adds to our familiar techniques of piping, guttering, channeling, canalling, and welling another set of practices that substitute co-existence for containment, collaboration for control. If water is the problem, management is not the answer. To make this argument I will mainly consider buildings by a single 20th century architect.

To demonstrate my co-existence thesis I will introduce a number of design ideas or thought-images: the building as a boat, a raft, and a receptacle; also, the soil as something akin to sea, and finally, human movement as a meander, like the ancient river with the same name. Each of these images will show how architecture can live with water as its most basic horizon: an unstinting source, as Alberti said, but also a limiting condition.

There is, perhaps, no more famous 20th century building than Le Corbusier's Villa Savoye at Poissy. Quite apart from the many familiar images, there is a less well-known free-hand drawing that can be seen to bear upon our theme. Anyone who has made the trip to Poissy will recall that the approach and departure from the building follow parallel lines that run between the front gate and the famous pilotis. The first thing one notices about the sketch I have in mind is that these lines of approach have been released from their parallelism and allowed to wave or wiggle a little, as if the terrain they cross were uneven, which of course it is not. Second, while the pilotis are visible in the sketch they are hardly prominent; Le Corbusier seems rather more insistent on the ripple that edges the lawn. Is it a lawn? I suppose the smudges we see should be read as tufts of grass, which means the corresponding verticals and arcs are un-leafed branches. Yet, when I first saw the drawing, I misread the lines of approach and departure as the wake of the building's forward progress, and the branching lines as wings of birds, gulls in fact— that Le Corbusier understood the precinct of his project as more or less aqueous.

If my sense of the Savoye site as sea-like strikes you as doubtful, I would ask you to suspend judgment until you read what he wrote about an even more famous building. The high point of the young architect's *Journey to the East* was his visit to the Acropolis in Athens.[5] The drawings are remarkable and the accompanying text is nothing less than stunning. In what seems a rather fevered struggle to name the destination of his voyage, he proposed a striking set of characterizations. Of the expect-

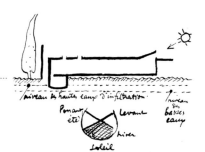

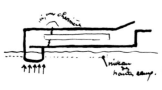

Le Corbusier, House on Lac Leman, Corseaux,
1923-4, buoyancy and movement of the house

Le Corbusier, House on Lac Leman, Corseaux, 1923-4, view from interior; sill, lintel, and water's edge horizons

edly topographical terms for the hilltop, he repeated "flat summit" most often.[6] Also unsurprising was a geometric rendering: the Parthenon appeared to him as a "yellow cube." To this geometry he ascribed governing rank with the term "sovereign cube," conflating topographical with political elevation. But the hill and its figure were also personified: it was a "gigantic apparition," an "unconquerable titan," and with reference to the bloody battles of Homeric myth, a "tragic carcass." But even more striking and relevant to my purpose are his maritime images, for he suggested that this building/block/boat was anchored in the midst of the sea, even though the Piraeus was well out of sight. The Acropolis was, he said, a "hull of rock," the Parthenon at night "a black marble pilot." This argues for governance once again, and renders the status of the governed as formless; in nautical terms, uncharted. Elsewhere in the text, a shift to textile imagery returned him to the problem of the horizon: the temple on the summit is a "dark knot" that binds together sky and sea. Of course, the horizon line in the distance did that too. Giving the "marble pilot" an outlook, he described the temple as a "contemplator of the sea;" it is, he said, a "block from another world," which places "man [whomever takes up its vantage] above the world," and if not elevated, at least afloat.

Vantage was also on his mind when he designed a house for his father and mother on the shores of Lake Geneva.[7] The 11 meter long horizontal window was the chief protagonist in the design of the house. His dad, he said, was a lover of nature. For that reason, it seems, near and far, or more concretely, the upper edge of the sill and water

line at the foot of the mountains were to be directly linked together by the lake in-between. The morning mist was undoubtedly part of this merge, thus positive, but rising damp also had negative consequences. In his little book on the house, Le Corbusier admitted that in its teen age years the house caught a cold. It was attacked by what he called "a strange affliction," a rather sizable crack from top to bottom.[8]

The fault was typical of houses on the lake, the result of seasonal water level changes and the shifting ground that resulted. Still, the water-tight cellar performed well, as if it were a little boat. When the waters rose, it floated, while the rest of the house did not. Unwilling to move from the water's edge—mom and dad liked the view—and proud of the boat, he installed a copper hinge on the roof, so the building-boat could freely rise and fall with the water, more or less like a dock, in harmony with seasonal rhythms. One does not have to approve or recommend this detail to see that it indicates one way that water and buildings can co-operate with one another by moving together. What is more, cooperation of this sort can occur in verticals as well as horizontals.

"Breathing walls" is the name Le Corbusier gave to the facades he designed after 1930. All manner of adjustable elements were invented to allow the building's "respiration." More broadly, this usage and the equipment it described suggest the need to rethink the old idea of buildings being inactive. The specific question is this: might a building's interactions with water bring it to life?

157

Le Corbusier, House on Lac Leman, Corseaux, 1923-4, elevation toward lake

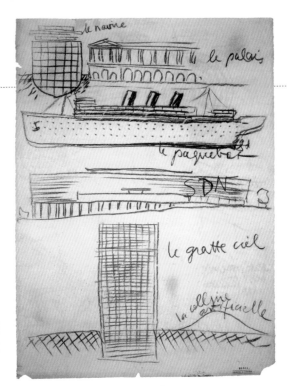

Le Corbusier, comparative study of Place de la Concorde, an ocean liner, the League of Nations, and an American skyscraper; from *Précisions sur un état présent de l'architecture et de l'urbanisme*, 1930

Boat-buildings were on Le Corbusier's mind throughout his career, as was the more basic problem of co-existing with the fluid substrate. In a lengthier study, one could describe several works that were designed to be at ease with watery terrain. For now, I will comment on just one: the Salvation Army Building in Paris, built in 1929, four years after the experiment on Lake Geneva.[9] I will begin anecdotally.

Years ago, in the Fall semester in my second year of architecture studies, I was given the assignment of producing a complete set of drawings of this building (plans, sections, elevations, and details). Of the many sheets I produced, the one that vexed me the most was the cross-section. The problem was the angle of the huge plane of glass, the largest such plane in Europe at the time, one that originally had very few openings. My concern was not the window's thermal performance, but its geometry, for it was plain from the very start that the building's front and back were not exactly parallel. Why? With a little research I found one of Le Corbusier's answers: he had to tilt the façade in order to stay under the height limit imposed on the project by local building codes. This also explains the set back of the upper floors for mothers with infants. The inclination through the full height saved him forty centimeters. The angle is slight, no more than a few degrees, more or less the same as the typical lean or list of boats at sea. That the project had a naval precedent is certain. Before Le Corbusier won the competition for their new building, the Salvation

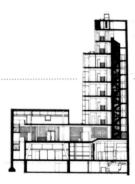

Le Corbusier, Salvation Army Building, Paris, 1929-33,
cross section (left) and east façade (right)

Army had given him the task of renovating their barge, the Louis Catherine, which had been in service on the Seine for years. Here, too, comparisons with the Lake Geneva project can be made, for the vessel was made out of reinforced concrete, and both the bunks and the long windows recall the accent on horizontals that made the parent's house so congenial to its flowing surrounds. Most decisive, though, is the inclination of the new building, the few degrees I noted. Just as the fluid in our inner ears keeps us upright, water level determines the horizon, it is the fundamental terrain that building boats occupy and represent.

BUILDING AS RAFT

At the outset of Le Corbusier's project for the Venice Hospital, he made a comment that seems to have governed the whole of the design. Looking at the Venetian landscape he said: "One cannot build high, it will be necessary to build without building. And then, it will be necessary to find the scale."[10] Clues to the height and the scale were provided by one of the city's greatest painters, Vittore Carpaccio, in his rendering of the Funeral of Saint Ursula, which Le Corbusier sketched in 1963. The height is set by the supports that raise the body above the fluctuations of the battle; scale was conferred by the horizon of bodies. These relationships can also be seen in the cross-section of the hospital, which was to never exceed a height of 13.6 meters—the elevation, Le Corbusier thought, of the Venetian rooftops and altane gar-

dens above the canals. All in all, his hospital was to be a network of enclosures, patios, and gardens. From above it appears to float, as if a raft, or series of them; in truth, however, the whole ensemble was to sit on hundreds of columns, as does Venice itself. The roof tiles above and waves below formed the outer limits of a richly stratified section. The public and service spaces were set at the level of the fondamenta, where the water and paving reach toward one another. The next major level positioned the patient rooms and beds above the treatment and public zones, with openings for air, light, and view. But the layering did not end there, as it did in contemporary and later mat buildings; Le Corbusier focused just as intently on the roof landscape, which included open air terraces, gardens, and attic spaces. Here the connection with the Venetian altane is explicit, particularly the use of the roof garden as an elevated ground plane, for flowers and food, of course, also the collection of rain water, and some particularly Venetian alchemy.

When Goethe visited Venice in the 18th century, he was especially impressed by the women with red hair sunning themselves on these elevated terraces. Special wide brimmed hats called solanas were devised—open at the top but expansive—to shelter the skin below the brim and expose the hair to color enhancing sunlight. To quicken the process, strange mixtures were added to the hair, lemon sometimes, also lye, sulfur unhappily, and salt water from the canals. In sum, the raft section allowed water below and above, with precious artifacts in-between.

159

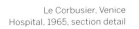
Le Corbusier, Venice
Hospital, 1965, section detail

Le Corbusier, diagram of
Carpaccio's *Funeral of Saint
Ursula*, c. 1964

Vittore Carpaccio, *Funeral of
Saint Ursula*, 1493

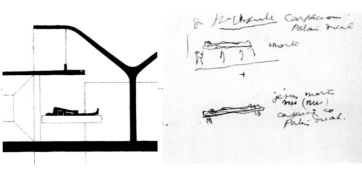

Le Corbusier, Unité d'Habitation,
Marseilles, 1947-52, roof swimming pool

BUILDING AS RECEPTICAL

With all that has been written about the elevated garden in the work of Le Corbusier, surprisingly little has been said about his use of the upper deck as a receptacle of water. Without doubt, the most elegant and instructive example of such a holding is the roof of the Millowner's Building in Ahmedabad.

The building's cross-section presents a fascinating thesis. Its base arises out of the Sabarmati River. While Le Corbusier used the word picturesque to describe the river, he also acknowledged its usefulness: the spectacle portrayed "cloth dyers washing and drying their cotton materials on the sand bed in the company of herons, cows, buffalo, and donkeys half immersed in water to keep cool." With an aqueous base as its first premise, the building rose toward the sky. The ramp leads to the entrance hall, which was open to the wind. The direct rays of the sun were meant to be broken by the grid of louvers that also gave the façade inhabitable depth. While the building had several practical and administrative purposes, it was essentially ceremonial. The route from below passed from the middle level to the upper deck on which the auditorium was encaved. Windowless, it received borrowed light from above, which is to say the underbelly of a sagging roof that was to serve as a receptacle garden, the ultimate destination of the architectural promenade. The basin's functions were primarily three: collecting, cooling, and centralizing. Water was essential for these purposes, as it was for the entire institution and

Le Corbusier, La Tourette, 1956-60, drain detail

Le Corbusier, Villa Sarabhai, 1955, roof
irrigation and drainage canal

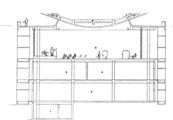

the culture it houses. Like the people and the land, the building waits on what it wants, ready to catch what falls, like the arms of a parent.

Describing his Villa Sarabhai in the same city, Le Corbusier observed that the country is tropical. That's hardly a newsflash; his next sentence was more interesting: "the monsoon rages for two months of the year and is an alternating combination of downpours and sunshine."[12] Also forceful were the winds. This explained, he said, the way the building was sited, also its sun breakers: "the Sarabhai House is situated according to the prevailing winds (in order to be traversed by currents of air), and its facades are furnished with brises-soleil."[13] Le Corbusier was particularly proud of the roof's construction and environmental performance. On top of half-cylinder vaults is a layer of earth that serves as both thermal insulation and the subsoil for grasses and local flowers. Anticipating the monsoon, water is given three outlets from the roof: an ingenious system of interlocking concrete canals, the wonderful "toboggan run" that empties into the pool, and a set of spouts that direct water into ground level receptacles. It appears the client's son gave the architect the idea for this dramatic incline; he, too, saw the building as a way of letting water give comfort to everyday life, although playfully, like a child, down the stairway two steps at a time. The house as a whole is an eloquent example of architecture at play in watery terrain.

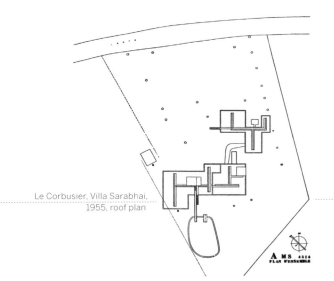

Le Corbusier, Villa Sarabhai,
1955, roof plan

161

Le Corbusier, Villa Sarabhai, 1955,
"toboggan" slide

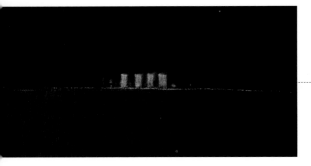

Le Corbusier, Skyscraper study for
Montevideo, 1929

SOIL AS WATER

Now I would like to turn to the water's edge, a limit found in most cities. Approaching the American shore for the first time, Le Corbusier recorded his impressions as follows: "Monday morning when my ship stopped at Quarantine, I saw a fantastic, almost mystic city rising up in the mist. But the ship moves forward and the apparition is transformed into an image of incredible brutality and savagery. Here is certainly the most prominent manifestation of the power of modern times. This brutality and this savagery do not displease me. It is thus that great enterprises begin: by strength."[14] At this moment, Le Corbusier is approaching New York City and describes his view in terms that are remarkably similar to those he used to describe the Acropolis—which is, of course, approached by boat, as the Piraeus is some distance away. Facing the New World, however, the night of the voyage was dispelled by the morning disclosure, for out of the mist Le Corbusier saw the ascent of a modern city. One could assume that from the promenade deck the shore would have been a line, a horizon, but nothing so definite was there. Le Corbusier used the term "vapor" to describe the city's foundation, as if it were formless. As the picture was sketched out more fully, he said nothing about the city's intermediate levels, focusing instead on what appeared above everything else.[15] In the sky, he saw articulate and distinct profiles. Up there, each of the city's buildings was a "banner in the sky," a "fireworks

rocket."[16] And there was something else: despite the striving of each for uniqueness, all of them had submitted to a "subjugating force." Unity or "grouping" is seen in every sky line. New York, he said, stands "above Manhattan like a rose-colored stone in the blue of a maritime sky, New York at night is like a limitless cluster of jewels. America is not small potatoes! In the last twenty years, facing the old continent, it has set the Jacob's ladder of the new times. It is a blow in the stomach that strikes you like a hurricane." The basic premise of all of it though was fluid and formless; both together, mist in support of crystals. But under the sun the shore was a line. Water is the sort of substrate that continually changes and remains the same: renewal is its potential, unwavering level is its promise. My main point is this: aqueous terrain is the horizon of all built horizons.

MOVEMENT AS MEANDER

Given his moral gloss on straight lines—direct means clear, forthright, and rational—the meander would seem to represent a fall from grace. In Le Corbusier's *Poem to the Right Angle* such a history is implied, but the meander is also shown to be decisive in nothing less than world formation: "the spring streams and rivers do the same. From a plane one sees them teeming in families on the deltas and estuaries of the Indus, the Madgalena or the

162

margins of California. Ideas, too, grope their way, tentative search in all directions to limit, fix the bounds to left and right. They touch one bank and then the other. Settle there? Run aground! The truth is present only in some spot where the current always seeks out its bed! . . Meander will live its adventure to its absurd consequence, moreover take its time, millennia if necessary. The inextricable bars the way, the incredible! But life must force a passage, burst the dam of vicissitude. It cuts through the meander, pierces the loops, sounding them out just where licentious passage made them meet. The current is straight once again… The law of meander is present in thought and man's enterprise forms renewed examples there, but the trajectory springs from the mind is projected by farsighted spirits beyond confusion."[17] Obviously, architecture, while not an actor on stage in this drama, is waiting in the wings. The key player is water, symbolized here as the first principle of movement and change, where it nourishes development and accelerates deterioration. Yet, water is not only amorphous; it is also precise, although it is always willing to take the shape of the container it enters. Essentially formless, it remains steadfastly dedicated to its own level, its horizon, which is also ours. Surely with these examples in mind we can imagine designs in which this most juvenile of elements—playful but obedient—can set the rules of the game no less firmly than our own desires.

Le Corbusier, A 4, *Milieu, Le Poeme de l'Angle Droit*, 1947-53

HERBERT DREISEITL
THINKING FLUID

IT IS HARD TO SAY HOW TO SEE WATER. THE STARTING POINT IS OFTEN SOMEWHERE BETWEEN ART, SCIENCE, ENGINEERING, AND PHILOSOPHY. WATER CAN BE WILD AND FRAGILE, OF A DELICATE BEAUTY ONE MOMENT, AND BRUTALLY DANGEROUS THE NEXT. THIS LIQUID PHENOMENON EXPRESSES ITSELF IN SILENT STILLNESS AND IN TURBULENCE. WATER DISPLAYS ITS INTERNAL STRUCTURE AND LOGIC MOST IN TRANSITIONS BETWEEN STAGNANCY AND MOVEMENT. IT TENDS TO DISAPPEAR IF WE TRY TO HOLD IT TIGHT; IT RUNS THROUGH OUR FINGERS, IS TASTELESS AND INVISIBLE. OFTEN, WHAT WE SEE IS MORE THE REFLECTION OF LIGHT THAN THE WATER ITSELF. TO UNDERSTAND THIS PERFORMANCE REQUIRES MORE THAN A STUDY OF THEORETICAL SCIENCES LIKE HYDROLOGY AND LIMNOLOGY. IT IS NOT JUST A CHEMICAL OR PHYSICAL FORMULA. TO REALLY SEE WATER, YOU HAVE TO WATCH ITS DYNAMIC MOVEMENTS, AND INTERACTIONS WITH LIGHT, AIR, AND EARTH.

In the book *Wasser bewegt, Phänomene und Experimente*, Haupt Verlag describes the inner structure of a very simple phenomenon like resistance in a water stream. When I started to work as an artist, I often did little experiments with water along with my students at university or with my professional teams. For example, I would let a little drop of water fall, and imagine that this drop makes a beautiful vortex. What would happen if this vortex encountered resistance? What imagination would arise? What is it to think with water?

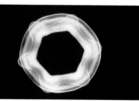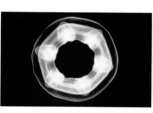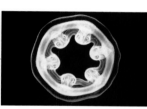

I started to work on larger projects, not only through computers, but also through real models at full scale. In Berlin, we tested different ways to create small waves and ripples with a thin layer of water running over flat surfaces. We then designed with these structures to create textured surfaces. When you see this project from up close, you think there is a river. It celebrates the rhythm, the movement, the quietness, and the position that water can have. When the surfaces that we designed are placed in the city, they create a civic space, an atmosphere, and an inspiration for people. They allow scenarios that invite people to act, to perform, and to make art. They inspire places where people can come together and perform; the city suddenly becomes a stage. Water encourages people to take action.

But this is still a designed place. We are not making a mountain stream; we are not trying to recreate a natural structure. We are translating nature into a design language. It has brought me more and more to the idea of working with infrastructures and using these infrastructures as design.

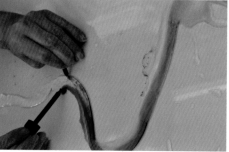

Potsdamer Platz, Berlin

McLaren Paragon Factory, London

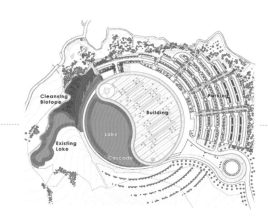

At the McLaren Factory in London, rainwater is an infrastructure used to cool down an entire plant. It is captured throughout the site, including the rooftops and the car parks and is cleaned in treatment trays and special cleansing systems. We designed a formal lake to hold this water, and from this lake we developed a circulation system that moves water through the fabric of the factory. Working at full scale, again, we used models to find the optimal structure to reduce the water's temperature. It was similar, in effect, to a cooling tower, but this tower was instead integrated into the entire plant structure. The temperature and the air conditioning of the entire building can be regulated completely with this captured water. In this way, the cascade structures become infrastructures for the building. But they are also a design feature, which surrounds the factory, making it beautiful, and producing a special sound.

Many people say this is luxurious and too expensive. I say it is an opportunity to design infrastructure that is multifunctional while engaging rain, surface, and ground waters. This infrastructure is about creating space to live, to perform, to listen; it makes the invisible visible. Water can be the starting point of reimagining urban infrastructure. All it requires is for us to cultivate a fluid imagination.

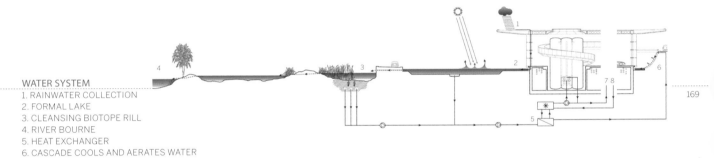

WATER SYSTEM

1. RAINWATER COLLECTION
2. FORMAL LAKE
3. CLEANSING BIOTOPE RILL
4. RIVER BOURNE
5. HEAT EXCHANGER
6. CASCADE COOLS AND AERATES WATER
7. SUPPLY TO CHILLED CEILINGS
8. HEATED WATER RETURN

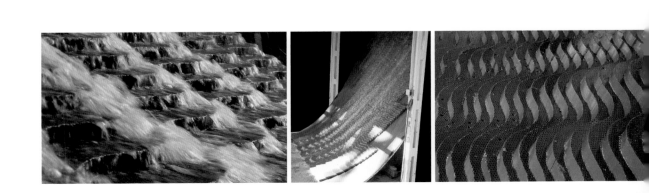

IÑAKI ECHEVERRIA & MARGARITA GUTIÉRREZ
SOFT ENGINEERING

STIGMATIZED FOR MORE THAN 30 YEARS, THE VALLEY OF MEXICO'S
METROPOLITAN ZONE (ZMVM) HAS AN OPPORTUNITY TO REINVENT ITSELF. IN
1971, A PRESIDENTIAL DECREE ORDERED THE CREATION OF THE TEXCOCO LAKE
COMMISSION, AND WAS SUCCESSFUL IN CREATING AND PROTECTING A LARGE
TERRITORIAL RESERVE. THIS RESERVE, LOCATED IN THE EASTERN OUTSKIRTS OF THE
ZMVM, AND FORMERLY OCCUPIED BY TEXCOCO LAKE, CAN BE RECLAIMED AS AN
ECOLOGICAL EDGE FOR THE CITY. IT CAN BE A NEW TERRITORY THAT INCORPORATES
NATURE, CULTURE, AND INFRASTRUCTURE: A CULTURAL ECOLOGY. WHEN BUILT,
THE TEXCOCO LAKE ECOLOGICAL PARK WILL BECOME THE LARGEST URBAN PARK IN
THE WORLD, REPRESENTING 11 PERCENT OF THE ENTIRE METROPOLITAN AREA AND
EXTENDING OVER 14,000 HECTARES (35,000 ACRES). THIS SPACE IS 23 TIMES THE SIZE
OF BOSQUE DE CHAPULTEPEC IN MEXICO CITY, 49 TIMES THE SIZE OF HYDE PARK
IN LONDON, AND 43 TIMES THE SIZE OF CENTRAL PARK IN NEW YORK. IT WILL JUMP-
START A PROCESS TO REDIRECT 500 YEARS OF HISTORICAL CONFLICT BETWEEN THE
CITY, WATER, AND THE ECOLOGY OF THE VALLEY.

XVI CENTURY

1824

1929

1941

1959

1970

1980

1990

Over the past century, the growth of the surrounding settlement has been exponential. Lands formerly occupied by Lake Texcoco are now inhabited by more than 20 million people.

SYSTEM OF LAKES: The basin of the Mexico City valley once incorporated a system of 5 lakes (Zumpango, Xaltoca, Xochimilco, Chalco, and Texcoco) which ranged from freshwater in the North to saltwater in the South. Due to their topographical relationships, these water bodies, which once covered 1,500 square km, all flowed towards lake Texcoco.

HISTORIC FORMATION

The ZMVM is located in the basin of the Mexico City valley. This area is part of a sequence of hydrological basins along the national territory, which creates a complicated relationship between the city and its geography, and especially with water, that has stood since the Spanish colonial era.

Until recently, a certain pathological relation with the Lake has prevailed in Mexico. In contrast to the symbiotic relation of Tenochtitlan (the early Aztec City) to its environment, there is a deep ignorance about cohabitation with water, which has gradually destroyed the valley's lakes. The inevitable result is an arid, swamp-like territory, confined in the unstable lakebed of Texcoco. Extreme heatstroke, flooding, sinking, and pollution caused by suspended particles and solid waste, are a daily reality of Mexico City.

This 500 year old geographical imbalance, together with the rapid urbanization of the ZMVM at rates that reached 10,000 inhabitants per day in the 70s and 80s has led to a "new geography" where the limit between the city and its territory is indistinguishable.

Texcoco Park

SINKING CITY

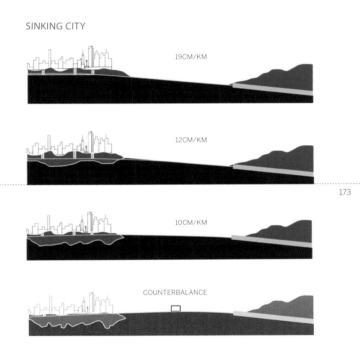

19CM/KM

12CM/KM

10CM/KM

COUNTERBALANCE

MEXICO CITY BASIN WATER BALANCE M³/S

AQUIFER RECHARGE	+ 31.6
EVAPORATION	- 159.4
RUNOFF	- 23.7
INDUSTRY	- 4.6
AGRICULTURE	- 12.6
CITY CONSUMPTION	- 64.7
WASTEWATER	- 50.4

Lake Texcoco has the opportunity to become a visible symbol for Mexico City of the role of nature in urban life. Intervention strategies aim to restore the site, allowing for long and short term processes that will foster the recovery of a lost ecosystem.

MATERIAL CONDITION

The Texcoco Lake area is a practically flat land with a high concentration of salt (sodium carbonate) and soda ash, that is polluted through nearby waste dumps and landfills. The ground has almost zero load-bearing capacity and a high tendency for water concentration both natural (rainfall runoffs) and artificial (Mexico City's drainage system). There are frequent health-threatening dust storms in part due to lack of vegetation and topographical variations.

The ground is almost impossible to re-vegetate due to its low density and extremely basic (11.0 pH) composition. The salty, soap-like sediment immediately dries-up almost every type of vegetation by sucking the water from its cells. Until now, just a few species have survived these extreme conditions, notably *Distichlis spicata* grass and the *Tamarix* tree.

Traditional methods of soil remediation are not viable here. To "wash-out" the sodium carbonate sediments from soil that is 70 meters deep requires a huge investment, an enormous amount of reactive materials (sulfuric acid and calcium), strenuous soil movements, high consumption of fresh water, a new drainage system, and a large area to store the washed sediments. And since evaporation levels exceed water infiltration, the salts in the lower layers of the soil would eventually rise to the surface to adversely affect any new vegetation.

Hydrology

Transitional Habitats

DISTICHLIS SPICATA

TAMARIX SPP.

MAKING NEW GROUND

How do you restore a site that's basically dead? The answer is simpler than one may think: you just forget about the salt, cover it up, and create new, healthy land on top of it. It all narrows down to material selection and an adequate layering system.

The first step is to stop sodium from rising. You begin with a layer of gravel, concrete debris or plastic waste; then a secondary, thinner layer of fine particle materials such as silt, sand and clay; and finally, a layer of topsoil comprising a mix of compost and treated sediments recovered from the city's drainage. It is like making a huge "plant pot" on top of a dead sea.

All these raw materials (plastics, organic waste, and concrete debris) are obtained from surrounding areas, triggering a self-sufficient and economically sustainable cycle. Also, with the addition of an appropriate drainage system, the waste water used to irrigate the land can be retrieved and reused; the layering system provides a slow filtering process that will eventually generate fresh water with a low content of salt.

This soil remediation system has had remarkable results in the laboratory. It has prevented sodium from reaching the surface and made land available for reforestation, revegetation, and reintroduction of endemic species (both fauna and flora). The aim is to recover a lost ecosystem, bringing into play a more robust, resilient, self-sustainable, adaptable, and flexible ground that will hold a rich diversity of wildlife habitats and botanical communities as well as places for recreation and relaxation.

PINE FOREST

FOREST

LACUSTRINE

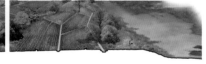

BORDER

PRAIRIE

+ **LAYER 3_**TOPSOIL WITH COMPOSTED
AND TREATED SEDIMENTS

+ **LAYER 2_**FINE PARTICLES INCLUDING
SILT, SAND, AND CLAY

+ **LAYER 1_**GRAVEL, CONCRETE DEBRIS,
OR PLASTIC WASTE

ARCHITECTURE IS PROCESS

The Texcoco Lake Ecological Park is and will be an ongoing investigation, constantly re-evaluated across multiple scenarios, where "fixed" designs are only understood as necessary means for communication. Just like a photograph of a fire, static images are merely a reference to many processes that change over time.

In reality, form will transform continuously through research. The water bodies will change radically through dry and rainy seasons. The ecology of the valley will be allowed to evolve and design to adapt to it. It is closer to an algorithm than to a garden or a building; it sets up a logic, with a certain degree of speculation.

Also, the project will operate on multiple scales simultaneously, to be specific, sensible, and variable yet vast, integrated, and continuous: a way for multiple publics to be considered in the decision-making process and for size to be a primary advantage.

Texcoco Park is ultimately a soft engineering project, one that acknowledges that making landscape infrastructure is a better way to negotiate the human need for dwelling and the capacity of the planet to sustain it.

Written in collaboration with Jonathan Hajar

FIRST SUCCESSION   SECOND SUCCESSION

LACUSTRINE

WETLANDS

STREAMS

SALINE GRASS

176 MEADOWS

BUFFER

RIPARIAN FOREST

CONIFER FOREST

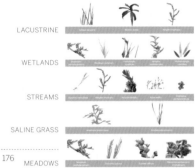
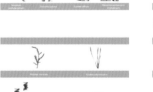
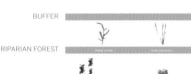

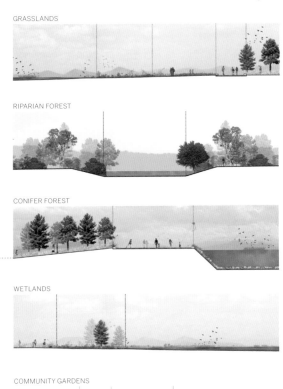

GRASSLANDS

RIPARIAN FOREST

CONIFER FOREST

WETLANDS

COMMUNITY GARDENS

The park will promote programs seldom seen in urban Mexico City, including sports fields, lakes and canals for boating and sailing, mountain biking, community gardening and walking trails, as well as areas for the observation of flora and fauna. In this way, the landscape becomes one of the most important pieces of infrastructure in the valley, one with the capacity to reconcile the city with its geography, incorporate hydrological cycles, eliminate the threat of floods, provide better health conditions for human populations, and contribute to the re-establishment of the native biota.

TILMAN LATZ
ENGINEERED WATERS

INFRASTRUCTURE PROJECTS—TRANSPORTATION ROUTES, DYKES, CANALS, DAMS, DEPOTS, POWER STATIONS, SOLAR FARMS AND WIND TURBINES, INDUSTRIAL PLANTS, BUSINESS PARKS AND AIRPORTS, LANDFILLS AND RECYCLING PLANTS—ARE GENERALLY DESIGNED TO BE TECHNICALLY ENHANCED BUT FUNCTIONALLY ISOLATED SYSTEMS WITH NO OTHER RELEVANCE FOR THE LIVING ENVIRONMENT. THEY TEND TO PRODUCE LARGE, UNATTRACTIVE, AND OFTEN UNUSABLE SPACES; THEY THREATEN URBAN LIFE WHEN THEY SHOULD BE INSTRUMENTAL IN FACILITATING AND SIMPLIFYING IT, AND THEY DIVIDE THE WORLD INTO NATURAL AND ARTIFICIAL, HEALTHY AND UNHEALTHY, BEAUTIFUL AND UGLY SPACES. THIS MUST CHANGE. AS DESIGNERS WE MUST UNDERSTAND THE ENGINEERING PRINCIPLES OF INFRASTRUCTURE AND ECOLOGICAL ASPIRATIONS OF CONTEMPORARY SOCIETY IN ORDER TO MAKE INFRASTRUCTURE THAT IS WORTH LIVING IN, OR THAT CAN AT THE VERY LEAST BE SEEN POSITIVELY. THIS IS NOT EASY. IT REQUIRES NOT JUST DESIGNING A NEW LANDSCAPE, BUT ALSO CHANGING ACQUIRED HABITS OF PERCEPTION. BUT WE MUST ALSO RECOGNIZE THE INHERENT POTENTIAL OFFERED BY MODERN INFRASTRUCTURE AND COMMUNICATE THIS TO THE POPULATION, DEFEND IT AGAINST TECHNOCRATIC MAXIMIZING DEMANDS, AND AGAINST ROMANTICISING PERCEPTUAL HABITS.

HIRIYA LANDFILL: Mystical Mountain

The Hiriya landfill came to be in 1952 on an agricultural plain southeast of Tel Aviv. It is between the Ayalon and Shapirim rivers just before their confluence. Thereafter, the Ayalon passes through the city in a canal alongside rail tracks and highways that severely restrict its carrying capacity and contribute to floods in Tel Aviv following the short period of winter rains.

The project is to rehabilitate the Hiriya landfill which was closed in 1999 for fear of polluting the rivers that washed against it in high waters and for the danger it posed to aircraft of Ben Gurion Airport due to the thousands of sea birds it attracted. But it is also a flood retention basin for the Shapirim and Ayalon rivers, as well as a park large and robust enough to incorporate safely the divergent interests of recreation-seeking visitors, flood control, nature conservation, politics, science, and the arts.

When the landfill was closed in 1999, it was nearly one kilometre in length, 87 metres high, and contained 16 million cubic metres of household waste.

Three levels mark the vertical dimension of the project: the sunken wadi with its streams, narrow paths, and low bridges; the main circulation network with ramps and bridges; and the Hiriya mountain and terrace at its base.

PRESERVING A MOUNTAIN

The Ayalon and Shapirim rivers are realigned to be more than 100 meters from the mountain, meandering freely through broad "wadis". The excavated material, plus several millions cubic metres of construction debris, is used to build a terrace around the base of the mountain, stabilizing it and retaining its unique form. Characteristic agricultural landscapes found in the locality will be planted on this terrace, mostly in the form of olive groves and orchards. They require little water, provide shade, are easy to maintain and perpetuate the traditional historic cultural landscape. This tree-covered space will hold a variety of recreational and sports activities.

181

PRESERVING WASTE

The mountain is sealed with a combination of natural and synthetic materials, and the biogas is safely extracted and utilized. Leachate seeping from its base is collected and treated in separate 'green sedimentation tanks'. A thin layer of recycled construction waste and clean soil stabilizes the outer skin of the mountain. This recycled material is produced in a plant on the eastern mountain slope, where a massive sheet pile wall secures a working platform against pressure from the mountain. The plant is one of Hiriya's visitor attractions and is currently being extended. Students, government officials, politicians, and the interested public from around Israel visit the site to learn about the sustainable treatment of waste and how to live with it.

182

SUMMER

HEAVY RAIN

20 YEAR FLOOD

100 YEAR FLOOD

Three landscape elements weave through the horizontal dimension of the project: agricultural grounds of groves and orchards, intensively used 'human corridors', and 'wild forest'.

WORKING WATERS

The mystical Hiriya mountain is within the 840-hectare Ariel Sharon Park, a park with a capacity to retain seven million cubic meters of highwaters from the Ayalon and Shapirim rivers and their tributaries. This capacity is made possible by excavations of retention basins up to nine metres deep and from 70 to 400 meters wide. The material from the excavation is used to raise the surface of the ground adjoining the basin, giving it a 2 percent gradient that is barely noticeable. The sides of the basin are steeper with cuts to accommodate access ramps and vistas. The resultant chain of polygonal soil wedges serves as the park's robust basic element, creating a tension between high plateaus and lowlands and introverted and extroverted spaces, and allowing various interpretations and uses.

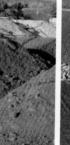

Hiriya Plateau   Tel Aviv in the Distance

ESTABLISHING VEGETATION

On the plateau atop the mountain and on the steep slopes are drought-resistant, mostly low, vegetation requiring little water and maintenance. Stormwater on the plateau is harvested in underground reservoirs during the rainy season, from where it is used to irrigate densely planted areas in dry periods. Much of the vegetation along the freely meandering Ayalon and Shapirim rivers is expected to establish spontaneously.

184

CONSTRUCTING AN OASIS

A sheltered depression in the centre of the mountain, once the site of a noisy and dusty waste disposal plant, is transformed into terraced slopes and an open 'spring water landscape' for intensive use. A solid concrete platform at its centre, where once large machines stood, is Hiriya's only stable area. It will accommodate central functions in the park and a café/restaurant. The vertical surfaces of this terraced depression are stabilized by traditional dry stone walls of recycled construction material. These

Drainage Pattern

The Belvedere

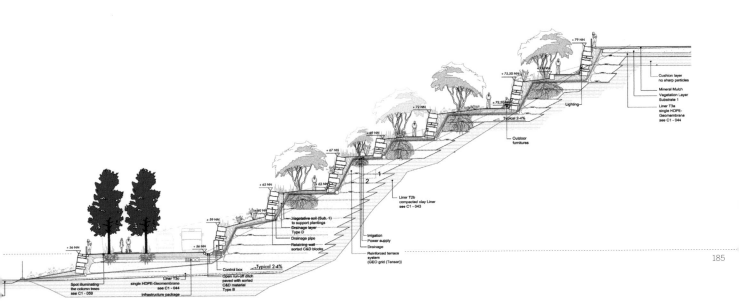

Cushion layer
no sharp particles

Mineral Mulch
Vegetation Layer
Substrate 1

Liner T3a
single HDPE-
Geomembrane
see C1 - 044

Lighting

Outdoor
furnitures

Typical 2-4%

Liner T2b
compacted clay Liner
see C1 - 043

Irrigation
Power supply
Drainage

Reinforced terrace
system
(GEO grid (Tensar))

Vegetative soil (Sub. 1)
to support plantings
Drainage layer
Type D

Drainage pipe

Retaining wall
sorted C&D blocks

Control box

Typical 2-4%

Spot illuminating
the column trees
see C1 - 059

Liner T3c
single HDPE-Geomembrane
see C1 - 044

Infrastructure package

Open run-off ditch
paved with sorted
C&D material
Type B

185

walls are able to adapt to movements in the mountain and provide the best conditions for the type of vegetation that is characteristic of the Mediterranean and for a variety of small-scale spaces. Buried layers of gravel serve as cool storage areas for rainwater used to top up small bodies of water throughout the year. A lush vegetation of palms and other trees, shrubs, aquatics, and flowering plants holds the centre of this oasis.

Adaptable walls respond to movements in the mountain as garbage settles over time. Made from recylced construction material, the walls create microclimates ideal for mediterranean vegetation.

PIETRO LAUREANO
THE OASIS EFFECT

MANY HAVE SAID THAT THE DESERT IS IN CONSTANT AGONY, YET, TWO BILLION PEOPLE LIVE IN DESERT AREAS TODAY. MOST ARE COMPLETELY RELIANT UPON WATER IMPORTED FROM EXTERNAL SOURCES, HOWEVER, IN DESERTS THERE REMAIN LANDSCAPES WHERE WATER NECESSITIES ARE RESOLVED LOCALLY. THESE ARE CALLED OASES. THEY ARE NOT A RESULT OF CHANCE; THEY DEPEND ON CAREFULLY DESIGNED AND SYMBIOTIC ACTIVITIES. THE EXISTENCE OF AN OASIS REPRESENTS A DYNAMIC ORGANIZATION AND MANAGEMENT OF DESERT ECOSYSTEMS, WHICH REALIZE NICHES AND MICROENVIRONMENTS IN AN OVERALL CYCLE OF ARIDITY THROUGH A COMPLEX OF HIGHLY ELABORATE KNOWLEDGE AND SKILLS. THEY ARE A REFLECTION OF A REFINED AWARENESS OF PLACE THAT CAN ONLY BE TRANSMITTED THROUGH TIME AND GENERATIONS, AND AN UNWRITTEN RECORD OF COOPERATION AND SYMBOLIC PRESENCE IN MUCH OF DESERT LIFE. IN OASES ARE CULTIVATED HUMANKIND'S MOST IMPORTANT SURVIVAL EXPERIENCES AND TESTED TECHNIQUES FOR GATHERING WATER, EVEN THOUGH, IN THESE LANDSCAPES, WATER IS RARELY SEEN. SO I SPEAK OF WATER, WHERE FOR MOST PEOPLE, WATER THERE IS NOT.

In the desert, a small amount of water is the difference between life and death. So to begin an oasis, people harvest water using the natural laws of the desert. A depression is dug and protected all around with dry palm leaves. Each night, humidity condenses and eventually saturates the desert sand with enough moisture to plant a date palm. This tree soon casts the shadows necessary for future cultivation, and an oasis is born. The palm is not a spontaneous plant; it is a product of human action, the result of domestication and cultivation. In its natural state, the palm is a bush without a trunk and branches. If the leaves are not cut, it will not grow into a tree, and will not produce shade. Oasis-makers remove the leaves in order to raise the tree, and inseminate them artificially with the flowers of male palms. The palm then creates not only shade, but also precious dates, which will attract organisms that eventually die and fertilize the ground below. Each palm that grows in the desert is a trace in a tested practice of careful nurturing and irrigation. This demonstrates that life depends on the contributions of different organisms; it is the fruit of symbiosis.

Over time, through diversified and complex techniques of water production, territorial planning, and micro-climate creation, palm groves may be extended, food crops may be grown, and green islands may be clustered among dunes or along the borders of salt depressions. Regardless of the scale, in each instance of oasis making, the same principal is at work.

This is the oasis effect: the establishment of a self-regulating, self-sustaining, and virtuous cycle.

OASIS EFFECT: Sand is both protection and resource; it is in continuous motion, but the formation of dunes is not accidental. Oases are developed in the shadow of the dunes, which shelter them from wind and provide moisture to palm groves.

DUNE BUILDING: This process exploits the desert's ecological laws: sand is transported by the wind; when an obstacle slows the power of the wind, grains of sand are released to the soil.

Dry palm leaves are progressively laid on top of the growing dune.

After a first deposition of sand, the accumulation grows steadily larger as more grains are captured.

Older dunes may reach up to 100 m in height.

A titanic deed is accomplished over generations: survival in a continuously changing dry sea of dunes.

MOTHER WELL

QANAT: These systems harvest three microflows: 5,000 year old rainfall migrating below the sands from the Saharan Atlas Mountains, local precipitation of less than 5 to 10 mm per year, and occult condensation. The layout of the water mine is skillfully calculated with a very slight slope to ensure that water runs smoothly towards the oasis and cultivated fields, but does not erode the channel.

PIETRO LAUREANO_THE OASIS EFFECT

There are many techniques to have water in the desert. Most are very nearly imperceptible phenomena but are fundamental to the ecology of the desert, such as occult precipitation. Occult precipitation is produced by the difference in temperature between day and night, which allows humidity to condense on the ground; this is what forms the hard crust of desert sands, which squeak when crushed. It is what enables the gazelle to drink by licking the night dew on wet stones. It is the cycle that allows beetles and lizards to absorb the moisture they need from the air. Prudently managed, occult precipitation is able to create significant water reserves.

This vital, yet often unseen source of water has been carefully cultivated with catchment tunnels known in Iran as qanat, in Morocco as khettara, and in Algeria as foggara. These are very complex systems of condensation, drainage, and capture formed by long, horizontal underground galleries, with orographically determined points of outlet in irrigated fields or oases. The route, therefore, must be carefully calculated so that water may flow without eroding the floor of the channel or transporting detritus and sand that could block it entirely. Vertical shafts are drilled every four to eight meters to connect the tunnel with the surface, and to allow removal of materials during the dig. Excavated earth is piled around these desert pores, creating characteristic mounds that mark the tunnel's path. The shafts, which may reach a depth of 150 m, have a specific role in this particular mechanism of water production. They regulate temperature and pressure, in addition to internal air circulation, to favor humidity absorption.

Qanat are not conduits that convey groundwater from springs or wells to an oasis from a distant extremity.

There are few, if any, natural springs in these desert areas. Rather, they are realized to capture along their lengths the microflows of water from within the rocks and sand in order to create open-air water. The catchment tunnels and shafts, through drainage, condensation, and aspiration, harvest atmospheric water vapor and store it in the subsoil before it disappears with the onset of the next day. Once trapped under the sands, this water becomes available to irrigate nearby palm groves or cultivated fields. Normally, humidity in the desert remains at a low level between 0 and 5 percent. In comparison, near Qanat, it may reach 80 percent. In this way, the tunnels work as production devices; as water mines. However, the palm groves feed back proactively by attracting and accumulating additional moisture that is eventually re-condensed in the catchment tunnels. This becomes a continuous autocatalytic water cycle. It is how in the most arid of environments, a salt lake, a desolate highland, a sterile canyon, can become a palm grove and an oasis of life.

In the desert, land does not have value; only the water is precious. In these areas, there is a complex system of managing and sharing water. When a father dies he leaves water to his sons, and his channels are re-directed to carry it to their respective fields. When people marry, they link their water. Through the distribution of inheritance, through marriage, or by purchase and sale, water quotas are broken up and put back together constantly, in an interlacing system of repartitions, links, and bypasses. In these complicated distribution networks, a pattern is created that visualizes family relationships, the state of property and the succession of generations. It is a diagram of kinship that is physically constructed by and

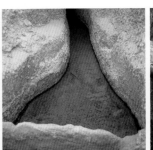

within the water system. As an invisible water landscape and as a garden of remembrance, the design of oases and irrigation systems is a record of history, written and erased with water. In such extreme situations, the oases people must work constantly to maintain their ecosystem.

When water depends on meticulous harvesting techniques and careful management and distribution systems, human survival is a direct result of cooperation. Without family alliances and mutualisms, oases cannot exist. The close link between human action and natural harmony imposes a series of interdictions, bonds, and prescripts, as even the most ordinary gestures help maintain the overall balance. The norms of tradition are accepted because they are written into nature itself. They arise from the tenacity of those who have found harmony with the harsh laws of the desert in order to obtain the bare resources necessary for life; water, above all, but also other means of subsistence; materials for building houses and humus for growing gardens; spiritual strength, collective knowledge, and mutual solidarity. The techniques and solutions adopted are equally aesthetic, symbolic, utilitarian, and fundamental to survival. Thus, in an oasis, the regular relationship between microcosm and macrocosm is not a metaphysical concept; it is a daily reality based on specific material needs. The correspondence between the self and the world establishes a covenant between culture and nature. Symbol and tradition become the witnesses and guardians of the harmony of the cosmos.

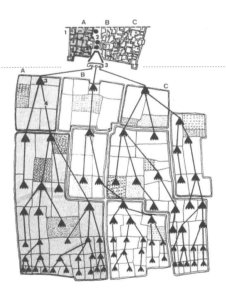

Using this vision and awareness, I have started to re-create oases that were completely abandoned in the Algerian Sahara. On the desert ground, we do not see anything other than desolate land. But, with aerial imagery, we were able to recognize the same patterns and graphs that we had seen on carpets and as symbols. These were the remains of abandoned catchment tunnels, canalizations, and gardens. When we walked on the soil early in the morning, the sand crusts showed traces of moisture

and humidity. Our sensitivity to this signal allowed us to recognize and individuate the ancient structures below. On the basis of our model, it has been possible to rebuild the ancient system, to restore the catchment tunnels, and water has come again. People have come back, have planted the palms, and have rebuilt the oases. A barren and neglected desert area now has water, palm groves, and cultivated fields.

In the oases, water is not a substance; it is a cycle. It is a landscape of water that we do not see, comprised of the water in the atmosphere, and the water that is in the ground. When we experience a drop of water, we don't perceive its true position in the overall progression relative to what came before and what will come after. However, oases are never isolated; their design is based on this cycle. Oases are a three-dimensional urbanism that considers the atmospheric, superficial, and the underground aspects of the settlement. Built up settlements form a continuum with the agro-pastoral space and its semi-nomadic and nomadic surroundings. These connections extend outward to link with the much broader, interregional area of nomads and of their great caravans and networks of trade routes. It is the fundamental cultivation of water, as a history, a symbiosis, and as a symbol that links these desert-dwellers to one another and to the ecology of the world beyond.

Modernity has asserted the inadequacy of the oasis in relation to progress. Yet, oasis making has existed as a vital and tenacious element of settlement in inhospitable environments for millennia. One might do better to ask how long the development model for large contemporary cities, which is based on the destruction of natural resources and overconsumption of water, will continue to last. The oasis carries a deep wisdom, and the torment that is a condition intrinsic to their existence is a wake-up call to the entire planet. Amid its thirst, erosion, and entropy, the desert holds the profound lesson that is the oasis; a wealth of knowledge and an experience that is indispensable to today's search for a new type of sustainability.

WATER RECORD: The pattern of water-sharing is memorized and reproduced in carpets and in the hairstyles of women. Through art, symbolism, and initiation, knowledge is transmitted, group cohesion is established, and a resilient community identity forms within its own built environment; in this way, an unseen landscape of water is constructed.

DIÉBÉDO FRANCIS KÉRÉ
TO HAVE WATER

IN BURKINA FASO, WHEN WE HAVE WATER, WE HAVE PROBLEMS.
THIS IS NOT TO SAY THAT WE HAVE WATER IN GREAT ABUNDANCE. RATHER, SINCE WE
DO NOT HAVE ACCESS TO THE SEA, FOR MUCH OF THE YEAR WE HAVE DROUGHT. THIS
TOO, IS A PROBLEM, AND LESS THAN 10 PERCENT OF THE POPULATION IS CONNECTED
TO THE WATER SUPPLY. TO HAVE WATER, MOST PEOPLE IN OUAGADOUGOU, THE CAPITAL
CITY, HAVE CLAY POTS, WHICH THEY WALK TO STORAGE TANKS OR DEEP WELLS.
IT DOESN'T MATTER IF YOU LIVE IN THE FORMAL OR INFORMAL PART OF THE CITY,
EVERYBODY SUFFERS THE SAME. IN MY COUNTRY, I HONESTLY DON'T KNOW HOW THE
TWO ARE DIFFERENT, EXCEPT THAT DURING THE RAINY SEASON, THE INFORMAL AREA
WILL BE DESTROYED THE MOST. IT IS EVEN WORSE IN THE RURAL ZONE, WHERE I GREW
UP. IN THIS PART OF THE WORLD, MOST PEOPLE HAVE NEVER HEARD OF ARCHITECTURE,
OR LANDSCAPE ARCHITECTURE, OR WATER ENGINEERING. REGARDLESS, THINGS ARE
ALWAYS BEING BUILT. TO MAKE THEIR HOMES, MOST PEOPLE USE CLAY, WHICH IS
LOCALLY AVAILABLE. WHILE WATER DESTROYS, IT IS ALSO USED TO MAKE CLAY, SO
PEOPLE CAN BUILD THEIR HOUSES AGAIN.

What I did was make a model. I am always the first to climb on top. The entire village was sitting and looking at me, hoping that it wouldn't break, because crash means 'bad technology' and no crash means 'okay wonderful, we will build it with you'.

MEN AND WOMEN, YOUNG AND OLD – ALL BROUGHT STONES TO MAKE A FOUNDATION FOR THE BUILDING. WITH A STRONG FOUNDATION, THERE IS NO FEAR OF WATER.

Primary School Gando, 2001

A typical school building in Burkina Faso holds more than 150 students. You can stand and touch the corrugated iron roof. When it is hot, I hope you can imagine the temperature inside. When it is cold, it is 40 degrees. It is not a place to teach children, believe me. So, how do you manage to build a school with new techniques in a village where most of the people are illiterate? How do you convince a community to adopt new techniques when they are not able to read?

You start by speaking. We met with the chief of the village, and then with the community. The youngest in the group always has to speak and explain. In a village like mine, when you are older you are very important—you are a library. It is not easy to convince the elders, but you need to, because it is the only way to succeed. You have to convince the people; you have to get them to trust in new things.

When I came to the village saying I was going to build a school, everybody was excited. When I told them, "I am going to build with clay," they said "Oh, what, clay for a school building? A clay building will be destroyed by rain. And a big building like that, of course, very quickly." But, I succeeded and the village allowed me to introduce traditional techniques in a modern building. I built this school for 120 children. After two years, I was forced to build an extension, because we had more than 300 new students.

In rural Burkina Faso, to have water is a problem. To collect and keep water from the rainy season into the dry season is very expensive. The dry season lasts eight months, when we have little rain. You can use an engine to drill, but it costs a lot of money, even more than a school building. After building the first school, when women had to carry water from six to ten kilometers on their heads, I made a well, about 60 meters deep. You cannot make this with your hands.

FIRST THE YOUNG GUYS, THEY STAND IN A QUEUE. THEY STAMP THE GROUND WITH THEIR FEET.

NEXT THEIR MOTHERS COME, AND DO THE HARDEST JOB.

THEY BEAT THE GROUND FOR HOURS AND HOURS WITH MALLETS AND WATER TO MAKE IT DENSE.

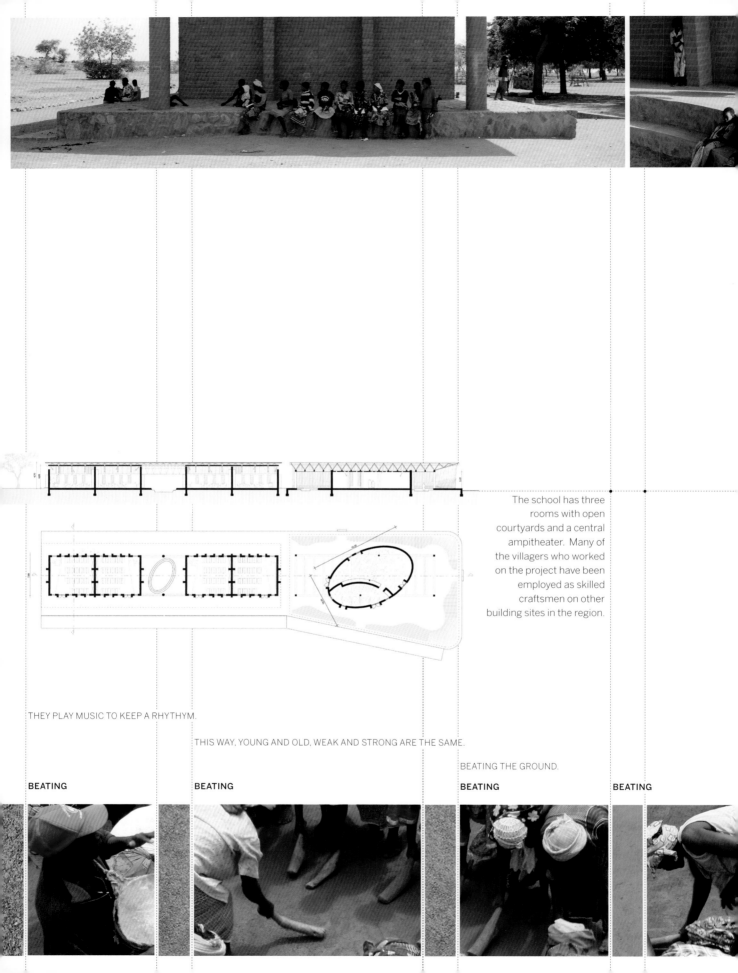

The school has three rooms with open courtyards and a central ampitheater. Many of the villagers who worked on the project have been employed as skilled craftsmen on other building sites in the region.

THEY PLAY MUSIC TO KEEP A RHYTHYM.

THIS WAY, YOUNG AND OLD, WEAK AND STRONG ARE THE SAME.

BEATING THE GROUND.

BEATING

BEATING

BEATING

BEATING

Compressed earth bricks were made from a
machine powered by two villagers with local
materials. By adding a small quantity of cement
(8%) the bricks are more stable and uniform.
We used very thin sixteen-millimeter rebar and
corrugated iron to make the roof. The triangular
shape of the girders was framed on site by
local craftsmen.

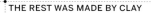

THE REST WAS MADE BY CLAY

199

THEN THE POLISHERS COME WITH SMOOTH STONES.

SOME GIVE WATER, OTHERS POLISH, ALWAYS SMOOTHING WITH THE STONES, ALWAYS ADDING WATER.

HOURS AND HOURS, CLAY, WATER AND THE POWER OF MY PEOPLE.

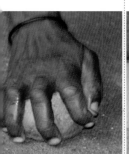

MANGO TREE PROJECT

In Burkina Faso, the hot and dry climate, and annual drought between October and June, makes it difficult for trees to survive. Daytime temperatures may reach 41°C and trees can provide much needed shade. Many choose to plant Eucalyptus trees, but they consume too much water and are too vulnerable to insects. Mango is more resilient and less sensitive to termites; it also gives shade and fruit.

Without conserving water, how can we use it in the dry season to create a good environment? We do not have engineering to store water throughout the year, and we do not have enough money to buy pipes. Maybe we could buy them once, but if they broke, the people would not be able to make repairs. Few, if any, have access to the country's water infrastructure. Outside the cities, it is even less.

In architecture, we are trained to look for solutions that are easily adapted by people. So, I am trying to grow a garden, to make an oasis in Gando, using primitive things. I began to think about clay pots, which are something that can be made in my home country, easily. Because we do not have wood to burn for energy, we use what comes after the cow eats. When the pots are finished, we put a little hole in bottom. We add water to the pots once a week, and then we wait. After I made several of these the villagers started to ask, "What is he doing? He

FOR A NEW TREE, A HOLE IS DUG AND FILLED WITH BONES AND MEAT.

ANTS COLONIZE THE HOLE AND STOP TERMITES FROM EATING THE YOUNG TREE.

TRADITIONAL CLAY POTS ARE PLACED NEXT TO THE TREE WITH DRIPPERS FACING THE ROOTS.

is taking this beautiful vase and breaking it!" In other parts of the world, it is called drip irrigation, and it allows young plants to grow. The school children started doing it and now every child has a tree. To start, the trees were small like them. Now, the trees are bigger than the children, and they proudly show off their plants. The children will grow with this technique. and it will become part of their daily life. We are using what we have, and it is not a complicated technology. I am trying to connect very primitive techniques with modern languages to develop new technologies that are easily adapted. I am using this approach in the area to collect water as an example for my people to do it. The older people, you cannot change them in my home country. They are convinced that they know everything. They will say to you, "look my son, I am so old, I do not need to know something else. Go and teach your brothers and sisters." What is important is to do something for my people. And that is what I am doing.

IRRIGATING DRIP BY DRIP

THE POTS PREVENT THE WATER FROM EVAPORATING, AND ONLY NEED TO BE FILLED ONCE A WEEK.

THIS GIVES THE PLANT A SMALL BUT CONSTANT SUPPLY OF WATER.

JOHN TODD
HEALING WATER

WHAT IS EVOLVING TODAY IN THE FACE OF THE ENVIRONMENTAL
CRISIS IS WHAT SOME PEOPLE CALL ECO-MIMETICS. IT IS THE ATTEMPT TO UNLOCK
NATURE'S OPERATING INSTRUCTIONS AND DECODE THEM TO THE POINT WERE YOU CAN
DIRECT THEM TO CARRY OUT WORK FOR SOCIETY—WHETHER THAT IS TREATING WASTE,
GENERATING FUELS, GROWING FOODS, OR RESTORING LANDSCAPES. **T**HE SEARCH FOR
THIS NEW LANGUAGE HAS REALLY BEEN THE GOAL OF MY LIFE. I HAVE FOUND THAT ONE
OF THE BEST WAYS TO LEARN IS TO GO TO REALLY NASTY PLACES. **F**OR EXAMPLE, THERE
WAS A POND ON **C**APE **C**OD NEAR WHERE I LIVE—IT WAS NOT LINED, JUST COARSE
SAND. **I**T WAS NEAR A LANDFILL AND IT HAD ALL OF THE TOP 15 NASTY ORGANIC
CHEMICALS AND HEAVY METALS THAT THE **EPA** WORRIES ABOUT. **T**HIS POND IS WHERE
THE TOWN DUMPED ALL OF ITS SEPTIC WASTE, EVEN THOUGH THIS TOXIC SITE IS JUST
8' ABOVE THE TOWN'S DRINKING WATER TABLE. **A**ND THE STORY IS SIMILAR IN MANY
PLACES IN THE WORLD. **S**O WHEN I COULDN'T FIND ANY TECHNOLOGIES TO TREAT THE
WATER IN THE POND BECAUSE IT WAS MORE CONCENTRATED AND MORE TOXIC THAN
SEWAGE, I BEGAN TO ASK THE QUESTION, WHAT CAN BE DONE HERE? THE ANSWER AS I
HAVE FOUND FREQUENTLY WAS TO BRING IN THE SUN.

Our primary idea was to create three dimensional ponds which would allow sunlight to penetrate. I think that without sunlight, what follows could never have happened in the same way that it did. The second idea was to admit, "I don't know enough to clean this water, no one on earth knows enough to clean this water, but the earth and its biological systems know how to clean this water." So I borrowed a diversity of flora and fauna from at least a dozen different landscapes; aquatic forms, salt marshes, ponds, streams, pig wallows, wet spots in forests and so on and added them to the solar-driven ponds. I had to make sure that all of the kingdoms of life were in those twenty-one ponds, because it is my personal theory, unproven, that life over the last five billion years has evolved together in concert; Darwin's view of evolution is correct, but it is only a tiny part of the whole story. As a result, I introduced into the ponds over a thousand species of organisms, including more than one hundred and fifty species of tiny, diminutive protozoans alone. This had the effect of creating twenty-one different, self-sustaining, co-evolving landscapes, which broke down and consumed waste separately from the one downstream. To feed the microorganisms, which did the real work of treating the organic waste, and to prevent noxious off gassing, I placed above the tanks a small, elevated aqueduct with plants that have an affinity for cracking apart organic compounds. I then pumped in the waste and waited to see what happened.

After 10 days, all the heavy metals we initially measured were removed 100 percent, except for one, which was removed 99.9 percent. Samples from the pond met drinking water standards for heavy metals and all priority pollutants. When the great biologist Lyn Margolis and her students examined the species assemblages in the tanks, they observed the same recognizable organisms coexisting in completely reorganized communities. Sunlight, and the great diversity I collected had recombined themselves to clean the polluted water. That is the power of the sun and all of the kingdoms of life working together.

SEASONAL GATHERING: I try to think about what kinds of sensitive life would live in the polluted environments we create. Then, I go find them. As a general rule, we choose from environments that are natural, polluted, and managed by humans. These range from feedlots to streams, ponds, and lakes. It is vital to return to these places for samples during each season. This ensures that the organisms in our machines will be adapted to seasonal differences in light and temperature, and can heal water throughout the year.

SOLAR DRIVEN PONDS: Strung like beads on a string, these mesocosms were developed on a recognition of the role of sunlight and photosynthesis. Each connected cell differs from the ones above and below, but all share biological linkages and exposure to the sun. The 10-day, solar-driven process involves overlapping phases of aeration, solid settlement, nutrient absorption, biofiltration, and ultimately clean water discharge. At various stages, water is recycled back upstream to create feedback loops and a more resilient cleansing process.

	INFLUENT (MG/L)						EFFLUENT (MG/L)
BOD_5	227						5.9
NH_3	16.3						0.4
NO_3	15.9						4.9
TOTAL SUSPENDED SOLIDS	213						5.3
CHEMICAL OXYGEN DEMAND	556						35.9
TOTAL NITROGEN	29.3						5.6

CAPE COD

METRICS OF CLEANSING

DAY 1   DAY 5   DAY 10   205

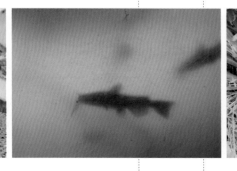

BUILDING DIVERSITY: Water is collected and pumped into clear-sided tanks in which a huge diveristy of aquatic life exists. Its function is to constantly culture and disseminate beneficial organisms into the polluted water. It is the genius of nature.

INFLUENT (MG/L)

400

300

200

100

0

206

M J S N J M M J S N J M M J S N J M M J

MONTH

A comparison of Total Suspended Solids for Influent (left) and Effluent (right) over a three year period. In each study, the performance in the winter time is as good as it is in the summer. By collecting highly adapted species which thrive during each season, different guilds of organisms perform regardless of temperature or light level.

VERMONT

EFFLUENT (MG/L)

400

300

200

100

0

M J S N J M M J S N J M M J S N J M M J S N J M M J
MONTH

In East Burlington, Vermont, we developed a similar system, which treated 80,000 gallons of sewage a day and employed over three hundred species of aquatic plants and a wide diversity of organisms from wild environments. Similar to our project on Cape Cod, the design is cellular in origin. Waste moves from tank to tank so local coevolution can take place. This project was sponsored by the EPA, which fully expected the design to break down and freeze in the wintertime. However, our studies have shown that the machine's performance in the winter is as good as it is in the summer. This is because we return to the wild every season of the year to collect organisms that are highly adapted to those specific light levels and temperatures. As a result, high-quality water is recycled back to Lake Champlain year round. In developing this project, our heads began to change.

Good ecological designers may consider technologies like clarifiers and sludge removal systems, which have inevitable by-products, incomplete designs. So, we introduced organisms that fed and thrived off the dead and dying bacteria from the end of the treatment process. We bought 10,000 fish for 99 cents apiece, fed them otherwise unusable organic waste, and sold them for 10 dollars each. In theory, at least, we are beginning to build an economy, not a cost. We are no longer waste treatment folks; we are farmers or nutrient ecology managers. The whole point is that a paradigm shift is taking place, where we are beginning to consider the ways waste treatment plants can be used to provide biological material both for repair of a particular region and to generate economic benefit.

POLLUTANTS: The Blackstone River Corridor, located in Grafton, MA is the oldest industrial corridor in North America. The main pollutant is Bunker C, or #6 Fuel oil. Over the last few centuries, oil storage units in the ground began to disintegrate and release oil into the canals. To clean up the oil, we are using a family of living technologies that utilize biodiversity to do creative work. We are finding the oil is being degraded by over 90 percent.

I've had a long interest in the planet's in-shore oceans. For a while, I was an oceanographer, though studying in-shore oceans around the world has been very saddening. Almost without exception, these landscapes support, or rather, supported, the world's most productive and greatest aquatic nurseries. As food scarcities grow worldwide, it is imperative to go back to our waterfronts and inshore oceans and get to work cleaning them up. So, I began on a somewhat quixotic scheme only a farmer-sailor would think of. It is a technology I call an Ocean Restorer. The first generation of Ocean Restorers to come from our drawing boards were floating structures with long, ribbon-like attachments that would be moored to the bottom of the ocean. Our plan was to have tidal currents move vast volumes of water past hanging ecological communities that were anchored to the Restorer platforms above. These communities would filter and produce oxygen for the water while contributing beneficial organisms to aid in oceanic purification cycles.

Then, the Gulf oil spill happened. We felt the Gulf needed Ocean Restorers that could be propelled through the water; this would dramatically increase the amount of pollution they could treat. Part ship, part biological community, these Ocean Restorers were catamarans that could move through ocean waters with ecological treatment technologies hanging between the two hulls. If we can achieve a relatively slow operating speed of three knots, due to the drag resistance of the suspended ecosystems, the Ocean Restorer could treat up to one billion gallons a day. We expect to have four distinct eco-technologies, inspired by and derived from four parent ecologies from inshore oceans. The first ecology is based on eelgrass communities that are the nurseries for so much of sea life. The second is an oyster reef community and it will have many species of clams, oysters, and other mollusks. The third one is an artificial kelp forest, and finally, the algal turf community, which is superb at sequestering heavy metals. Our dream for the Ocean Restorers is to create a culture of ocean stewardship that assists the seas in restoring the great oceanic bounty with which they used to bless us.

OCEAN RESTORER: This ocean-going vessel supports four eco-mimetic technologies between twin hulls, including eelgrass; oyster reef, kelp forest, and algal turf communities. sailing at three knots, the ocean restorer may cleanse up to one billion gallons of water a day, while supporting and gathering new organic life.

Endangered Inshore Oceans

JOHN TODD_HEALING WATERS

Drinking water, a lot of people don't have it and a lot of people die from it. With a group of my graduate students and colleagues, we have begun to comb the world for organisms that produce such powerful antibiotics that they can take contaminated surface waters and render them safe. Our idea is to start small and stay small, potentially at the scale of the individual household. We have two modest projects: one in Haiti and one with refugees at the Thai Burma border. One of the organisms that we are employing in our little ecological technology is *Pleurotus osteatus*, a fungus that has some remarkable purification properties. Every week in our search for organisms to help purify water, some new candidate comes up. We are working with five-gallon buckets and starting with a well known technology: sand filtration. Its already well documented that the micro-pores in sand filters can support highly diverse microbial communities that are very effective at purifying water. In fact, the water in these systems is clean enough to grow a variety of working ecological "toppings" like *Mentha aquatica* or *P. osteatus*, in addition to the microorganisms in their various substrates. One of the great rationales for these small systems with these particular organisms, which are somehow friendly and familiar, is that they would be able to be employed more widely in communities with high rates of illiteracy. The idea is perhaps to create a recipe for potable water that would allow so many of these children who die to live. We hope to soon have a working prototype that we can trust in the field. One of the things we most concern ourselves with is the relationship and transfer between new information and community-based technologies. It is a very humbling and very complex process. Wherever we look, we find almost an infinite and rapidly expanding universe of possibilities. In this era of collapsing resources, materials, and fuels, we are simultaneously moving into a new world of informational richness. While we are frequently constrained by materials and resources, we are still able to think the impossible, and to create a truly symbiotic relationship between ourselves and the natural world.

DRINKING WATER: *Mentha aquatica* produces extremely powerful antibiotics and in a short period of time can kill things like strep, staph and other bacterial pathogens in drinking water.

Pleurotus Ostreatus

MUSHROOM FILTERS: Designed to work at the scale of the individual household, these filters employ locally-available materials and community-based technologies to provide potable drinking water. Sand filtration functions by creating tortuous pathways which trap solids or other suspended sediments as they are drawn through the system by gravity. The addition of species, such as oyster mushrooms further purify the water by contributing natural compounds which kill bacterial pathogens including streptococcus and staphylococcus.

APPENDIX

PARTICIPANTS

KAZI ASHRAF: Ashraf is a professor at the University of Hawaii at Manoa, and director of the Urban Design Action Group (UDAG) in Dhaka, Bangladesh. His recent publications include *The Hermit's Hut: Architecture and Asceticism in India* (University of Hawaii Press, 2013), and *Designing Dhaka: A Manifesto for a Better City* (LOKA, 2012).

ILA BERMAN: Berman is a principal of Scaleshift design and the O'Donovan Director of the University of Waterloo School of Architecture. She is an architect, theorist, and curator of architecture and urbanism. Her research investigates the relationship between culture, the environment, and the evolution of contemporary material and spatial practices. Berman's work includes *URBANbuild local global*, and *New Orleans: Urban Operations for a Future City* and the forthcoming book: *Expanded Field*. She is the recipient of an AIGA award and Communication Arts Award of Excellence.

WILLIAM BRAHAM: Braham is the director of the Master of Environmental Building Design program and the TC Chan Center for Building Simulation and Energy Studies at the School of Design, University of Pennsylvania. His most recent projects include the Carbon Reduction Action Plan for the University of Pennsylvania and the book *Architecture and Energy: Performance and Style* (Routledge, 2013).

LINDSAY BREMNER: Bremner is the director of Architectural Research at the University of Westminster in London, having formally taught at Temple University in Philadelphia and the University of the Witwatersrand in Johannesburg. She is an award-winning architect and writer and has published, lectured, and exhibited widely on the post-apartheid transformation of Johannesburg. She is engaged in two on-going research projects: *Geo-architecture,* which investigates relations between geology, politics and architecture and *Folded Ocean,* which researches the organizational and spatial logics of the Indian Ocean world.

TEDDY CRUZ: Cruz is a professor in Public Culture and Urbanism in the Visual Arts department at University of California, San Diego, where he directs the Center for Urban Ecologies. Cruz was the recipient of the Rome Prize in Architecture and the first James Stirling Memorial Lecture on the City Prize. His work has been exhibited at MoMA in New York City.

DILIP DA CUNHA: Da Cunha is an architect and planner. He is Adjunct Professor at the School of Design, University of Pennsylvania. With his partner Anuradha Mathur, he is currently working on a project titled *The Invention of Rivers*. It stems from questioning the natural status given to rivers and the imaging and imagining that this assumption has inspired. They are authors of *Mississippi Floods: Designing a Shifting Landscape,* (Yale University Press, 2001); *Deccan Traverses: The Making of Bangalore's Terrain* (Rupa & Co., 2006); and *Soak: Mumbai in an Estuary* (National Gallery of Modern Art / Rupa & Co., 2009).

HERBERT DREISEITL: Dreiseitl is director of the Liveable Cities Lab at the Ramboll Group, he is founder of Atelier Dreiseitl and a 2011 Loeb Fellow at the Harvard Graduate School of Design. As a water artist, landscape architect, and interdisciplinary planner, Dreiseitl's internationally recognized design projects include the Tanner Springs Park in Portland, Oregon (2010), and the Bishan – Ang Mo Kio Park in Singapore (2012). He is currently working on the Copenhagen Strategic Flood Masterplan (2013).

IÑAKI ECHEVERRIA: Echeverria founded his eponymous design firm in 2008. Since then, the office has been awarded a number of important public and private commissions, including the Parque Lago Texcoco (35,000 acres), the Papalote Children's Museum in Monterrey, diverse projects for Liverpool,the largest luxury retailer in Mexico and other public and private commissions. Echeverria is Professor of Design at the Universidad Iberoamericana, Director of the Berlin Summer Workshop at the Aedes Network Campus Berlin, and was recently awarded a Gold Medal at the Puerto Vallarta Biennale.

NATALY GATTEGNO: Gattegno is a principal of Future Cities Lab, an experimental design and research office based in San Francisco, California that has been awarded the Architectural League of New York Young Architect Prize and the Van Alen New York Prize. Future Cities Lab has been widely exhibited most recently at the San Francisco Museum of Modern Art and the Yerba Buena Center for the Arts. Gattegno is a faculty member at the California College of the Arts.

MARGARITA EUGENIA GUTIÉRREZ: Gutiérrez is the founder of the Biogeochemistry Group, and is currently a professor in the school of chemistry at the National Autonomous University of Mexico (UNAM), where she teaches on the chemistry of inorganics, soils, and hazardous wastes. She has coordinated over 60 projects for the mining industry, in addition to a cooperative project between Germany and Mexico for the management of hazardous waste between 2002 and 2006. Gutiérrez was a visiting professor at the University of Maryland College Park in 2001.

ANNA HERINGER: Heringer was a Loeb Fellow at the Harvard Graduate School of Design and the honorary Professor of the UNESCO Chair Earthen Architecture Programme. Her work in Rudrapur, Bangladesh, in partnership with Eiki Roswag, received the Aga Khan Award for architecture. Heringer is also the 2011 recipient of the Global Award for Sustainable Architecture.

ALISON HIRSCH: Hirsch is an assistant professor of Landscape Architecture at the University of Southern California. She is the co-founder of foreground design agency, a transdisciplinary practice working between the fields of architecture, landscape architecture, urbanism, and the visual arts. Hirsch is the author of *City Choreographer: Lawrence Halprin in Urban Renewal America* (University of Minnesota Press, March 2014).

WALTER HOOD: Hood is an Oakland, California based environmental designer, artist, and educator. He is a professor at the University of California, Berkeley's Landscape Architecture and Environmental Design Department, which he chaired from 1998 to 2002. His studio practice, Hood Design, has been engaged in environmental and landscape design, urban design, art installations, and research commissions since 1992.

PETER HUTTON: Peter Hutton is an experimental filmmaker who has made over 20 films, including silent film studies of cities, landscapes, and seacapes through out the world. He has taught at Hampshire College , SUNY Purchase, Harvard University, and currently at Bard College. Hutton's work has been presented in major museums and festival both in the US and in Europe. In 2008 the Museum of Modern Art presented a retrospective on Hutton's work. His film *Study of A River*, which was presented at the Terrain of Water conference, was selected by the Library of Congress in 2009 for permanent preservation.

DOUGLAS JEROLMACK: Jerolmack is an associate professor in the Department of Earth and Environmental Science at the University of Pennsylvania. Jerolmack created the Penn Sediment Dynamics Laboratory, and was the first recipient of the American Geophysical Union's Luna B. Leopold Young Scientist Award in 2010.

DIÉBÉDO FRANCIS KÉRÉ: Kéré is the principal of Kéré Architecture and is a Professor at the Accademia di Architettura in Mendriso. His Primary School in Gando project (2001) received the Aga Khan award for Architecture, while his recent projects include a school extension, library, and Woman's Association Center (also in Gando). Kéré is also the winner of an urban design competition for a former barracks terrain in Manheim, Germany.

TILMAN LATZ: Latz is a landscape architect and architect and is the head of Latz+Partner, an international landscape architecture firm based in Kranzberg, Germany. He is a guest professor at the University Kassel, has taught studios at the University of Pennsylvania School of Design, has been a guest critic on a number of juries, and has given professional and educational lectures for audiences around the world.

PIETRO LAUREANO: Laureano is an architect and urban planner, and a UNESCO Consultant for arid regions, water management, Islamic civilization, and endangered ecosystems. Laureano is founder of the IPOGEA Centre for Studies on Traditional Knowledge and the International Traditional Knowledge Institute, based in Florence, Italy.

DAVID LEATHERBARROW: Leatherbarrow is a professor of Architecture at the University of Pennsylvania, where he also serves as Chairman of the Graduate Group in Architecture. He is the author of scholarly publications including: *Architecture Oriented Otherwise* (Princeton Architectural Press, 2009), *Topographical Stories: Studies in Architecture and Landscape Architecture* (University of Pennsylvania Press, 2013), and *On Weathering: The Life and Time of Buildings*, co-authored with Mohsen Mostafavi (MIT, 1993).

ANURADHA MATHUR: Mathur an architect and landscape architect, is professor of Landscape Architecture at the School of Design, University of Pennsylvania. She and her partner Dilip da Cunha are currently working on a project titled 'Structures of Coastal Resilience' for Norfolk, VA funded by the Rockefeller Foundation. They are authors of *Mississippi Floods: Designing a Shifting Landscape*, (Yale University Press, 2001); *Deccan Traverses: The Making of Bangalore's Terrain* (Rupa & Co., 2006); and *Soak: Mumbai in an Estuary* (National Gallery of Modern Art / Rupa & Co., 2009).

REBEKAH MEEKS: Meeks is a multidisciplinary designer located in Fayetteville, Arkansas. She graduated with a MLA from the University of Pennsylvania in 2012 and a BArch from the Fay Jones School of Architecture in 2008.

ELIZABETH MOSSOP: Mossop is a landscape architect and urban planner. She is a founding principal of Spackman Mossop and Michaels landscape architects in the US and Australia. She is a professor and former director of the Robert Reich School of Landscape Architecture at Louisiana State University where she is director of the Urban Landscape Lab and a member of the Executive Committee of the Coastal Sustainability Studio.

SIMON RICHTER: Richter is professor of Germanic Languages and Literatures at the University of Pennsylvania and past president of the Goethe Society of North America. Richter's many publications include *Missing the Breast: Gender, Fantasy and the Body in the German Enlightenment* (University of Washington Press, 2006) and *Women, Pleasure, Film: What Lolas Want* (Palgrave, 2013). Richter's current research focuses on the cultural history of sustainability in Germany and Northwestern Europe.

ANNE WHISTON SPIRN: Whiston Spirn is an author, landscape architect, photographer, and a professor in the department of Landscape Architecture and Planning at the Massachusetts Institute of Technology. Spirn is the former Chair of Landscape Architecture and Regional Planning at the University of Pennsylvania, and has been a director of the West Philadelphia Landscape Project since 1987. She was the 2007 John Simon Guggenheim Memorial Foundation Fellowship recipient in the Social Sciences.

JOHN TODD: Todd is a professor emeritus of Natural Resources at the Rubenstein School of Environmental and Natural Resources at the University of Vermont, and a Fellow at the Gund Institute for Ecological Economics. He is the founder and president of Ocean Arks International and a principal of John Todd Ecological Design, Inc. based in Woods Hole, Massachusetts. Todd is the 2008 winner of the International Buckminster Fuller Challenge, and was named a "Hero of the Earth" by Time Magazine in 1999.

MARION WEISS: Weiss is the Graham Chair professor of Architecture at the University of Pennsylvania and a founding partner of WEISS/MANFREDI, a multidisciplinary design firm in New York. Her firm's projects include the Olympic Sculpture Park: Seattle Art Museum, Brooklyn Botanic Garden Visitor Center, Barnard College Diana Center, and the University of Pennsylvania Singh Center for Nanotechnology. Two monographs on their work have been published by Princeton Architectural Press and a new monograph in Korean and English by Pro Architect was recently released in autumn 2012.

CHRISTIAN WERTHMANN: Werthmann is a professor of Landscape Architecture and Design at the Leibniz University Hannover, and was the 2010 recipient of the Hans Fischer Senior Fellowship of the Technical University in Munich. His studio research report, titled *Tactical Operations in the Informal City* received the 2010 Award in Communication Excellence by the ASLA. Werthmann's most recent investigations are concerned with landscape based strategies for low income communities living in high risk areas.

MATTHEW WIENER: Wiener is currently pursuing a masters degree in landscape architecture at the School of Design, University of Pennsylvania. He graduated from Vassar College in 2009 with a B.A. in environmental science. Under Anuradha Mathur and Dilip da Cunha, Wiener is working on a project titled 'Structures of Coastal Resilience' for Norfolk, VA funded by the Rockefeller Foundation.

KONGJIAN YU: Yu is a visiting design critic in Landscape Architecture at the Harvard Graduate School of Design, in addition to the founder and Dean of the College of Architecture and Landscape Architecture at Peking University. Yu is also the Founder, President and Principal of Turenscape, an international design firm whose projects have received awards that include the 2009 ULI Global Award for Excellence, ten ASLA Awards including two Awards of Excellence in general design.

ENDNOTES

ANURADHA MATHUR / DILIP DA CUNHA_WATERS EVERYWHERE

[1] *Meteorologica* (Cambridge MA: Harvard University Press, 1952), Book II, Ch. II, 133 and Book I, Ch. IX, 69, 71

[2] Luna B. Leopold, *A View of the River* (Cambridge MA: Harvard University Press, 1994), 1

[3] Charles H. Kahn, *Anaximander and the Origins of Greek Cosmology* (New York: Columbia University Press, 1960), 81

[4] James S. Romm, *The Edges of the Earth in Ancient Thought: Geography, Exploration, and Fiction* (Princeton: Princeton University Press, 1992), 10-11

[5] Steven Schultz and Jay A. Leitch, "Floods and Flooding," in Stanley W. Trimble (ed.), *Encyclopedia of Water Science* (Boca Raton: CRC Press 2008), Vol. 1

[6] Niccolò Machiavelli, *The Prince,* (New York: Oxford University Press, 1984)

[7] *Book of Ecclesiastes* in the Bible, New International Version (1984), Chapter I, verse 7.

[8] Seneca, *Naturales Quaestiones* Book III, 4.1-6.1, translated by Thomas H. Corcoran (Cambridge, MA: Harvard University Press, 1971), Vol. 7, 217

[9] Frank Dawson Adams, "The Origin of Springs and Rivers," *The Birth and Development of the Geological Sciences* (Baltimore: The Williams & Wilkins Company, 1938), 460

[10] Herodotus, *The Histories,* Book II: 97, translated by Aubrey de Sélincourt (London: Penguin Books, 2003), 132

[11] This is pointed out by Diodorus Siculus: "Herodotus says that the size of the Nile at its swelling is its natural one, but that as the sun travels over Libya in the winter it draws up to itself from the Nile a great amount of moisture, and this is the reason why at that season the river becomes smaller than its natural size." *Diodorus of Sicily* with an English Translation by C.H. Oldfather, Book I.38.8 (New York: G.P. Putnam's Sons, 1933), Vol. 1, 135

[12] *The New Encyclopædia Britannica* (Encyclopædia Britannica Inc., 2007), Vol. 26, 843

LINDSAY BREMNER_MUDDY LOGICS

[1] Anuradha Banerjee, *Environment Population and Human Settlements of Sundarban Delta* (New Delhi: Concept Publishing, 1998).

[2] William Langewiesche, *The Outlaw Sea* (New York: North Point, 2004); Alfred Nijkirk, "Shipbreaking USA," *Recycling International*, March 2006, http://www.environmental-expert.com/Files/6496/articles/6415/Shipbreaking.pdf; "American Ship Breaking. It All Comes Apart at the Bottom of America," *The Lay of the Land, Center for Land Use Interpretation*, Spring 2010, http://www.clui.org/lotl/pdf/33_spring2010_color-200dpi.pdf; and "Annex 3 Dismantling Sites in Europe and the OECD," *sgmer.gouv.fr*, http://www.sgmer.gouv.fr/IMG/pdf/ Annex_3_Dismantling_site_in_Europe_and_OECD.pdf [accessed March 10, 2011]. The United Kingdom, United States and the Netherlands were the major shipbreaking nations until after World War II. In the nineteen fifties, shipbreaking yards opened in Belgium, followed by Spain, Greece, the former Yugoslavia, Mexico, Colombia, Japan and Taiwan. By the nineteen sixties, Taiwan was the leading shipbreaking country, with yards clustered around Kaohsuing. These closed in 1986, following a fatal explosion and the South Asian nations took over as the worlds primary ship breakers The United States still operates two ship breaking yards – at Chesapeake Virginia, and Brownsville Texas, where ships from the three federal Ghost Fleets (surplus ships built in the 1950's and held in reserve to be activated in times of war) are taken apart. In Europe, yards still operate in the ports of Gand in Belgium, Scheepssloperij in the Netherlands, Grenaa and Esburg in Denmark and Klaipeda in Lithuania.

[3] http://www.greenpeace.org/india/campaigns/toxics-free-future/ship-breaking [accessed April 09, 2012]. The world's major ship breaking yards today are at Gadani Beach in Pakistan, Alang in India, Aligia in Turkey, Bhatiary (just north of Chittagong) in Bangladesh and Panyu City, Guangdong, and Xiagang in the Yangtze delta in China.

[4] http://en.wikipedia.org/wiki/Gadani_ship-breaking_yard# History [accessed April 09, 2010].

[5] M. Maruf Hossain and Mohammad Mahmudul Islam, "Shipbreaking Activities and its Impact on the Coastal Zone of Chittagong, Bangladesh: Towards Sustainable Management," *Young Power in Social Action*, http://www.ypsa.org/publications/Impact.pdf [accessed December 12, 2011].

[6] Ataur Rahman and A. Z. M. Tabarak Ullah, "Ship Breaking, A Background Paper," *International Labor Organization's Sectoral Activities Programme*, Dhaka 1999, http://ilo-mirror.library.cornell.edu/public/english/protection/safework/sectors/shipbrk/shpbreak.htm [accessed April 08, 2010] and Syed Tashfin Chowdhury, "Bangladesh shipbreakers survive headwinds," *Asian Times*, March 01, 2011, http://www.atimes.com/atimes/South_Asia/MC01Df02.html [accessed March 28, 2011]. This number has increased dramatically to 108, since the 2008 economic recession. In 2009, about 2.4 million tons of iron were obtained from ships scrapped in Bangladesh, compared with 650,000 tons from 2007 to 2008 and 1.22 million tons in 2006. Opportunities are set to increase further as the European Union completes a phase-out of single-hull tankers operating in its waters.

[7] Aage Bjorn Andersen, Erik Bjornbom and Terje Sverud, *Technical Report DNV RN 590, Decommissioning of Ships, Environmental Standards, Ship-breaking Practices / On-site Assessment, Bangladesh Chittagong Report No. 2000 3158, Revision No. 01* (Hovik, Norway: Det Norske Veritas, 2000).

[8] Gary Cohn and Will Englund, Baltimore Sun, "The Shipbreakers," *Pulitzer Prize for Investigative Reporting,* 1998, http://www.pulitzer.org/works/1998-Investigative-Reporting [accessed February 23, 2010].

[9] Jacob Baynham, "Muddy Waters. Are US shipping companies still selling their clunkers to the toxic scrap yards of South Asia?" *slate.com*, September 18, 2009, http://www.slate.com/id/2228712/pagenum/all/ [accessed February 22, 2010] and Rajesh Joshi, "US Environmental Agency to let Anders sail," *Basel Action Network, ban.org*, August 28, 2009, http://www.ban.org/ban_news/2009/090828_usepa_to_let_anders_sail.html [accessed February 22, 2010]. The Jones Act (Merchant Marine Act of 1920, Section 27) forbids sale of United States government ships to foreign companies and the Toxic Substances Control Act (TSCA) forbids the export or the distribution in commerce of polychlorinated biphenyls (PCBs), which are highly toxic compounds of chlorine and benzene and were once widely used in ship construction.

[10] 97 percent of the ships that are taken apart in Bangladesh are recycled.

[11] Jennifer Ashraf, "Sunset Splendour at Bhatiary," *The Daily Star Home* 2, 49, June 14, 2005, http://www.thedailystar.net/lifestyle/2005/06/02/page02.htm [accessed April 09, 2010].

[12] "Sitakunda Upzala," *Banglapedia.org*, 2006, http://www.banglapedia.org/httpdocs/HT/S_0420.HTM [accessed April 10, 2010]. It has two hundred and eighty mosques, eight mazars, forty nine Hindu temples, four ashrams, and three Buddhist temples.

[13] "Sitakunda Upzala," *Banglapedia.org*, 2006, http://www.banglapedia.org/httpdocs/HT/S_0420.HTM [accessed April 10, 2010].

[14] Group: 01(Warrior), "Report on the Impact of the Small Scale Real Estate Business on the Urbanization Patterns of Third World Cities: A Case Study on Chittagong Division," *scribd.com*, December 20, 2009, http://www.scribd.com/doc/24494329/The-Impact-of-the-Small-Scale-Real-Estate-Business-On [accessed April 10, 2010].

[15] Aage Bjorn Andersen, Erik Bjornbom and Terje Sverud, *Technical Report DNV RN 590, Decommissioning of Ships, Environmental Standards, Ship-breaking Practices / On-site Assessment, Bangladesh Chittagong Report No. 2000 3158, Revision No. 01* (Hovik, Norway: Det Norske Veritas, 2000).

[16] Greenpeace and International Federation for Human Rights in co-operation with Young Power for Social Action, "End of Life Ships – The Human Cost of Breaking Ships," *fidh.org*, 2005, http://www.fidh.org/END-OF-LIFE-SHIPS-THE-HUMAN-COST-OF-BREAKING [accessed April 10, 2010]. Workers come from Nandail (north of Kishorganj), Saria Kandi (near Bogra) Chandan Baisha, Dac Bangla and Kolni Bari (south of Saria Kandi).

[17] For details of the relations between the industry and government ministries and departments, and the structuring of the industry see Ataur Rahman and A. Z. M. Tabarak Ullah, "Ship Breaking, A Background Paper," *International Labor Organization's Sectoral Activities Programme*, Dhaka 1999, http://ilo-mirror.library.cornell.edu/public/english/protection/safework/sectors/shipbrk/shpbreak.htm [accessed April 08, 2010].

214

[18] Brian Foote and Joseph Yoder, "Big Ball of Mud," *laputan.org*, August 28, 2001, http://www.laputan.org/mud/mud/html [accessed November 15, 2010].
[19] Ibid.,2.
[20] Ibid.
[21] Ibid, 9.
[22] Ibid, 5.
[23] *Bangladesh Environmental Lawyers Association*. http://www.belabangla.org/ [accessed 10 December 2011].
[24] "Bangladesh Environment Conservation Act, Act 1 of 1995. Section 12." PI-COM, http://www.picom.gov.bd/pdf/env1995.pdf and "Bangladesh Factories Act, 1965, Act 4 of 1965." *International Labor Organization*. http://www.ilo.org/dyn/natlex/docs/WEBTEXT/47346/65073/E65BGD01.htm [accessed 10 December 2011].
[25] M. Maruf Hossain and Mohammad Mahmudul Islam, "Shipbreaking Activities and its Impact on the Coastal Zone of Chittagong, Bangladesh: Towards Sustainable management," *Young Power in Social Action*, http://www.ypsa.org/publications/Impact.pdf [accessed December 12, 2011]. Lack of occupational health and safety standards, training or personal protection result in high levels of exposure by workers to accidents and they or their families are paid limited or no compensation when they are injured or killed. Workers are subjected to extended working hours, less than minimum wages, and are not permitted to form trade unions and the use of child labor is common.
[26] "Import Policy Order 2009-2012." DITP, http://www.depthai.go.th/DEP/DOC/53/53002565.pdf [accessed 10 December 2011]. This included Import Policy Order 2009-2012, which required that ships be pre-cleaned before entering Bangladesh. Ministry of Commerce, Government of the People's Republic of Bangladesh.
[27] Maria Sarraff et.al. "Ship Breaking and Recycling Industry in Pakistan." World Bank Report No 58275-SAS, 17. *The World Bank*, http://siteresources.worldbank.org/SOUTHASIAEXT/Resources/223546-1296680097256/Shipbreaking.pdf [accessed 12 December 2011].
[28] Syed Tashfin Chowdhury, "Bangladesh shipbreakers survive headwinds," *Asian Times*, March 01, 2011, http://www.atimes.com/atimes/South_Asia/MC01Df02.html [accessed March 28, 2011].

NATALY GATTEGNO_AQUEOUS TERRITORIES
[1] R Chevallier, 'The Greco-Roman Conception of the North from Pytheas to Tacitus', *Arctic*, Vol 37, No 4, December 1984, 341.

TERRA INCOGNITA, AURORA, GLACIARIUM, HYDRAMAX
Design: Jason Kelly Johnson & Nataly Gattegno
Project Team: Carrie Norman, Thomas Kelley
Project Collaborators: Noah Keating, Troy Rogers
Assistants: Kezia Ofiesh, Paul Fromm, Sarah Fugate, Hank Byron, Taylor Burgess, Ed Yung, Ben Fey, Dayoung Shin, Kyle Kugler, Jim Staddon, Gin Harr, Yuki Staddon, Matt Young, Brad DeVries, Kyle Sturgeon.
Map Resources: The University of Michigan Map Library
Photography: Zechariah Vincent
Support: The Van Alen Institute, The University of Michigan TCAUP, Graham Foundation for Advanced Studies in the Fine Arts Grant, Columbia University Avery CNC Fabrication Lab, NYC College of Technology - CityTech

HYDRAMAX
Design: Jason Kelly Johnson & Nataly Gattegno
Project Manager: Ripon DeLeon; Project Interns: Gavin Johns, Cameron Eng
Collaborative Sponsor: MIGA Motor Company (Dr. Mark Gummin)

ALISON HIRSCH_IMAGING CHANGE
[1] Robert E. Cook, "Do Landscapes Learn? Ecology's 'New Paradigm' and Design in Landscape Architecture," in Michel Conan, ed., *Environmentalism in Landscape Architecture*, (Washington, DC: Dumbarton Oaks, 2000). 119-120.
[2] Halprin defines "Wildness" in his essay "Wildness as Art," in an unpublished book manuscript, *Environment as Art Experience* (1974). He begins, "Wildness or wild nature, if you will, is where we can perceive the pure world and react to it in a state of unmodified as yet by our technological changes. It is the last pure stronghold on earth of 'what is', without our value system imposed… 'Wildness' is a state of being… an effable quality existing in those places in our world in which humans have not made changes… in which natural forces have created all that exists without our intervention. It is not nature but 'nature unaffected by humans' that creates the quality of wildness. Wildness is different than wilderness – wilderness is a place, an area, a situation in which wildness may exist. Wildness is the quality, the experience, the essence of wilderness… Everything we are has origins in wildness. And only there can we see *undisturbed process at work*…" (Halprin Archives, 014.I.B.2302). Emphasis in original.
[3] Yet like his predecessors, he also hoped to generate forms that would resist cultural obsolescence - that would sustain relevance despite the forward march of time.
[4] Kevin Starr, *Americans and the California Dream*, 1850-1915 (New York: Oxford University Press, 1973), 180.
[5] "Dance Deck in the Woods," *Impulse* (1956), 24.
[6] John Dewey, *Art as Experience* (New York, Minton, Balch & Co., 1934), 15-16.
[7] Marshall Berman, *All That is Solid Melts into Air: The Experience of Modernity* (London: Penguin Books, 1988), 348.

ANNE WHISTON SPIRN_RESTORING WATER
Parts of this essay are adapted from "Restoring Mill Creek: Landscape Literacy, Environmental Justice, and City Planning and Design," *Landscape Research* 30:5 (July 2005): 359-377 (available at http://www.annewhiston-spirn.com/pdf/SpirnMillCreek2005.pdf). For more on the West Philadelphia Project and for the photographs featured here, as well as others, see: www.annewhistonspirn.com and www.wplp.net.

KONGJIAN YU_COMPLETE WATER
1. See Kongjian Yu and Dihua Li, *The Road to Urban Landscape: Talks to Mayors* (Beijing: China Architecture & Building Press, 2003). Published only in Chinese.
2. Chen Kelin, Lü Yong, and Zhang Xiaohong, "No Water Without Wetland," *China Environment and Development Review* (2004), 296–309. See also John McAlister, "China's Water Crisis," Deutsche Bank China Expert Series, March 22, 2005.
3. Kongjian Yu, "Elegy to Water," editorial, LA China 12, October 4, 2010, 20–24.

SIMON RICHTER_THE HYDROLOGICAL MOMENT
[1] J. W. von Goethe, *Faust*, lines 11,559-11,856, my translation.
[2] Oswald Spengler, *The Decline of the West* (New York: A. A. Knopf, 1939).
[3] The 2008 Veerman Commission of the Netherlands recommends increasing flood plains along the built up shorelines of the Maas and Rhine by 10%. This entails an aggressive use of eminent domain.
[4] Gaston Bachelard, *Water and Dreams: An Essay on the Imagination of Matter* (Dallas: Pegasus Foundation, 1983), 6.
[5] Philippe Ariès, *The Hour of Our Death* (New York: Oxford University Press, 1991).
[6] Sigmund Freud, *New Introductory Lectures on Psychoanalysis* (New York: W. W. Norton, 1965), 71.
7 Bruno Bettelheim, *Freud and Man's Soul* (New York: A. A. Knopf, 1983), 64.

CHRISTIAN WERTHMANN_POLLUTION + PROPAGANDA
The author would like to acknowledge Joseph Claghorn for editorial work, and Fernando de Mello Franco and Giselle Mendonça for historical image sourcing.

MARION WEISS_CULTURAL WATERMARKS
Museum of the Earth
1999-2003
Client: Paleontological Research Institution
Site Design / Architecture: WEISS/MANFREDI Architecture/Landscape/Urbanism

215

Marion Weiss and Michael A. Manfredi (Design Partners), Christopher Ballentine (Project Manager); Lauren Crahan and Armando Petruccelli (Project Architects), Michael Blasberg, Christopher Kimball, Christopher Payne, and Giselle Sperber
Structural Engineering: Weidlinger Associates Consulting Engineers
MEPFP Engineering: MG Engineering P.C.
Civil Engineering: T.G. Miller, P.C.
Landscape/Horticulture: Elemental Landscapes
Lighting Design: Brandston Partnership Inc.
Exhibition Design: Weiss/Manfredi (Entry Hall) and Jeff Kennedy Associates (Exhibition Hall)
Cost Estimator: AMIS Inc.
Owner's Representative: John Fontana, P.E.
General Contractor: Hueber Breuer Construction Co., Inc.

Olympic Sculpture Park
2001-2007
Client: Seattle Art Museum
Competition Winner:
WEISS/MANFREDI Architecture/Landscape/Urbanism
Site Design / Architecture: WEISS/MANFREDI Architecture/Landscape/Urbanism
Marion Weiss and Michael A. Manfredi (Design Partners), Christopher Ballentine (Project Manager), Todd Hoehn and Yehre Suh (Project Architects), Patrick Armacost, Michael Blasberg, Beatrice Eleazar, Hamilton Hadden, Mike Harshman, Mustapha Jundi, John Peek, and Akari Takebayashi. Competition and Exhibition team: Lauren Crahan, Kian Goh, Justin Kwok, Lee Lim and Yehre Suh,
Structural and Civil Engineering: Magnusson Klemencic Associates
Mechanical and Electrical Engineering: ABACUS Engineered Systems
Lighting Design: Brandston Partnership Inc.
Geotechnical Engineering: Hart Crowser
Environmental: Aspect Consulting
Aquatic Engineering: Anchor Environmental
Graphics: Pentagram
Security and AV/IT: ARUP
Catering & Food Service: Bon Appetit
Kitchen: JLR Design
Retail: Doyle + Associates
Architectural Site Representation: Owens Richards Architects, pllc
Project Management: Barrientos LLC
General Contractor: Sellen Construction

McCann Residence
2004-2011
Client: Joseph and Anne McCann
Area: 4,900sf
Site Design / Architecture: WEISS/MANFREDI Architecture/Landscape/Urbanism
Marion Weiss and Michael A. Manfredi (Design Partners); Hamilton Hadden, Michael Blasberg (Project Architects)
Architect Consultant: Michael DeCandia Architects
Michael DeCandia (Design Partner); John Cunniffe (Project Architect)
Civil Engineer: Thomas W. Skrable, PE

Brooklyn Botanic Garden
2004-2012
Architect & Site Design: WEISS/MANFREDI Architecture/Landscape/Urbanism
Michael A. Manfredi, FAIA and Marion Weiss, FAIA (Design Partners); Armando Petruccelli, RA (Project Manager); Hamilton Hadden, RA, Justin Kwok, LEED-AP, Michael Steiner, LEED-AP (Project Architects); Christopher Ballentine, Cheryl Baxter, Michael Blasberg, RA, Paúl Duston-Muñoz (Project Team); Patrick Armacost, Jeremy Babel, Caroline Emerson, Eleonora Flammina, Kian Goh, Michael Harshman, Aaron Hollis, Hanul Kim, Hyoung-Gul

Kook, Lee Lim, Jonathan Schwartz, Na Sun, Jie Tian, Yoonsun Yang (Additional Team Members)
Consultant Team
Structural and Civil Engineering Consultant: Weidlinger Associates Consulting Engineers
MEPFP/IT Engineering Consultant: Jaros, Baum & Bolles Consulting Engineers
Geothermal/Geotechnical Engineering Consultant: Langan Engineering and Environmental Services Landscape: HM White Site Architecture
Lighting Design Consultant: Brandston Partnership Inc.
Cost Estimator: AMIS Inc.
Environmental Consultant: Viridian Energy & Environmental, LLC
Retail Consultant: Jeanne Giordano Ltd.
AV/Acoustics/Security Consultant: Cerami & Associates, Inc
Security Consultant: TM Technology Partners
Food Service Consultant: Ricca Newmark Design
Curtain Wall Consultant: R.A. Heintges & Associates
Code & Life Safety: Code Consultants, Inc.
Traffic Consultant: Sam Schwartz LLC
Construction Manager: The Liro Group
General Contractor: E.W. Howell

WILLIAM BRAHAM_WASTE, WORK, & WORTH
[1] Charles Dickens, "Philadelphia," *American Notes and Pictures from Italy* (London: Chapman and Hall, 1874), Chapter VII.
[2] Water and Sewage Works, *Municipal Engineering*, Vol. 18, January-June, 1900. 119.
[3] Randal C. Archibold, "From Sewage, Added Water for Drinking," *New York Times* (November 27, 2007). http://www.nytimes.com/2007/11/27/us/27conserve.html, [accessed April 15, 2013].
[4] A. Buenfil, *Emergy Evaluation of Water* (Unpublished PhD Dissertation, University of Florida, 2001).

DAVID LEATHERBARROW_HORIZON OF ALL HORIZONS
[1] Leon Battista Alberti, *On the Art of Building in Ten Books* (Cambridge, MA: The MIT Press, 1988).
[2] This observation follows those made by Francis Ponge, in poem called "Water," in *The Voice of Things* (New York: McGraw-Hill, 1974).
[3] W.H. Auden, *Thank you Fog* (Random House, 1974).
[4] With the western coast of Ireland as her topic, shore life has been studied fully and beautifully by Anna Ryan, in *Where Land Meets Sea* (Farnham, Surrey: Ashgate Publishing, 2012). For the American context, see Anuradha Mathur and Dilip da Cunha, *Mississippi Floods: Designing a Shifting Landscape* (New Haven, CT: Yale University Press, 2001).
[5] Le Corbusier, *Journey to the East* (Cambridge, MA: MIT Press 2007).
[6] Ibid.
[7] Still the best account of this wonderful building is Bruno Reichlin, "The Pros and Cons of the Horizontal Window," *Daidalos*. But see also Le Corbusier's own report: *Une Petite Maison* (Zurich, Switzerland: Birkhäuser Architecture 1954).
[8] *Une Petite Maison* (Zurich, Switzerland: Birkhäuser Architecture 1954).
[9] The most thorough study to date on this building is Brian Brace Taylor, *The Salvation Army Building*
[10] Hashim Sarkis, *The Mat Building*, (Prestel Publishing, 2002). 23
[11] Le Corbusier, *Oeuvre Complete (Fondation Le Corbusier, 1995)*.
[12] Le Corbusier, *Oeuvre Complete (Fondation Le Corbusier, 1995)*.
[13] Ibid.
[14] Le Corbusier, *When the Cathedrals Were White* (New York: McGraw-Hill, 1964).
[15] I describe this encounter a little more fully in a chapter called "Skylines," in *Architecture Oriented Otherwise* (New York: Princeton Architectural Press, 2009).
[16] Le Corbusier *When the Cathedrals Were White*, (New York: McGraw-Hill, 1964).
[17] Le Corbusier, *Poem to the Right Angle* (Fondation Le Corbusier, 1989)

IÑAKI ECHEVERRIA/MARGARITA EUGENIA GUTIÉRREZ_
SOFT ENGINEERING

Aguilar, Adrián Guillermo (2006) *Las grandes aglomeraciones y su periferia regional*. Experiencias en Latinoamérica y España, México DF, Porrúa.

Aguilar, Adrián Guillermo y Escamilla, Irma, (1999) *Problems of megacities: Social inequalities, environmental risk and urban governance*, México DF, Instituto de Geografía UNAM.

2G Revista internacional de arquitectura No. 18, (2001). Arquitectura y energía, Barcelona, Gustavo Gili, SA.

Balcells, Conxita y Bru, Josepa (2002) *Al lado de/Alongside*, Barcelona, Gustavo Gili, SA

Bitácora Arquitectura., (2000). Numero 3: la ciudad de México hacia el siglo XXI, México DF, Facultad de Arquitectura UNAM.

Cruickshank García, Gerardo., (1994). *Proyecto Lago de Texcoco. Rescate hidrológico*, México DF, Grupo Impresor MANSUA S.A. de C.V.

Czerniak, Julia y Hargreaves, George., (2007) *Large Parks*, New York, Princeton Architectural Press.

Echeverria, Iñaki. + Plunz, Richard (2000). *A Gardener's Logic*. New York, Praxis

Echeverria, Iñaki., (2008). *Proyecto Parque Bicentenario*, México DF.

Glaeser, Edward. (2011) *Triumph of the city: How our greatest invention makes us Richer, Smarter, Greener, Healthier and Happier*. USA, The Penguin Press

Gonzáles, Aragón y Jorge, Cortés Delgado, José Luis., (2004). *Corpus Urbanístico de México en España*, México DF, Fundación Santillana.

Graz Architecture magazine. (2008). *Emerging realities*, Viena, GAM.

Kirkwood, Niall. (2001). *Manufactured sites. Rethinking the Post-Industrial landscape*, Londres y New York, Spon Press.

Lot, Antonio, Novelo, Alejandro y Esparza, Elvia., (2004). *Iconografía y estudio de plantas acuáticas de la ciudad de México y sus alrededores*, México DF, Universidad Nacional Autónoma de México.

Molinari, Luca. (2000). *West 8*, Milano, Skira editores S.p.A

Plunz, Richard y Culligan, Patricia (2007) *Eco-Gowanus: Urban Remediation by design*, New York, GSAPP.

Quaderns: d'arquitectura i urbanisme No. 233, (2002) *Tierra usada-Used Land*, Barcelona, Editorial Gustavo Gili, SA.

Rosell, Quim., (2001). *Después de/afterwards*, Barcelona, Gustavo Gili, SA.

Verwijnen, Jan y Lehtovuori, Panu., (1993). *Creative cities. Cultural industries, urban development and the information society*, Helsinki, UIAH Publications.

Waldheim, Charles, (2007). *The Landscape Urbanism Reader*, New York, Princeton Architectural Press.

IMAGES

ANURADHA MATHUR/DILIP DA CUNHA: **Unless otherwise noted, all images credited to and © Anuradha Mathur and Dilip da Cunha.**

Additional Credits: S1-TH (1) James Rennell, "The Delta of the Ganges," *A Bengal Atlas* (1781) [Library of Congress] (1781): S2-TH (1) Hecataeus' Map in Edward Herbert Bunbury, *A History of Ancient Geography Among the Greeks and Romans from the Earliest Ages til the Fall of the Roman Empire,* Vol. 1 (London: John Murray, 1883), S2-TH (2) cr. Annenberg Rare Book & Manuscript Library, University of Pennsylvania, Tabula ex Marino Sanuto in William Vincent, *The Commerce and Navigation of the Ancients in the Indian Ocean* (London: T. Cadell and W. Davies, 1807), S2-TH (3) Levee break in 1927 flood of the Mississippi River, S2-TH (4) G.W. Colton, *Mountains & Rivers,* Published by J.H. Colton & Co. NY (Detail), S2-MH (1) The Hydrologic Cycle, Robert E. Horton, "The Field, Scope, and Status of the Science of Hydrology," *Transactions of the Geophysical Union,* Vol. 12, 1931, S3-TH (1) cr. British Library, Thomas Daniell, Dusasumade Gaut, at Benares, *Oriental Scenery: Twenty four Views in Hindoostan* (1796), S3-TH (2) cr. Annenberg Rare Book & Manuscript Library, University of Pennsylvania, Robert Hyde Colebrooke, "Chart of the River Ganges from Colgong to Hurrisonker; Exhibiting the State of Its Islands and Sands During the Dry Season of 1796-7," in *Asiatic Researches* Volume 7, 1803, S4-TH (1) "Distribution of Project Flood," From P.A. Feringa and W. Schweizer, *One Hundred Years Improvement on the Lower Mississippi River* (Vicksburg, MS: Mississippi River Commission, 1952), S5-TH (1) Jean Nicolas Bellin, Detail, *Carte reduite de la Presque Isle de l'Inde,* 1766, S6-TH (1) Pedro and Jorge Reinel and Lopo Homem 1519 Chart of the Indian Ocean (Detail) in *Atlas Miller* (Barcelona: M. Moleiro, 2003), S6-TH (2) Jean Nicolas Bellin, *Carte Reduite de la Presque Isle de l'inde,* 1766. Detail., S6-TH (3) Thomas Jefferys, The East Indies with the Roads, 1768. Detail., S6-TH (4) Guillarme de L'Isle, *Carte des Cotes de Malabar et de Coromandel,* 1735. Detail., S6-TH (5) Levee in 1927 flood of the Mississippi River. S6-BH (1) Indian mound in 1927 flood of the Mississippi River.

TEDDY CRUZ: **Unless otherwise noted, all images credited to and © Anuradha Mathur and Dilip da Cunha.**

Additional Credits: © Teddy Cruz: S1-TH (1), S1-BH (1), S2-MH (1), S2-MH (2), S2-MH (3), S2-MH (4), S2-MH (5), S3-MH (1), S3-MH (2), S4-MH (1), S4-MH (2), S4-MH (3), S4-MH (4), S4-MH (5), S4-MH (6), S4-MH (7).

LINDSAY BREMNER: **All images © Lindsay Bremner.**

NATALY GATTEGNO: **All images © Future Cities Lab.**

ANNE WHISTON SPIRN: **Unless otherwise noted, all images credited to and © Anne Whiston Spirn:** cr. West Philadelphia Landscape Project (WPLP): S1-BH (1) S2-MH (2), S2-BH (3), S2-BH (4), S3-TH (1), S4-BH (2), S4-TH (1); cr. WPLP/David Moses: S3-MH (1), S3-MH (1), S3-MH (3), S3-MH (4); cr. WPLP/Sulzberger Middle School: S2-BH (5); cr. WPLP/Justin Parish: S3-BH (1); cr. WPLP/Cleveland Pickett: S3-BH (3); cr. WPLP/Dean Holloway: S3-BH (4); cr. Eric Husta and Steven Sattler: S4-MH (2), S4-MH (3); cr. Allison Hu and Florence Guiraud Doughty: S4-BH (1); cr. Elizabeth Ramaccia: S4-BH (3)

Addtional Credits: © Philadelphia Water Department: S2-TH-(1); © Urban Archives, Temple University: S2-TH-(3). S2-TH (2).

ALISON HIRSCH: **Unless otherwise noted, all images © Lawrence Halprin Collection, The Architectural Archives, University of Pennsylvania:**

Additional Credits: © Maude Dorr: S2-TH (1), S2-TH (2), S2-TH (3), S2-TH (4), S2-TH (5), S2-TH (6); © Eeo Stubblefield (1998): S4-BH (1) Title: Anna Halprin Sand Series #20 Still Dance Created by Eeo Stubblefield, S4-BH (2) Title: Anna Halprin Driftwood Series #12 Stilldance created by Eeo Stubblefield.

KONGJIAN YU: **All images © Kongjian Yu**

SIMON RICHTER: © **AP Images:** S3-MH (1); © **Andy Taylor:** S2-TH (5), S2-TH (6), S3-TH (1); cr. Nederlands Instituut voor Beeld en Geluid: S3-BH (1),

S3-BH (2), S3-BH (3), S3-BH (4), S3-BH (5), S3-BH (6), S3-BH (7), S3-BH (8), S3-BH (9), S3-BH (10), S3-BH (11), S3-BH (12), S3-BH (13), S3-BH (14), S3-BH (15); cr. New Land Lelystad, Photo Collection New Land Management Wieringermeer, J. Potuyt: S4-BH (2).

DOUG JEROLMACK: © **Nicole Kahn:** S1 - TH (1), S2-TH (1), S2-TH (2), S2-TH (3), S2-TH (4), S2-TH (5), S3-TH (2) with Doug Jerolmack, S4-TH (1), S4-TH (2), S4-TH (3); © **Meredith Reitz:** S1 - BH (1), S2-BH (1), S2-BH (2), S3-BH (1), S3-BH (2), S4-MH (1); S4-BH (1), S4-BH (2); © **Louisiana Universities Marine Consortium:** S3-MH (1).

Additional Credits: United States Army Corps of Engineers cr. Norman R. Moore: S2-MH (1).

ELIZABETH MOSSOP: **Unless otherwise noted, all images credited to and © Elizabeth Mossop:** cr. Kristi Cheramie: S1-TH (1), S2-TH (1), S2 - TH (4), S2 - TH (3); cr. Christopher Hall: S2-TH (2), S2-BH (5), S2-BH (6), S3-MH (1), S4-TH (2); cr. L9 Center for Sustainable Engagement and Development: S3-BH (1), S3-BH (2), S3-BH (3), S3-BH (4); cr. Coastal Sustainability Studio: S2 - TH (5), S2 - TH (6), S2 - TH (7), S2-MH (1), S2-MH (2), S2-BH (1), S2-BH (7), S3-TH (2), S3-TH (3), S3-TH (4), S3-TH (5), S3-MH (2), S4-TH (3), S4-MH (1), S4-MH (2).

Additional Credits: cr. Marvin Nauman/FEMA: S2-BH (3), S2-BH (4).

WALTER HOOD: **Unless otherwise noted, all images credited to and © Walter Hood/Hood Design:** S3-TH (6) cr. Tim Mollette-Parks,

Additional Credits: © **Studio for Spatial Practice:** S4-MH (3), S4-MH (4), S4-MH (5), S4-MH (6); **Courtesy of Spoleto Festival USA, Charleston, South Carolina:** Photo cr. Walter Hood, Artist cr. Kendra Hamilton, Walter Hood, Ernesto Pujol, Frances Whitehead, S1-BH (1), S2-BH (2); Photo cr. Ernesto Pujol, Artist cr. Ernesto Pujol and Walter Hood, S2-BH (1), S2-BH (3) S2-BH (4).

KAZI ASHRAF: **Unless otherwise noted, all images credited to and © Rebekah Meeks.**

Additional Credits: © **Kazi Ashraf:** S2-MH (1), S2-MH (2), S2-MH (3), S2-MH (4), S2-MH (5), S2-MH (6), S2-MH (7), S2-MH (8), S2-MH (9), S2-MH (10), S2-MH (11), S2-MH (12), S2-MH (13), S2-MH (14), S4-MH (1) cr. Schiffino and Barber, Ashraf Studio, Temple University.

PETER HUTTON: **All images © Peter Hutton:** *At Sea* (2004) and *Two Rivers* (2002).

ILA BERMAN: **Unless otherwise noted, all images credited to and © Ila Berman/Scaleshift.**

Additional Credits: © **Chris Austin:** S1 - TH (1), S4-TH (1), S4-TH (2), S4-TH (3), S4-TH (4), S4-TH (5), S4-TH (6), S5-TH (1), S5-BH (1), S5-BH (2), S5-BH (3), S5-BH (4), S5-BH (5); © **County of Inyo, Eastern California Museum:** S2-TH (2), S2-TH (3), S2-TH (4); © **John Monnat:** S2-BH (1), S2-BH (2); © **Barry Lehrman:** S4-BH (1), S5-TH; cr. U.S. Lib of Congress, Jet Lowe Hist. Engineering Record: S4-TH (7).

CHRISTIAN WERTHMANN: **Unless otherwise noted, all images credited to and © Christian Werthmann/Harvard GSD Studio:** cr. Tomas Amorin: S2-TH (1); cr. Katie Powell: S2-TH (4) cr. Joseph Claghorn: S2-TH (7), S3-TH (1).

Additional Credits: © **Nelson Kon:** S1-BH (1), © **Fabio Knoll:** S4-TH (1), S4-TH (2), S4-TH (3), S4-TH (4); © **Philip Snow:** S4-BH (1).

MARION WEISS: **Unless otherwise noted, all images credited to and © WEISS/MANFREDI:** cr. Paul Warchol: S1-TH (1), S2-TH (1), S2-TH (2), S2-TH (5), S3-TH (1), S3-TH (2), S3-TH (3), S3-TH (4), S1-TH (1), S3-TH (7) cr. Bruce Moore: S3-TH (5).

Additional Credits: cr. United States Geological Survey: S2-BH (3); © **Jeff**

218